THE USBORNE

INTERNET-LINKED

ESSENTIAL
ATLAS
OF THE WORLD

Stephanie Turnbull

Designers: Stephen Moncrieff and Helen Wood

Consultant cartographic editor: Craig Asquith

Cartography by European Map Graphics Ltd
Map design by Laura Fearn and Keith Newell

SCHOLASTIC INC.

New York Toronto London Auckland Sydney
Mexico City New Delhi Hong Kong Buenos Aires

CONTENTS

This page: African elephants graze on plains south of the Sahara Desert.

Title page: Evening sunlight shines on Mount Rainier, in Washington, northwestern U.S.A.

Endpapers: This picture of the world at night has been made by combining many satellite images.

INTERNET LINKS

This book contains descriptions of many interesting websites where you can find out more about maps and places around the world. For links to these sites, go to the Usborne Quicklinks Website at **www.usborne-quicklinks.com** and enter the keywords "essential atlas". There you will find links to take you to all the sites.

Site availability

The links on the Usborne Quicklinks Website will be reviewed and updated regularly. If any sites become unavailable, we will, if possible, replace them with suitable alternatives.

Occasionally, you may get a message saying that a website is unavailable. This may be temporary, so try again a few hours later, or even the next day.

Internet links

For links to all the websites described in this book, go to **www.usborne-quicklinks.com** and enter the keywords "essential atlas".

Help

For general help and advice on using the Internet, go to the Usborne Quicklinks Website and click on "Net Help".

To find out more about using your web browser, click on your browser's Help menu and choose "Contents and Index". You'll find a searchable dictionary containing tips on how to find your way around the Internet easily.

What you need

The websites described in this book can be accessed using a standard home computer and a web browser (the software that enables you to display information from the Internet). Here's a list of the basic requirements:

- A PC with Microsoft® Windows® 98 or a later version, or a Macintosh computer with System 9.0 or later

- 64Mb RAM

- A web browser such as Microsoft® Internet Explorer 5, or Netscape® 6, or later versions

- Connection to the Internet via a modem (preferably 56kbps) or a faster digital or cable line

- An account with an Internet Service Provider (ISP)

- A sound card to hear sound files

Computer not essential

If you don't have use of the Internet, don't worry. This atlas is a complete, self-contained reference book on its own.

Extras

Some websites need additional free programs, called plug-ins, to play sounds, or to show videos, animations or 3-D images. If you go to a site and you do not have the necessary plug-in, a message should come up on the screen.

There is usually a button on the site that you can click on to download the plug-in. Alternatively, go to Usborne Quicklinks and click on "Net Help". There you can find links to download plug-ins. Here is a list of plug-ins that you might need:

- **QuickTime** – lets you play video clips.

- **RealOne™ Player** – lets you play video clips and sound files.

- **Flash™** – lets you play animations.

- **Shockwave®** – lets you play animations and enjoy interactive sites.

Computer viruses

A computer virus is a program that can damage your computer. A virus can get into your computer when you download programs from the Internet, or in an attachment (an extra file) that arrives with an email. We strongly recommend that you buy anti-virus software to protect your computer and that you update the software regularly. You can buy anti-virus software at computer stores or download it from the Internet. To find out more about viruses, go to Usborne Quicklinks and click on "Net Help".

Internet safety

When using the Internet, make sure you follow these simple safety rules.

- Ask your parent's or guardian's permission before you connect to the Internet. They can then stay nearby if they think they should do so.

- If you write a message in a website guest book or on a website message board, do not include your email address, real name, address or telephone number.

- If a website asks you to log in or register by typing your name or email address, ask the permission of an adult first.

- If you receive email from someone you don't know, tell an adult and do not reply to the email.

- Never arrange to meet anyone you have talked to on the Internet.

Note for parents

The websites described in this book are regularly checked and reviewed by Usborne editors and the links in Usborne Quicklinks are updated. However, the content of a website may change at any time and Usborne Publishing is not responsible for the content of any website other than its own.

We recommend that children are supervised while on the Internet, that they do not use Internet chat rooms and that you use Internet filtering software to block unsuitable material. Please ensure that your children follow the safety guidelines above. For more information, go to the Net Help area on the Usborne Quicklinks Website at **www.usborne-quicklinks.com**

MAPS AND ATLASES

An atlas is a collection of maps, along with useful information about the areas shown. The maps in this atlas cover the whole world and are grouped by continent.

What maps show

A map is an image that represents an area of the Earth's surface, usually from above. Unlike a photograph, which shows exactly what an area looks like, a map can show features of the area in a clear, simplified way. It can also give different information, such as place names. Symbols are often used to mark features such as volcanoes and waterfalls.

Which way is up?

Although the Earth doesn't have a top and a bottom, north is usually at the top of maps. But it is sometimes more convenient to reposition a map, so north might not necessarily be at the top. Some maps have a compass symbol that indicates where north lies.

Wolf volcano

Darwin volcano

San Salvador

Fernandina

Alcedo volcano

La Cumbre volcano

Santa Cruz

Isabela

Sierra Negra volcano

Cerro Azul volcano

This simple map of the central Galapagos Islands names the main islands and their volcanoes.

Floreana

This is a satellite image of part of the Galapagos Islands. Using the map on this page, can you identify the islands shown in the satellite photo?

Physical and political

Physical maps indicate natural features such as mountains, deserts, rivers and lakes. Political maps focus on the division of the Earth's surface into different countries. Look on pages 16–17 for a political map of the world, and on pages 18–19 for a physical map. Most of the maps in this atlas show physical features as well as country borders, cities and towns.

Using satellites

Today, scientists can make more accurate maps of the world than ever before, using information from artificial satellites in space. These devices travel around, or orbit, the Earth, and send back pictures of its surface. Satellite images provide detailed views of the Earth, and are often artificially shaded to highlight certain features, for example forests or deserts, so they are easier to see. They are used for a variety of purposes, such as monitoring weather conditions and natural hazards.

Map scales

The size of a map in relation to the area it shows is called its scale. Some maps have a scale bar, which is a rule with measurements. It tells you how many miles or km are represented by a certain distance on the map. Other maps show these relative distances just as numbers. For example, the figure 1:100 means that 1cm on the map represents 100cm on the Earth's surface.

The scale of a map depends on its purpose. A map showing the whole world is on a very small scale, but a town plan is on a much larger scale so that features such as roads can be shown clearly.

Internet links

For links to the following websites, go to **www.usborne-quicklinks.com**

Website 1 Find physical and political maps of different countries.

Website 2 Look at detailed satellite pictures of any part of the world.

This illustration shows a satellite that monitors weather conditions on Earth. It collects data using powerful radar.

1:80,000,000

| 0 | 1,000 | 2,000 | 3,000km |

| 0 | 1,000 | 2,000 miles |

This map of Europe is on a small scale so that it all fits onto one small map.

1:7,000,000

| 0 | 100 | 200 | 300km |

| 0 | 100 | 200 miles |

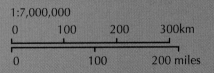

This map of Denmark is on a larger scale to show more detail.

DIVIDING LINES

The Earth is divided up with imaginary lines that help us measure distances and find where places are. There are two sets of lines, called latitude and longitude.

This arctic fox lives in northern Canada, very near the Arctic Circle line of latitude.

Latitude lines

Lines of latitude run around the globe. They are parallel to each other and get shorter the closer they are to the two poles. The latitude line that runs around the middle of the Earth is called the Equator. It is the most important line of latitude as all other lines are measured north or south of it.

Latitude lines

Longitude lines

This drawing of the Earth shows some of the main latitude and longitude lines.

Longitude lines

Lines of longitude run from the North Pole to the South Pole. All the lines are the same length, and they all meet at the North and South Poles.

The most important line of longitude is the Prime Meridian Line, which runs through Greenwich, in England. All other lines of longitude are measured east or west of this line.

Other lines

The Equator is not the only named line of latitude. The Tropic of Cancer is a line north of the Equator. The Tropic of Capricorn is at the same distance south of the Equator. Between these lines are the hottest, wettest parts of the world. This region is called the tropics.

The Arctic Circle is a latitude line far north of the Equator. The area north of this includes the North Pole and is called the Arctic. On the other side of the globe is the Antarctic Circle. The area south of this includes the South Pole and is known as the Antarctic.

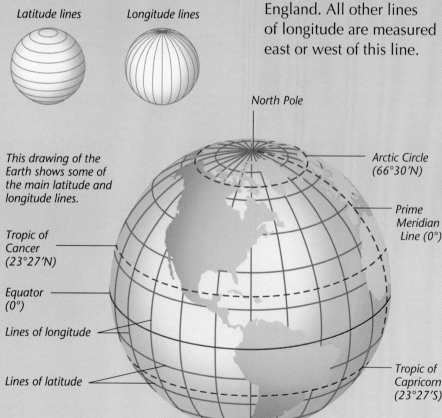

North Pole

Arctic Circle (66°30'N)

Prime Meridian Line (0°)

Tropic of Cancer (23°27'N)

Equator (0°)

Lines of longitude

Lines of latitude

Tropic of Capricorn (23°27'S)

Internet link

For a link to a website where you can find out more about the Earth's lines of latitude and longitude, and test your knowledge with a great latitude and longitude quiz, go to **www.usborne-quicklinks.com**

Using the lines

Lines of latitude and longitude are measured in degrees (°). The positions of places are described according to which lines of latitude and longitude are nearest to them. For example, a place with a location of 50°S and 100°E has a latitude 50 degrees south of the Equator, and a longitude 100 degrees east of the Prime Meridian Line.

Exact locations

The distance between degrees is divided up to give even more precise measurements. Each degree is divided into 60 minutes ('), and each minute is divided into 60 seconds ("). The subdivisions allow us to locate any place on Earth. For example, the city of New York, U.S.A., is at 40°42′51″N and 74°00′23″W.

The steamy rainforests of Malaysia lie near the Equator. Many apes, like the one shown here, live in these rainforests.

Using a grid

Lines of latitude and longitude form grids on maps. The maps in this book look similar to the one on the left. The columns that run from top to bottom are formed by lines of longitude and marked with letters. The rows running across the page are formed by lines of latitude and are numbered.

This is a map of New Zealand, with a grid formed by lines of latitude and longitude.

All the places listed in the map index on page 98 have a letter and a number reference that tell you where to find them on a particular page. For example, on the map on the left, the city of Christchurch would have a grid reference of C3.

HOW MAPS ARE MADE

The process of making maps is called cartography. Map-makers, or cartographers, compile each map by gathering information about the area and representing it as an image as accurately as possible.

Internet link

For a link to a website where you can see examples of all kinds of different map projections, including cylindrical, conical and azimuthal projections, go to **www.usborne-quicklinks.com**

Creating maps

Many sources are used to create maps. These include satellite images and aerial photographs. Cartographers often visit the area to be mapped, where they take many extra measurements.

In addition, cartographers use statistics, such as population figures, from censuses and other documents. As the maps are being made, many people check them to make sure they are accurate and up to date.

Map projections

Cartographers can't draw maps that show the world exactly as it is, because it is impossible to show a curved surface on a flat map without distorting (stretching or squashing) some areas. A representation of the Earth on a map is called a projection. Projections are worked out using complex mathematics.

There are three basic types of projections – cylindrical, conical and azimuthal, but there are also variations on these. They all distort the Earth's surface in some way, either by altering the shapes or sizes of areas of land or the distance between places.

A cartographer uses an electronic distance measurer to check the measurements of an area of land.

Cylindrical projections

A cylindrical projection is similar to the image created by wrapping a piece of paper around a globe to form a cylinder and then shining a light inside the globe. The shapes of countries would be projected onto the paper. Near the middle they would be accurate, but farther away they would be distorted.

Cartographers often alter the basic cylindrical projection to make the distortion less obvious in certain areas, but they can never make a map that is completely accurate.

This picture of a piece of paper wrapped around a globe illustrates how a cylindrical projection is made.

Below is a type of cylindrical projection called the Mercator projection, which was invented in 1596 by a cartographer named Gerardus Mercator. It makes countries the right shape, but makes those near the poles too big.

This cylindrical projection makes countries the right size in relation to each other, but some parts are too long. The projection was created in 1973 by Arno Peters. It is called the Peters Projection.

Conical projections

A conical projection is similar to the image you would get if you wrapped a cone of paper around part of a globe, then shone a light inside the globe. Where the cone touches the globe, the projection will be most accurate.

This picture of a cone of paper over a globe illustrates how a conical projection is made.

This is a conical projection. The land nearest the top is the most distorted in shape.

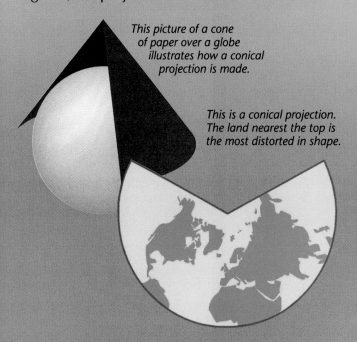

Azimuthal projections

An azimuthal projection is like an image made by holding paper in front of a globe, and shining a light through it. Land projected onto the middle of the paper would be accurate, but areas farther away would be distorted.

This picture of a piece of paper placed in front of a globe illustrates how an azimuthal projection is made.

This is an azimuthal projection. The farther away land is from the middle, the more distorted it is.

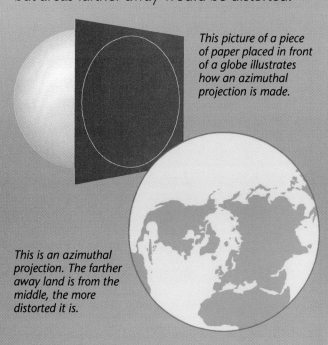

THEMATIC MAPS

Maps that represent information on particular themes, like the ones on these pages, are known as thematic maps. They help you to identify patterns and make comparisons between the features of different areas.

Earth's resources

The Earth contains all kinds of useful resources. Rocks and minerals can be used as building materials, and fuels such as coal, oil and gas contain energy that can be turned into heat and electricity.

Countries with large amounts of natural resources can become very rich. For example, Saudi Arabia, in western Asia, has large oil and gas reserves, which it exports all over the world.

This is an oil field, where oil is extracted from the ground using pumps. It is then piped to refineries and turned into products such as motor fuel.

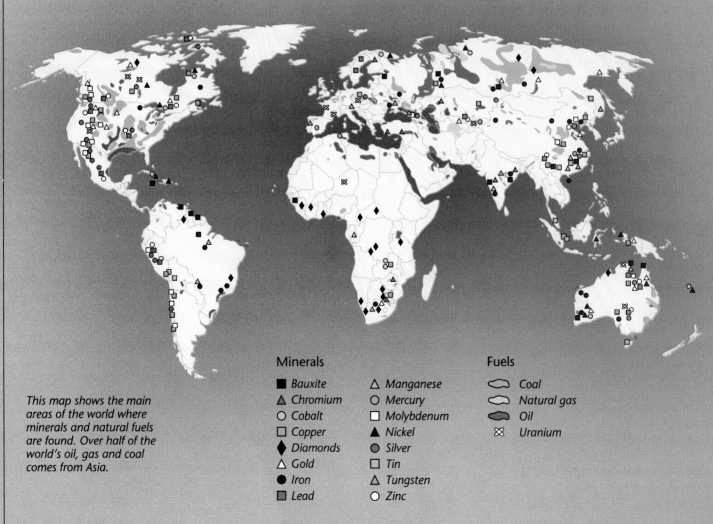

This map shows the main areas of the world where minerals and natural fuels are found. Over half of the world's oil, gas and coal comes from Asia.

Minerals

■ Bauxite	△ Manganese
▲ Chromium	○ Mercury
○ Cobalt	□ Molybdenum
□ Copper	▲ Nickel
◆ Diamonds	● Silver
△ Gold	□ Tin
● Iron	△ Tungsten
▨ Lead	○ Zinc

Fuels

⌒ Coal
⌒ Natural gas
◗ Oil
⊗ Uranium

Different climates

The long-term or typical pattern of weather in a particular area is known as its climate. Climates vary across the world and depend largely on each area's latitude. The hottest parts of the world are those closest to the Equator.

Climate is also affected by other factors, such as wind and the height of the land. Oceans influence climate too – places near the sea normally have a milder, wetter climate than areas farther inland.

On this map, land is divided into five climate types. Dry areas are generally hot, but temperatures there can fall very low too. Some dry places, such as the Gobi Desert in eastern Asia, are extremely cold in winter.

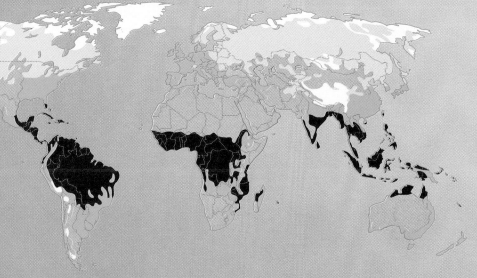

- ☐ Polar
- ☐ Cold
- ☐ Temperate
- ☐ Dry
- ■ Tropical

World population

There are more than six billion people in the world, and the population is still growing. Experts think it may reach more than nine billion by 2050. The number of people living in a given area is known as its population density. Europe and Asia are the most densely populated continents in the world. About a third of the world's population lives in China and India alone.

Internet link

For a link to a website where you can discover how many people there were on Earth when you were born, and find out about the effects of population growth, go to **www.usborne-quicklinks.com**

This map shows the average population density by country. The shading indicates the number of people per sq km (0.386 sq miles).

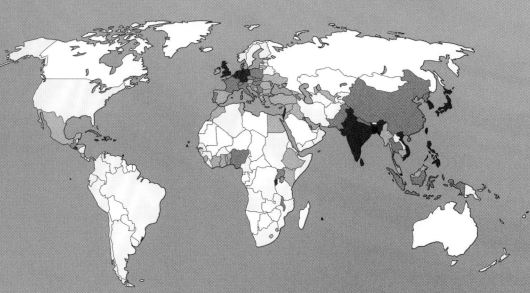

- ■ Over 500 people
- ■ 200–500 people
- ■ 100–200 people
- ☐ 50–100 people
- ☐ 10–50 people
- ☐ Fewer than 10 people

HOW TO USE THE MAPS

Each continent section in this atlas begins with a political map showing the whole continent. The rest of the maps are larger scale maps showing the various parts of the continent in more detail.

Political maps

The shading on the political maps in this atlas is there to help you see clearly the different countries that make up each continent. The main purpose of these maps is to show country borders and capital cities. Alongside them there are facts and figures about the continents and their features.

This is a section of the political map of South America. You can see the whole map on pages 28–29.

Environmental maps

The majority of the maps in this atlas are environmental maps, like the one on the right. The shading on these maps shows different types of land, or environments, such as desert, mountain or wetland.

The main key on the opposite page shows what the different shading means. It also shows the symbols used to represent towns, cities and other features. There is a smaller key on each environmental map repeating the most important information from this key.

Finding places

To find a particular place or feature on the environmental maps, look up its name in the index on pages 98–111. Its page number and grid reference is given next to the name. You can find out how to use the grid on page 9.

The map on the right is part of the environmental map of the U.S.A. The numbered labels at the top explain some important features of these maps.

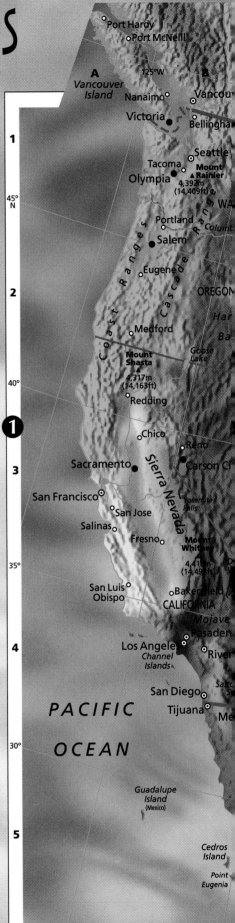

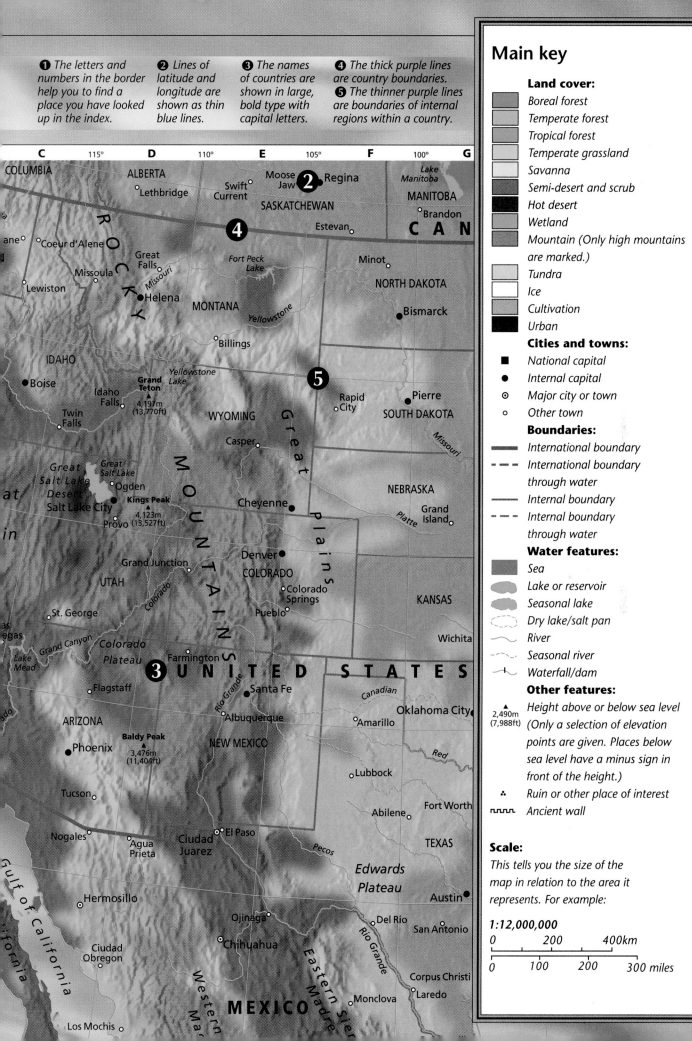

① *The letters and numbers in the border help you to find a place you have looked up in the index.*

② *Lines of latitude and longitude are shown as thin blue lines.*

③ *The names of countries are shown in large, bold type with capital letters.*

④ *The thick purple lines are country boundaries.*

⑤ *The thinner purple lines are boundaries of internal regions within a country.*

Main key

Land cover:

- Boreal forest
- Temperate forest
- Tropical forest
- Temperate grassland
- Savanna
- Semi-desert and scrub
- Hot desert
- Wetland
- Mountain (Only high mountains are marked.)
- Tundra
- Ice
- Cultivation
- Urban

Cities and towns:

- ■ National capital
- ● Internal capital
- ⊙ Major city or town
- ○ Other town

Boundaries:

- International boundary
- International boundary through water
- Internal boundary
- Internal boundary through water

Water features:

- Sea
- Lake or reservoir
- Seasonal lake
- Dry lake/salt pan
- River
- Seasonal river
- Waterfall/dam

Other features:

- ▲ 2,490m (7,988ft) *Height above or below sea level (Only a selection of elevation points are given. Places below sea level have a minus sign in front of the height.)*
- ⁕ Ruin or other place of interest
- ⊓⊓⊓ Ancient wall

Scale:

This tells you the size of the map in relation to the area it represents. For example:

1:12,000,000

0   200   400km

0   100   200   300 miles

GREENLAND
(Denmark)

ICELAND

NOR

ALASKA
(U.S.A.)

Arctic Circle

CANADA

UNITED
KINGDOM

DENM

IRELAND

NEX

BELG

LU

SW

FRANC

UNITED STATES
OF AMERICA

Azores
(Portugal)

PORTUGAL

MOROCCO

TUN

Tropic of Cancer

Canary Islands
(Spain)

ALGER

Hawaiian
Islands
(U.S.A.)

WESTERN SAHARA
(Morocco)

20°
N

THE BAHAMAS

MEXICO

CUBA

DOMINICAN
REPUBLIC

MALI

NIC

HAITI

CAPE VERDE

BELIZE

JAMAICA

SENEGAL

GUATEMALA

HONDURAS

Caribbean Sea

DOMINICA

THE GAMBIA
GUINEA-BISSAU

BURKINA
FASO

EL SALVADOR

NICARAGUA

BENIN

GUINEA

TOGO

NIGE

COSTA RICA

TRINIDAD AND TOBAGO

SIERRA LEONE

GHANA

PANAMA

VENEZUELA

GUYANA

LIBERIA

EQUATO

PACIFIC

SURINAM

GU

COLOMBIA

FRENCH GUIANA
(France)

SAO TOME AND
PRINCIPE

OCEAN

Galapagos Islands
(Ecuador)

Equator

ECUADOR

ATLANTIC

KIRIBATI

OCEAN

BRAZIL

Cook
Islands
(New Zealand)

PERU

French
Polynesia
(France)

BOLIVIA

20°
S

Tropic of Capricorn

Pitcairn
Islands
(U.K.)

PARAGUAY

CHILE

URUGUAY

ARGENTINA

1:80,000,000

0   1,000   2,000   3,000   4,000 5,000km

0   1,000   2,000   3,000 miles

Falkland Islands
(U.K.)

South Georgia
(U.K.)

40°

Antarctic Circle

Weddell
Sea

80°

160°   140°   120°   100°   80°   60°   40°   20° W   0°

160° 140° 120° 100° 80° 60° 40° 20° W

80°

Beaufort Sea

Victoria Island

Queen Elizabeth Islands

Ellesmere Island

Baffin Bay

Greenland

Greenland Sea

Arctic Circle

Alaska

Mount McKinley
▲
6,194m
(20,321ft)

Yukon

Baffin Island

Iceland

60°

Gulf of Alaska

Hudson Bay

Labrador Sea

British Isles

No...
...Se...

Aleutian Islands

Rocky Mountains

Great plains

NORTH AMERICA

Great Lakes

Appalachian Mountains

Newfoundland

40°

Azores

Canary Islands

Atlas Mount...

Tropic of Cancer

Mississippi

Gulf of Mexico

20°
N

Hawaiian Islands

Cuba

Greater Antilles

West Indies

Lesser Antilles

Cape Verde Islands

Caribbean Sea

Guiana Highlands

0°
Equator

Galapagos Islands

Amazon Basin *Amazon*

Selvas

ATLANTIC

P o l y n e s i a

PACIFIC

OCEAN

Andes

SOUTH AMERICA

OCEAN

Tahiti

20°
S

Tropic of Capricorn

...Desert

Easter Island

Aconcagua
6,959m
(22,831ft)

Pampas

40°

Patagonia

1:80,000,000

0   1,000   2,000   3,000   4,000 5,000km

Falkland Islands

0   1,000   2,000   3,000 miles

South Georgia

Cape Horn

60°

Antarctic Circle

Antarctic Peninsula

Weddell Sea

80°

160° 140° 120° 100° 80° 60° 40° 20° W

ARCTIC OCEAN

Svalbard
North Cape
Barents Sea
Novaya Zemlya
Kara Sea
Severnaya Zemlya
Laptev Sea
New Siberia Islands
80°
East Siberian Sea
Arctic Circle
60°

Scandinavia
North European Plain
Ural Mountains
Ob
Yenisey
Siberia
Verkhoyansk Range
Sea of Okhotsk
Kamchatka Peninsula

EUROPE
Danube
Black Sea
Volga
Mount Elbrus
5,642m
(18,510ft)
Aral Sea
Caspian Sea
ASIA
Altai Mountains
Lake Baikal
Gobi Desert
Huang He (Yellow)
Hokkaido
Sea of Japan
Honshu
40°

Mediterranean Sea
Zagros Mountains
Himalayas
Ganges
Mount Everest
8,850m
(29,035ft)
Chang Jiang (Yangtze)
Yellow Sea
East China Sea
Taiwan
Tropic of Cancer
20° N

Red Sea
Arabian Peninsula
Arabian Sea
Deccan Plateau
Bay of Bengal
Mekong
South China Sea
Philippine Islands
Micronesia
PACIFIC OCEAN

AFRICA
Ethiopian Highlands
Sri Lanka
Celebes Sea
Borneo
OCEAN

Lake Victoria
Congo Basin
Kilimanjaro
5,895m
(19,340ft)
Seychelles
INDIAN
Sumatra
Greater Sunda Islands
Java
New Guinea
Mount Wilhelm
4,509m
(14,793ft)
Melanesia
Solomon Islands
Equator

Rift Valley
Comoro Islands
OCEAN
Lesser Sunda Islands
Arafura Sea
Coral Sea

Namib Desert
Kalahari Desert
Madagascar
Mauritius
Reunion
Great Sandy Desert
Great Barrier Reef
New Caledonia
Fiji Islands
20° S
Tropic of Capricorn

Drakensberg
AUSTRALASIA AND OCEANIA
Great Victoria Desert
Great Dividing Range
Tasman Sea
North Island
40°

Cape of Good Hope
Kerguelen Islands
Tasmania
South Island

SOUTHERN OCEAN
60°
Antarctic Circle

ANTARCTICA
See page 15 for key.
80°

20° E   40°   60°   80°   100°   120°   140°   160°   180°

NORTH AMERICA

The name "North America" can be used to mean several different things. In this atlas, North America includes Greenland, Canada, the U.S.A., the Caribbean, and the countries of Central America, which run along the narrow strip of land between the U.S.A. and South America. The continent has over 20 countries, including Canada, the second-largest country in the world.

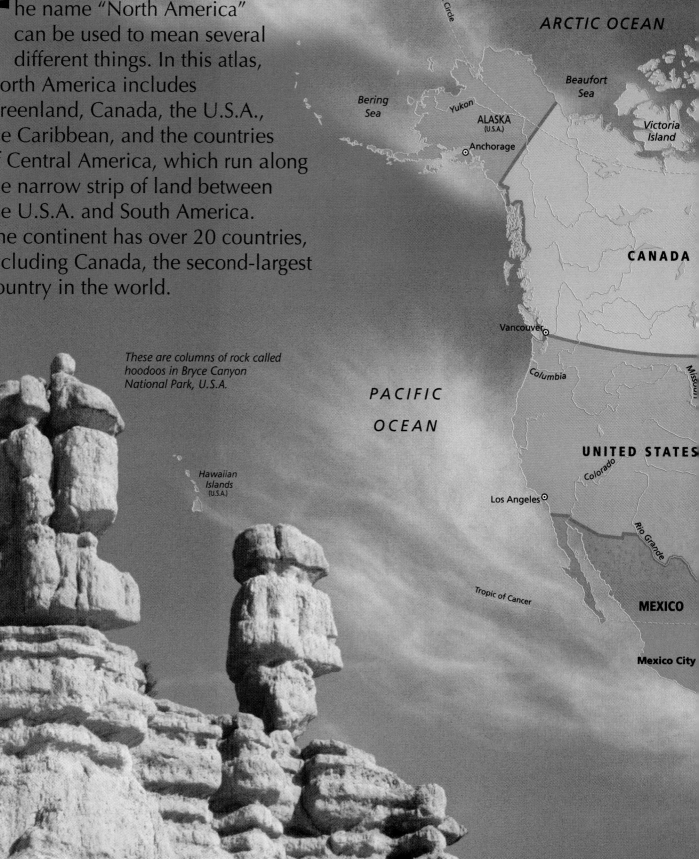

These are columns of rock called hoodoos in Bryce Canyon National Park, U.S.A.

Arctic Circle

ARCTIC OCEAN

Beaufort Sea

Bering Sea

Yukon

ALASKA
(U.S.A.)

Anchorage

Victoria Island

CANADA

Vancouver

Columbia

Missouri

PACIFIC OCEAN

Hawaiian Islands
(U.S.A.)

UNITED STATES

Colorado

Los Angeles

Rio Grande

Tropic of Cancer

MEXICO

Mexico City

The shading on this map is there to help you see clearly the different countries that make up the continent.

Ilesmere
land

GREENLAND
(Denmark)

Arctic Circle

ueen
zabeth
ands

Baffin
Island

Godthab

Hudson
Bay

Newfoundland

St. Lawrence

Montreal
Ottawa

Great
Lakes

Chicago

New York

Washington D.C.

F AMERICA

Mississippi

Houston

THE
BAHAMAS

Tropic of Cancer

Gulf of
Mexico

Havana
CUBA

Puerto Rico
(U.S.A.)

Guadeloupe
(France)

HAITI

DOMINICAN
REPUBLIC

DOMINICA
Martinique (France)

BARBADOS

JAMAICA

TRINIDAD
AND TOBAGO

BELIZE

Caribbean Sea

GUATEMALA

HONDURAS

EL SALVADOR

NICARAGUA

COSTA RICA

PANAMA

ATLANTIC

OCEAN

Internet link

For a link to a website where you can find out about the history and geography of each U.S. state, go to
www.usborne-quicklinks.com

Facts

Total land area 22,656,190 sq km (8,745,289 sq miles)

Total population 487 million

Biggest city Mexico City, Mexico

Biggest country Canada *9,970,610 sq km (3,849,653 sq miles)*

Smallest country Saint Kitts and Nevis *269 sq km (104 sq miles)*

Highest mountain Mount McKinley, Alaska, U.S.A. *6,194m (20,321ft)*

Longest river Mississippi/Missouri, U.S.A. *6,019km (3,741 miles)*

Biggest lake Lake Superior, between the U.S.A. and Canada *82,414 sq km (31,820 sq miles)*

Highest waterfall Yosemite Falls, on the Yosemite Creek, California, U.S.A. *739m (2,425ft)*

Biggest desert Great Basin Desert, U.S.A. *492,000 sq km (190,000 sq miles)*

Biggest island Greenland *2,175,600 sq km (840,000 sq miles)*

Main mineral deposits Silver, gold, copper, lead, zinc, graphite, molybdenum, nickel

Main fuel deposits Oil, coal, natural gas, uranium

The bald eagle is the national bird of the U.S.A. It is not really bald, but has white feathers on its head.

21

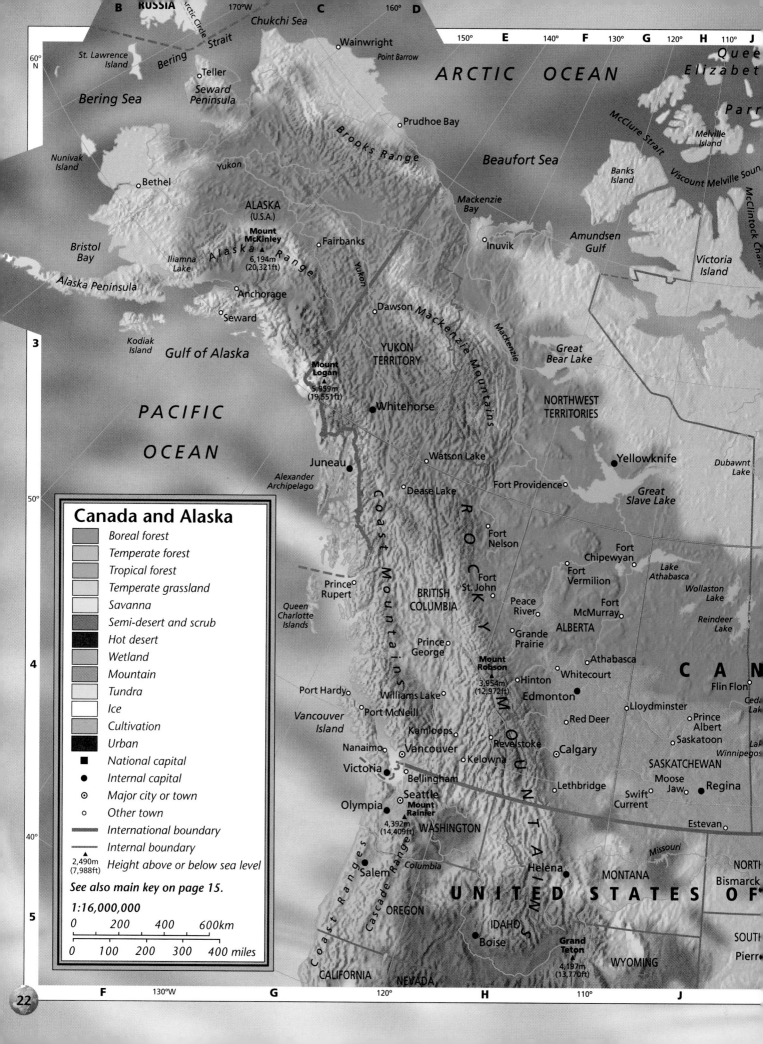

Coordinates (top): K 90° L 80° M 70° N 60° P 50° Q 40° R 30° S

Inset map (Aleutian Islands):

A 180° B 170°W C

Bering Sea

Shishaldin Volcano
2,857m
(9,372ft) ▲ Unimak Island

Attu Island
Near Islands

A l e u t i a n   I s l a n d s

Fox Islands
Unalaska Island

Andreanof Islands

Umnak Island

Rat Islands

Atka Island

Umnak Island

Same scale as main map

55°N

Main map labels:

Ellesmere Island

Islands

Devon Island

Baffin Bay

Lancaster Sound

Somerset Island

Boothia Peninsula

Gulf of Boothia

Baffin Island

Cumberland Peninsula

Nettilling Lake

Davis Strait

GREENLAND
(Denmark)

Cape Farewell

Labrador Sea

ATLANTIC OCEAN

Melville Peninsula

Foxe Basin

Foxe Peninsula

Amadjuak Lake

Iqaluit

Southampton Island

Hudson Strait

Cape Chidley

NUNAVUT

Ivujivik

Ungava Peninsula

Ungava Bay

Nain

Makkovik

Cartwright

Kuujjuaq

NEWFOUNDLAND

All islands within Hudson Bay, James Bay and Ungava Bay lie within Nunavut.

Inukjuak

Happy Valley-Goose Bay

Smallwood Reservoir

Churchill Falls

Churchill

Hudson Bay

Belcher Islands

Labrador City

Gander

St. John's

Newfoundland

Fort Severn

La Grande Reservoir

QUEBEC

Manicouagan Reservoir

Anticosti Island

Corner Brook

MANITOBA

Thompson

James Bay

Radisson

Baie-Comeau

Gaspe

St. Pierre and Miquelon (France)

Gulf of St. Lawrence

Sydney

Lake Winnipeg

Fort Albany

Waskaganish

Lake Mistassini

Chicoutimi

Bathurst

Edmundston

PRINCE EDWARD ISLAND

Moncton

Charlottetown

Grand Rapids

ONTARIO

NEW BRUNSWICK

Halifax

winnipeg

Lake anitoba

Val-d'Or

Quebec

Fredericton

Saint John

NOVA SCOTIA

innipeg

Lake of the Woods

Dryden

Lake Nipigon

Kirkland Lake

Trois-Rivieres

MAINE

Yarmouth

Kenora

Marathon

Montreal

St. Lawrence

Augusta

DAKOTA

Thunder Bay

Lake Superior

Ottawa

Montpelier

NEW HAMPSHIRE

Concord

MINNESOTA

Sudbury

North Bay

Boston

MERICA

Sault Ste. Marie

Huntsville

Kingston

VERMONT

Albany

MASSACHUSETTS

Providence

St. Paul

MICHIGAN

Owen Sound

Lake Ontario

NEW YORK

Hartford

RHODE ISLAND

Minneapolis

WISCONSIN

Lake Huron

Toronto

Niagara Falls

CONNECTICUT

Madison

Mississippi

Lansing

Hamilton

Lake Erie

Harrisburg

New York

Trenton

NEW JERSEY

Lake Michigan

London

Buffalo

Philadelphia

DAKOTA

Detroit

Erie

PENNSYLVANIA

Dover

Chicago

ILLINOIS

Windsor

Cleveland

Pittsburgh

Annapolis

DELAWARE

INDIANA

OHIO

Columbus

Washington D.C.

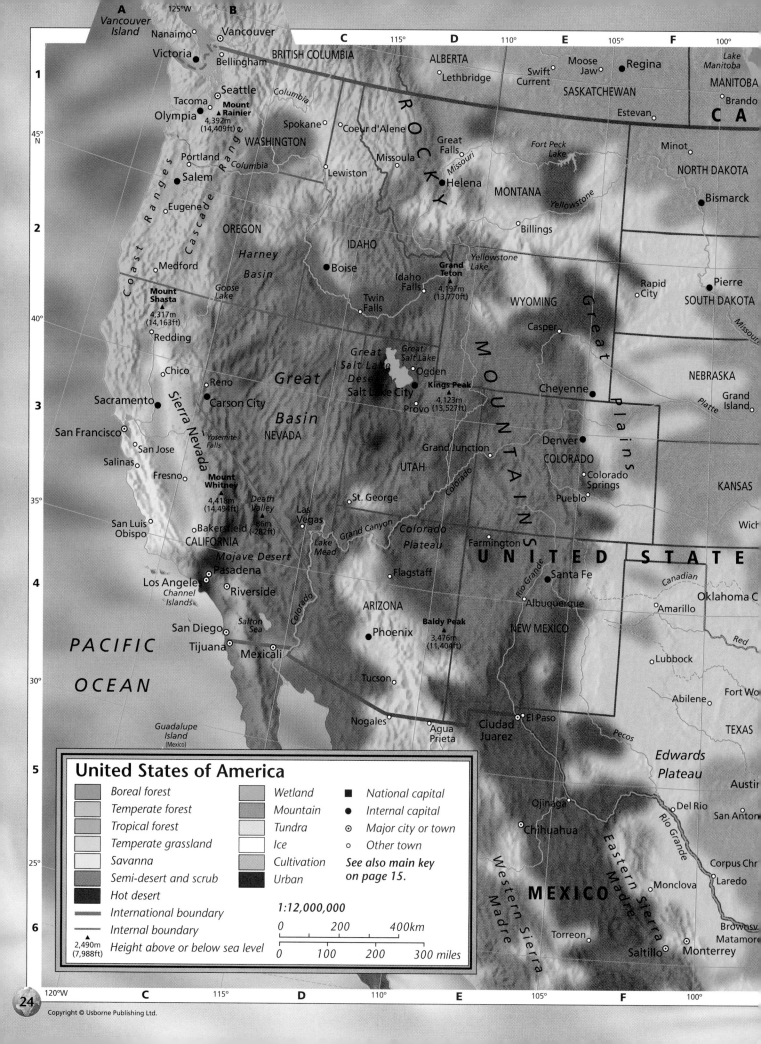

H 95° 90° J 85° K 80° L 75° M 70° N 65°

1

Chicoutimi · Bathurst

Lake Winnipeg · Edmundston

·nnipeg · Kenora · Dryden · ONTARIO · NEW BRUNSWICK

Lake Nipigon · Gouin Reservoir · QUEBEC

D · A · Lake of the Woods · Marathon · Val-d'Or · Quebec · Fredericton

·and Forks · Thunder Bay · Kirkland Lake · Trois-Rivieres · MAINE · Saint John

·argo · Duluth · Cabonga Reservoir · Ottawa · Montreal · St. Stephen · 45° N

Sault Ste. Marie · Sudbury · St. Lawrence · Bangor

MINNESOTA · North Bay · Huntsville · Montpelier · NEW HAMPSHIRE · Portland · Augusta · Gulf of Maine · 2

Owen Sound · Kingston · NEW YORK · Concord · Boston

Minneapolis · St. Paul · Lake Huron · Toronto · Lake Ontario · Albany · MASSACHUSETTS · Cape Cod

Green Bay · MICHIGAN · Hamilton · Syracuse · Springfield · Providence

WISCONSIN · Mississippi · Grand Rapids · London · Niagara Falls · Rochester · Hartford · RHODE ISLAND · 40°

·oux Falls · Milwaukee · Lansing · Buffalo · Jamestown · CONNECTICUT

Madison · Lake Michigan · Detroit · Lake Erie · Erie · Newark · New York

Sioux City · Rockford · Windsor · Toledo · Cleveland · PENNSYLVANIA · Trenton · Philadelphia

Cedar Rapids · Chicago · South Bend · Fort Wayne · Pittsburgh · Harrisburg · NEW JERSEY · Atlantic City

·Omaha · Des Moines · IOWA · Peoria · INDIANA · OHIO · Columbus · Baltimore · Dover · DELAWARE · 3

Lincoln · ILLINOIS · Indianapolis · Cincinnati · WEST VIRGINIA · MARYLAND · Annapolis

Quincy · Springfield · Ohio · Frankfort · Charleston · Washington D.C.

·Kansas City · Jefferson City · St. Louis · Evansville · Lexington · VIRGINIA · Charlottesville · Richmond

·opeka · MISSOURI · Cape Girardeau · KENTUCKY · Roanoke · Virginia Beach · 35°

Springfield · Kentucky Lake · Knoxville · Greensboro · Raleigh · Cape Hatteras

·rkansas · OF · A M E R I C A · Ozark Plateau · Nashville · Tennessee · NORTH CAROLINA · ATLANTIC · 4

·Tulsa · Jonesboro · TENNESSEE · Chattanooga · Appalachian Mountains · Charlotte

OKLAHOMA · Little Rock · Memphis · Huntsville · Clark Hill Lake · Columbia · OCEAN

·Dallas · ARKANSAS · Tupelo · Birmingham · Atlanta · SOUTH CAROLINA

Texarkana · Greenville · Tuscaloosa · Macon · Charleston

Shreveport · MISSISSIPPI · Meridian · ALABAMA · GEORGIA · Columbus · Savannah

·aco · Vicksburg · Jackson · Montgomery · Albany

Sam Rayburn Reservoir · LOUISIANA · Hattiesburg · Valdosta · Jacksonville

Beaumont · Toledo Bend Reservoir · Baton Rouge · Mobile · Tallahassee · Daytona Beach

·ouston · Galveston · New Orleans · Pensacola · Apalachee Bay · Orlando · Cape Canaveral

Mississippi Delta · FLORIDA · Grand Bahama · THE BAHAMAS · 25°

Gulf of Mexico · Tampa · St. Petersburg · Lake Okeechobee · Freeport City · Abaco · Eleuthera

Fort Lauderdale · Nassau · Cat Island

Key West · The Everglades · Miami · Andros · Tropic of Cancer · 6

Florida Keys · Long Island

Straits of Florida · Acklins Island

H 95° 90° J · Matanzas · CUBA · Santa Clara · Ciego de Avila · 75°

Havana · Cienfuegos · Camaguey · 25

Pinar del Rio · 80°

Hawaiian Islands inset:
160°W · Same scale as main map

Hawaiian Islands

Kauai · Oahu · Molokai

Honolulu · Kahului · Maui · 7 · 30°

HAWAII (U.S.A.) · 4,205m (13,796ft)▲ · 20°N

20°N · Hilo

PACIFIC OCEAN · 8

160°W · P · Hawaii · 155°

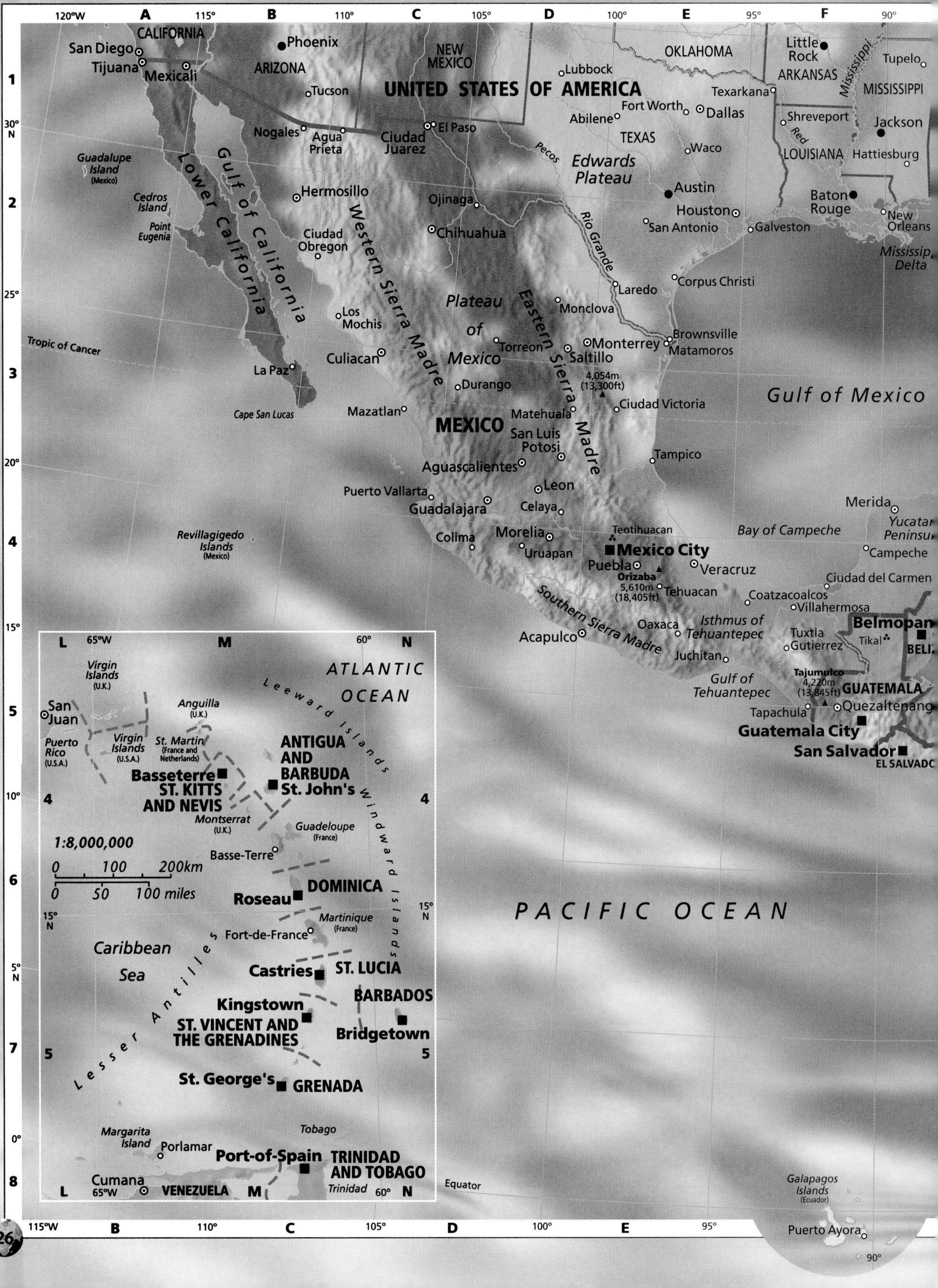
120°W
A
115°
B
110°
C
105°
D
100°
E
95°
F
90°
1
2
3
4
5
6
7
8
30° N
25°
20°
15°
10°
5° N
0°
CALIFORNIA
San Diego
Tijuana
Mexicali
Phoenix
ARIZONA
Tucson
NEW MEXICO
UNITED STATES OF AMERICA
OKLAHOMA
Lubbock
Little Rock
ARKANSAS
Mississippi
Tupelo
MISSISSIPPI
Texarkana
Fort Worth
Dallas
Abilene
TEXAS
Shreveport
Red
Jackson
LOUISIANA
Hattiesburg
Nogales
Agua Prieta
Ciudad Juarez
El Paso
Pecos
Edwards Plateau
Waco
Guadalupe Island (Mexico)
Cedros Island
Point Eugenia
Lower California
Gulf of California
Hermosillo
Western Sierra Madre
Ojinaga
Chihuahua
Rio Grande
Austin
Houston
San Antonio
Galveston
Baton Rouge
New Orleans
Mississippi Delta
Ciudad Obregon
Corpus Christi
Laredo
Plateau of Mexico
Eastern Sierra Madre
Monclova
Los Mochis
Tropic of Cancer
Torreon
Monterrey
Saltillo
Brownsville
Matamoros
Culiacan
La Paz
Durango
4,054m (13,300ft)
Ciudad Victoria
Gulf of Mexico
Cape San Lucas
Mazatlan
Matehuala
MEXICO
San Luis Potosi
Tampico
Aguascalientes
Leon
Puerto Vallarta
Guadalajara
Celaya
Merida
Revillagigedo Islands (Mexico)
Colima
Morelia
Uruapan
Teotihuacan
Mexico City
Bay of Campeche
Yucatan Peninsula
Campeche
Puebla
Orizaba
5,610m (18,405ft)
Veracruz
Tehuacan
Ciudad del Carmen
Coatzacoalcos
Villahermosa
Southern Sierra Madre
Acapulco
Oaxaca
Isthmus of Tehuantepec
Tuxtla Gutierrez
Tikal
Belmopan
BELIZE
Juchitan
Gulf of Tehuantepec
Tajumulco 4,220m (13,845ft)
GUATEMALA
Tapachula
Quezaltenango
Guatemala City
San Salvador
EL SALVADOR
PACIFIC OCEAN
L
65°W
M
60°
N
Virgin Islands (U.K.)
ATLANTIC OCEAN
Leeward Islands
San Juan
Anguilla (U.K.)
Puerto Rico (U.S.A.)
Virgin Islands (U.S.A.)
St. Martin (France and Netherlands)
ANTIGUA AND BARBUDA
St. John's
Basseterre
ST. KITTS AND NEVIS
Montserrat (U.K.)
Windward Islands
Guadeloupe (France)
1:8,000,000
0 100 200km
0 50 100 miles
Basse-Terre
DOMINICA
Roseau
15° N
Martinique (France)
Fort-de-France
Caribbean Sea
Lesser Antilles
Castries
ST. LUCIA
Kingstown
BARBADOS
ST. VINCENT AND THE GRENADINES
Bridgetown
St. George's
GRENADA
Tobago
Margarita Island
Porlamar
Port-of-Spain
TRINIDAD AND TOBAGO
Cumana
VENEZUELA
Trinidad
Equator
Galapagos Islands (Ecuador)
115°W
Puerto Ayora
90°

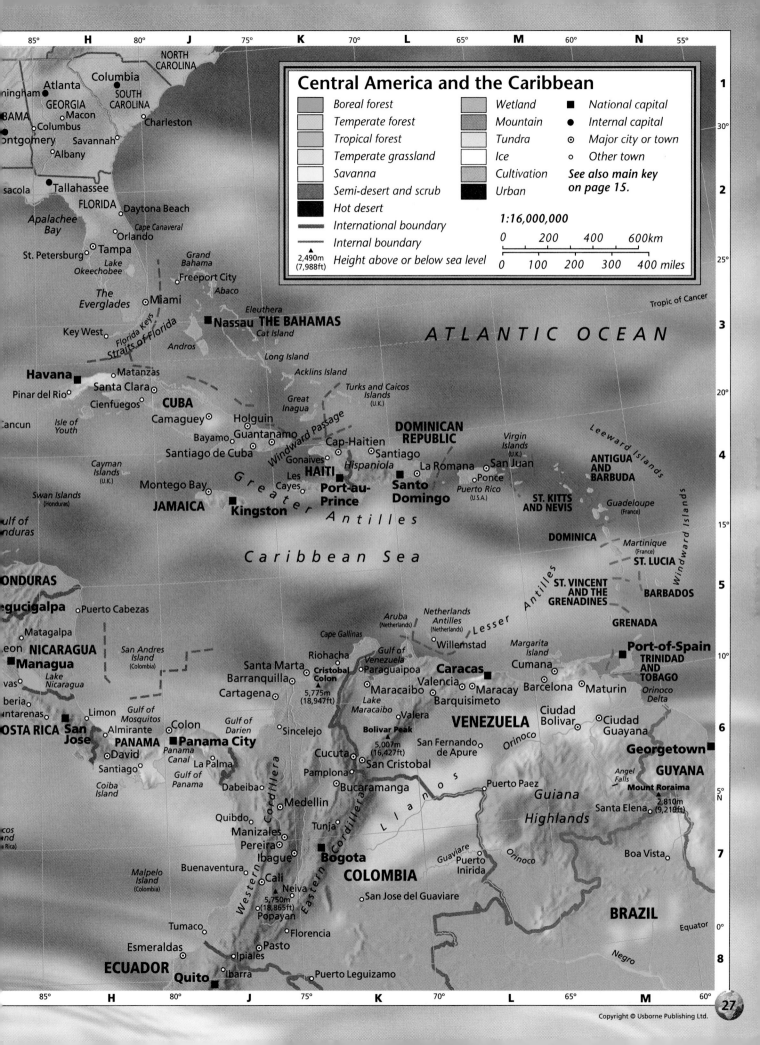

SOUTH AMERICA

South America is made up of 12 independent countries, along with French Guiana, which belongs to France. The continent's biggest and most industrialized country is Brazil, which covers about half of the total land. Brazil is also home to half of South America's population.

This is a guanaco. Guanacos are members of the camel family that live in South America. Guanaco hair is used to make textiles.

Caribbean Sea

Caracas

VENEZUELA

Medellin○ ■ Bogota

COLOMBIA Orinoco

Equator

Galapagos
Islands
(Ecuador)

Quito
ECUADOR
Guayaquil○

Mar

PERU

Lima ■

BOLIVIA
La Paz ■

■ Sucr

Tropic of Capricorn

CHILE

PACIFIC

OCEAN

Santiago ■ ○Mendoza

ARGENTI

Cape Horn

Drake Passa

The shading on this map is there to help you see clearly the different countries that make up the continent.

orgetown
Paramaribo
ANA ■ Cayenne
URINAM FRENCH
GUIANA
(France)

azon

Equator

Recife

B R A Z I L

■ Brasilia

Belo Horizonte

Parana

RAGUAY

Sao Paulo Rio de Janeiro

Asuncion

Tropic of Capricorn

Porto Alegre

RUGUAY
Montevideo
enos Aires

ATLANTIC

OCEAN

alkland Islands
(U.K.)

Internet link

For a link to a website where you can discover the sights and sounds of the Amazon rainforest, go to
www.usborne-quicklinks.com

This is a red-eyed tree frog. These frogs live in rainforests in South and Central America.

Facts

Total land area 17,866,130 sq km (6,898,113 sq miles)

Total population 346 million

Biggest city Sao Paulo, Brazil

Biggest country Brazil 8,547,400 sq km (3,300,151 sq miles)

Smallest country Surinam 163,270 sq km (63,039 sq miles)

Highest mountain Aconcagua, Argentina 6,959m (22,831ft)

Longest river Amazon, mainly in Brazil 6,440km (4,000 miles)

Biggest lake Lake Maracaibo, Venezuela 13,312 sq km (5,140 sq miles)

Highest waterfall Angel Falls, on the Churun River, Venezuela 979m (3,212ft)

Biggest desert Patagonian Desert, Argentina 673,000 sq km (260,000 sq miles)

Biggest island Tierra del Fuego 46,360 sq km (17,900 sq miles)

Main mineral deposits Copper, tin, molybdenum, bauxite, emeralds

Main fuel deposits Oil, coal

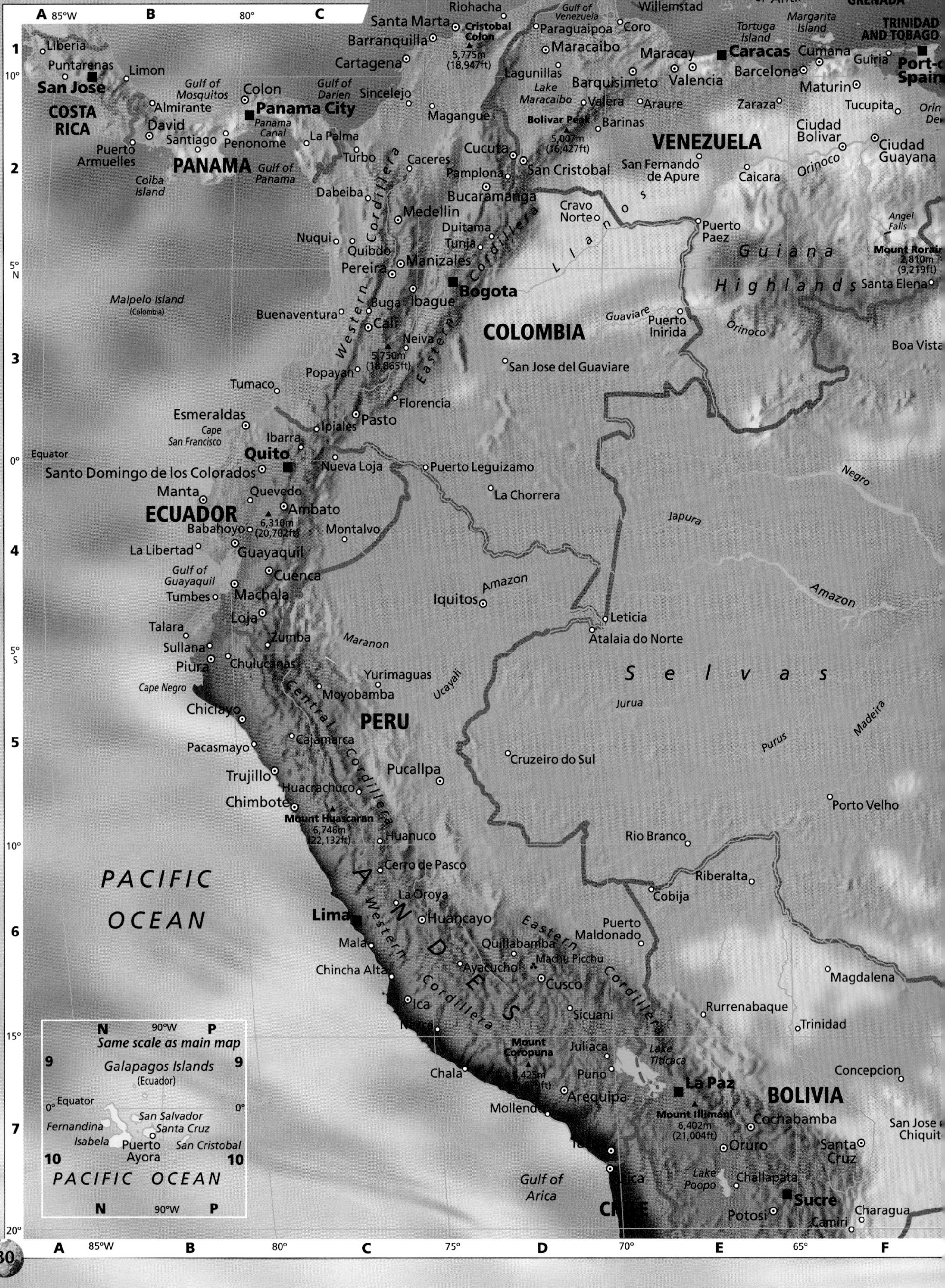
A 85°W
B
80°
C
75°
D
70°
E
65°
F
1
2
3
4
5
6
7
10°
5° N
0°
5° S
10°
15°
20°
Equator
Cape Gallinas
Aruba (Netherlands)
Netherlands Antilles (Netherlands)
Lesser Antilles
GRENADA
TRINIDAD AND TOBAGO
Port-of-Spain
Riohacha
Willemstad
Gulf of Venezuela
Coro
Paraguaipoa
Santa Marta
Cristobal Colon
5,775m (18,947ft)
Barranquilla
Cartagena
Maracaibo
Lagunillas
Lake Maracaibo
Barquisimeto
Maracay
Valencia
Caracas
Tortuga Island
Margarita Island
Cumana
Barcelona
Guiria
Maturin
Tucupita
Zaraza
Araure
Valera
Barinas
Bolivar Peak
5,007m (16,427ft)
VENEZUELA
Ciudad Bolivar
Ciudad Guayana
Orinoco
Caicara
San Fernando de Apure
San Cristobal
Cucuta
Pamplona
Bucaramanga
Cravo Norte
Llanos
Puerto Paez
Angel Falls
Mount Roraima
2,810m (9,219ft)
Guiana Highlands
Santa Elena
Liberia
Puntarenas
San Jose
Limon
COSTA RICA
Gulf of Mosquitos
Almirante
Colon
Panama City
Panama Canal
Gulf of Darien
Sincelejo
Magangue
David
Santiago
Penonome
Puerto Armuelles
PANAMA
Gulf of Panama
Coiba Island
La Palma
Turbo
Caceres
Dabeiba
Medellin
Duitama
Tunja
Nuqui
Quibdo
Pereira
Manizales
Bogota
Malpelo Island (Colombia)
Buenaventura
Buga
Ibague
Cali
Western Cordillera
Central Cordillera
Eastern Cordillera
Neiva
5,750m (18,865ft)
COLOMBIA
Guaviare
Puerto Inirida
Orinoco
Boa Vista
Popayan
San Jose del Guaviare
Tumaco
Florencia
Pasto
Ipiales
Esmeraldas
Cape San Francisco
Ibarra
Quito
Nueva Loja
Puerto Leguizamo
Santo Domingo de los Colorados
Negro
Manta
Quevedo
La Chorrera
Ambato
ECUADOR
6,310m (20,702ft)
Babahoyo
Montalvo
Japura
La Libertad
Guayaquil
Gulf of Guayaquil
Cuenca
Amazon
Tumbes
Machala
Iquitos
Loja
Leticia
Talara
Atalaia do Norte
Zumba
Maranon
Sullana
Piura
Chulucanas
Selvas
Cape Negro
Yurimaguas
Ucayali
Moyobamba
Jurua
Chiclayo
PERU
Madeira
Cajamarca
Purus
Pacasmayo
Cruzeiro do Sul
Pucallpa
Trujillo
Huacrachuco
Porto Velho
Chimbote
Mount Huascaran
6,746m (22,132ft)
Huanuco
Rio Branco
PACIFIC OCEAN
Cerro de Pasco
Riberalta
ANDES
La Oroya
Cobija
Lima
Huancayo
Puerto Maldonado
Mala
Quillabamba
Machu Picchu
Chincha Alta
Ayacucho
Cusco
Magdalena
Ica
Sicuani
Rurrenabaque
Nazca
Trinidad
Mount Coropuna
Juliaca
Lake Titicaca
Chala
Puno
Concepcion
Arequipa
La Paz
BOLIVIA
Mollendo
Mount Illimani
6,402m (21,004ft)
Cochabamba
San Jose de Chiquitos
Oruro
Santa Cruz
Gulf of Arica
Lake Poopo
Challapata
Sucre
Arica
CHILE
Potosi
Charagua
Camiri
N
90°W
P
Same scale as main map
9
Galapagos Islands (Ecuador)
0° Equator
San Salvador
Fernandina
Santa Cruz
Isabela
Puerto Ayora
San Cristobal
10
PACIFIC OCEAN

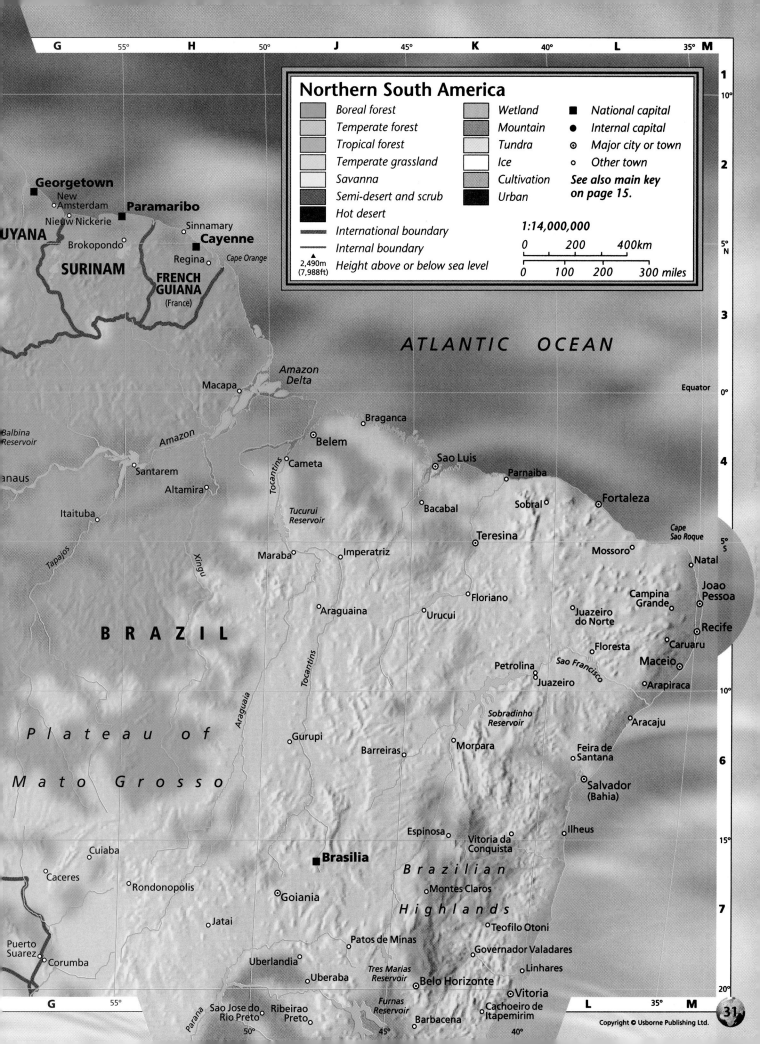

Northern South America

Boreal forest	Wetland	■	National capital
Temperate forest	Mountain	●	Internal capital
Tropical forest	Tundra	⊙	Major city or town
Temperate grassland	Ice	○	Other town
Savanna	Cultivation		
Semi-desert and scrub	Urban		
Hot desert			

See also main key on page 15.

International boundary
Internal boundary

▲ 2,490m (7,988ft) Height above or below sea level

1:14,000,000

0   200   400km

0   100   200   300 miles

ATLANTIC OCEAN

Georgetown
New Amsterdam
Nieuw Nickerie
UYANA
Brokopondo
SURINAM
Paramaribo
Sinnamary
Cayenne
Regina
Cape Orange
FRENCH GUIANA (France)

Equator

Macapa
Amazon Delta

Balbina Reservoir
Amazon
anaus
Santarem
Altamira
Itaituba
Tapajos

Cameta
Belem
Braganca
Sao Luis
Parnaiba
Sobral
Fortaleza
Cape Sao Roque

Tocantins
Bacabal
Teresina
Mossoro
Natal

Tucurui Reservoir
Maraba
Imperatriz
Floriano
Urucui
Campina Grande
Joao Pessoa

Xingu
Araguaina
Juazeiro do Norte
Recife
Floresta
Caruaru

BRAZIL

Tocantins
Petrolina
Juazeiro
Sao Francisco
Maceio
Arapiraca

Araguaia
Gurupi
Barreiras
Morpara
Sobradinho Reservoir
Aracaju

Plateau of
Mato Grosso
Feira de Santana

Salvador (Bahia)

Espinosa
Vitoria da Conquista
Ilheus

Cuiaba
Caceres
Rondonopolis
Brasilia
Brazilian
Montes Claros
Highlands

Jatai
Goiania

Teofilo Otoni

Puerto Suarez
Corumba

Patos de Minas
Governador Valadares
Linhares

Uberlandia
Uberaba
Tres Marias Reservoir
Belo Horizonte
Vitoria
Cachoeiro de Itapemirim

Parana
Sao Jose do Rio Preto
Ribeirao Preto
Furnas Reservoir
Barbacena

Grid coordinates (top)
1   2   3   4   5   6

10°S   15°   20°   25°   30°

Grid rows (left)
L   K   J   H   G   F   E   D

40°   45°   50°   55°   60°   65°   70°W

Countries
PERU
BOLIVIA
BRAZIL
PARAGUAY
URUGUAY
CHILE
Buenos

Major labels
Plateau of Mato Grosso
Brazilian Highlands
Gran Chaco
ANDES
Atacama Desert
Tropic of Capricorn
Tropic of

Cities and features
Sobradinho Reservoir
Feira de Santana
Ilheus
Vitoria da Conquista
Morpara
Espinosa
Teofilo Otoni
Linhares
Montes Claros
Governador Valadares
Cachoeiro de Itapemirim
Campos
Barreiras
Vitoria
Belo Horizonte
Barbacena
Juiz de Fora
Macae
Nova Iguacu
Rio de Janeiro
Brasilia
Tres Marias Reservoir
Furnas Reservoir
Mount Aguilhas Negras 2,787m (9,144ft)
Sao Paulo
Patos de Minas
Pocos de Caldas
Goiania
Uberaba
Ribeirao Preto
Araraquara
Campinas
Tocantins
Gurupi
Uberlandia
Sao Jose do Rio Preto
Presidente Prudente
Marilia
Itapetininga
Curitiba
Paranagua
Jatai
Londrina
Guarapuava
Itajai
Florianopolis
Araguaia
Rondonopolis
Campo Grande
Dourados
Ponta Pora
Cascavel
Foz do Iguacu
Eldorado
Passo Fundo
Santa Maria
Caxias do Sul
Criciuma
Porto Alegre
Patos Lagoon
Rio Grande
Caceres
Cuiaba
Corumba
Puerto Suarez
Concepcion
Iguacu Falls
Ciudad del Este
Posadas
Uruguaiana
Bage
Pelotas
Melo
Mirim Lake
Minas
San Jose de Chiquitos
Santa Cruz
Pedro Juan Caballero
Paraguay
Asuncion
Villarrica
Encarnacion
Rivera
Tacuarembo
Paysandu
Durazno
Trinidad
Magdalena
Concepcion
PARAGUAY
Formosa
Corrientes
Reconquista
Concordia
Salto
Gualeguaychu
San Nicolas de los Arroyos
Santa Fe
Cochabamba
Sucre
Camiri
Charagua
Pilcomayo
Tartagal
San Salvador de Jujuy
San Miguel de Tucuman
Santiago del Estero
Salado
Parana
San Francisco
Venado Tuerto
Rosario
Villa Maria
Rufino
Rio Branco
Riberalta
Cobija
Puerto Maldonado
Rurrenabaque
La Paz
Mount Illimani 6,402m (21,004ft)
Lake Titicaca
Lake Poopo
Oruro
Challapata
Potosi
Uyuni
Tupiza
Tarija
Camiri
Salta
Catamarca
La Rioja
Cordoba
Merlo
San Luis
Villa Mercedes
Juliaca
Puno
Tacna
Arica
Iquique
Pica
Calama
San Pedro de Atacama
Antofagasta
Mount Ojos del Salado 6,908m (22,664ft)
Aconcagua 6,959m (22,831ft)
San Juan
Mendoza
Taltal
Chanaral
Copiapo
Vallenar
Coquimbo
Ovalle
Illapel
Valparaiso
Santiago
Rancagua
Ollague
Oruro
Rio Cuarto
San Jose
Challapata
Goiania

Page number
32

Southern South America

Boreal forest
Temperate forest
Tropical forest
Temperate grassland
Savanna
Semi-desert and scrub
Hot desert
Wetland
Mountain
Tundra
Ice
Cultivation
Urban

■ National capital
● Internal capital
◉ Major city or town
○ Other town
━ International boundary
━ Internal boundary
▲ 2,490m (7,988ft) Height above or below sea level

See also main key on page 15.

1:14,000,000

0   100   200   300   400km
0   100   200   300 miles

ARGENTINA

ANDES

Pampas

ATLANTIC OCEAN

PACIFIC OCEAN

SOUTHERN OCEAN

Linares
Chillan
Concepcion
Los Angeles
Victoria
Temuco
Valdivia
Osorno
Puerto Montt
Chiloe Island
Quellon
Chonos Archipelago
Coihaique
Mount San Valentin 4,058m (13,313ft)
Gulf of Penas
Wellington Island
Puerto Natales
Punta Arenas
Porvenir
Tierra del Fuego
Ushuaia
Cape Horn
Drake Passage

Santa Rosa
Zapala
Neuquen
General Roca
Esquel
Colorado
San Antonio Oeste
Viedma
Bahia Blanca
Tres Arroyos
Blanca Bay
Gulf of San Matias
Valdes Peninsula
Rawson
Gulf of San Jorge
Comodoro Rivadavia
Cape Tres Puntas
Puerto Deseado
San Julian
Lake Buenos Aires
Lake Viedma
Lake Argentino
Grande Bay
Rio Gallegos
Strait of Magellan
Rio Grande
Olavarria
Tandil
Dolores
Necochea
Mar del Plata
Cape San Antonio

Falkland Islands (U.K.)
East Falkland
West Falkland
Stanley

South Georgia (U.K.)
Grytviken

South Sandwich Islands (U.K.)

South Orkney Islands (U.K.)

South Shetland Islands (U.K.)
King George Island
Elephant Island

AUSTRALASIA AND OCEANIA

Australasia is made up of Australia, New Zealand and Papua New Guinea. Oceania is a collection of over 20,000 islands stretching out into the Pacific Ocean.

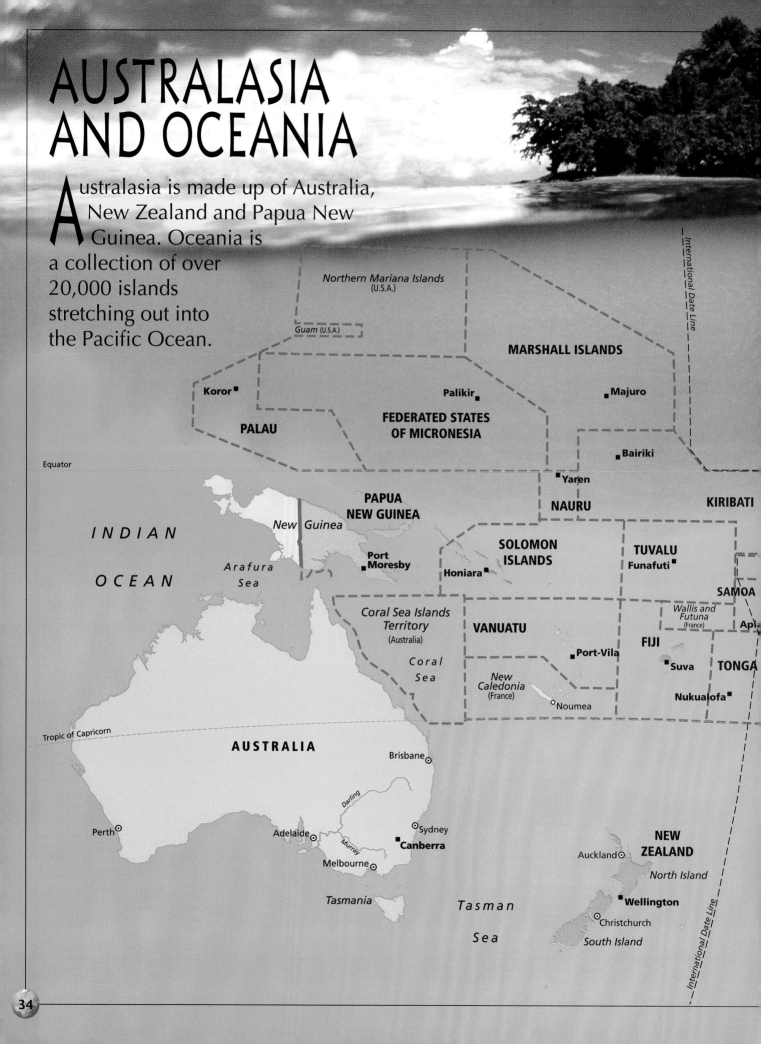

International Date Line

Northern Mariana Islands (U.S.A.)

Guam (U.S.A.)

MARSHALL ISLANDS

Koror ■
PALAU

Palikir ■
FEDERATED STATES OF MICRONESIA

■ Majuro

■ Bairiki

Equator

■ Yaren
NAURU

KIRIBATI

INDIAN

OCEAN

New Guinea

PAPUA NEW GUINEA

Port ■ Moresby

Arafura Sea

SOLOMON ISLANDS

Honiara ■

TUVALU
Funafuti ■

SAMOA

Wallis and Futuna (France)

Apia ■

Coral Sea Islands Territory (Australia)

VANUATU

Coral Sea

New Caledonia (France)

Port-Vila ■

FIJI

■ Suva

TONGA

Nuku'alofa ■

○ Noumea

Tropic of Capricorn

AUSTRALIA

Brisbane ○

Darling

Perth ○

Adelaide ○

Murray

○ Sydney

■ **Canberra**

Melbourne ○

Tasmania

Tasman Sea

NEW ZEALAND

Auckland ○

North Island

■ **Wellington**

○ Christchurch

South Island

International Date Line

This small island belongs to Papua New Guinea.

PACIFIC OCEAN

The shading on this map is there to help you see clearly the different countries that make up the continent.

Line Islands

Equator

okelau
(N Zealand)

American
Samoa
(U.S.A.)

Marquesas
Islands

Niue
(New Zealand)

Society
Islands

French
Polynesia
(France)

Cook Islands
(New Zealand)

Pitcairn Islands
(U.K.)

Tropic of Capricorn

Internet link

For a link to a website where you can take a virtual tour of New Zealand and find out all about its sights, cities and landscape, go to **www.usborne-quicklinks.com**

Facts

Total land area 8,564,400 sq km (3,306,715 sq miles)

Total population 31 million

Biggest city Sydney, Australia

Biggest country Australia 7,686,850 sq km (2,967,124 sq miles)

Smallest country Nauru 21 sq km (8 sq miles)

Highest mountain Mount Wilhelm, Papua New Guinea 4,509m (14,793ft)

Longest river Murray/Darling River, Australia 3,718km (2,310 miles)

Biggest lake Lake Eyre, Australia 9,000 sq km (3,470 sq miles)

Highest waterfall Sutherland Falls, on the Arthur River, New Zealand 580m (1,904ft)

Biggest desert Great Victoria Desert, Australia 388,500 sq km (150,000 sq miles)

Biggest island New Guinea 800,000 sq km (309,000 sq miles) (Australia is counted as a continental land mass and not as an island.)

Main mineral deposits Iron, nickel, precious stones, lead, bauxite

Main fuel deposits Oil, coal, uranium

The Moorish idol fish is found in shallow waters throughout the Pacific. It has very bold stripes and a long, distinctive snout.

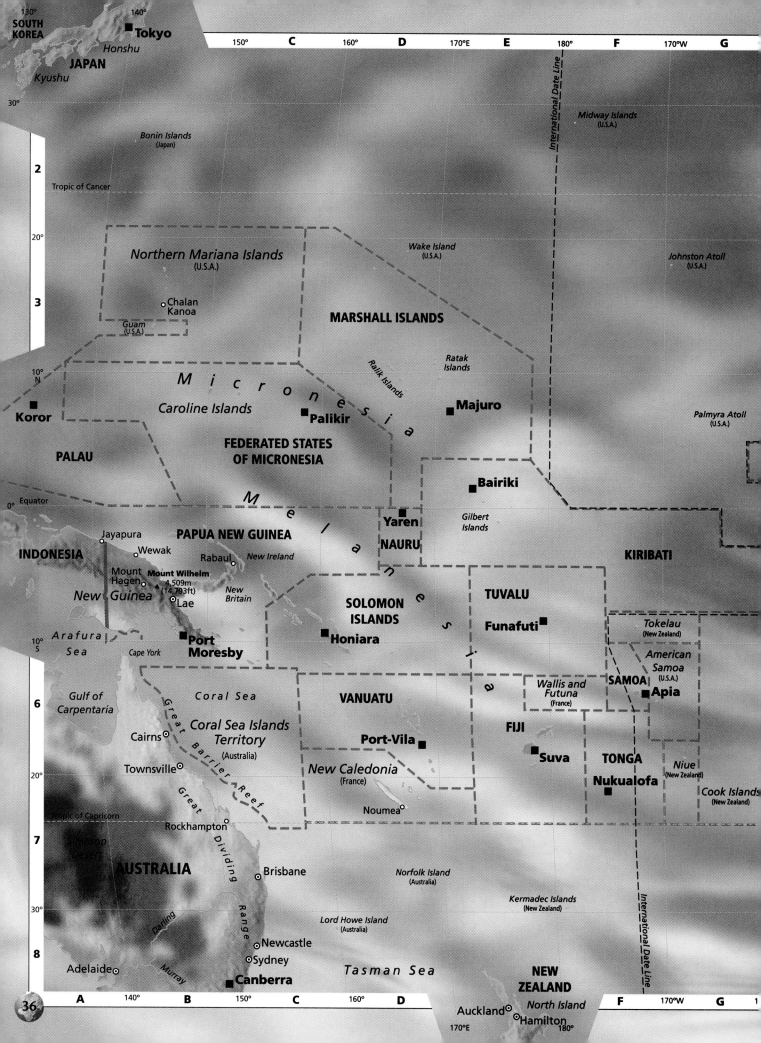

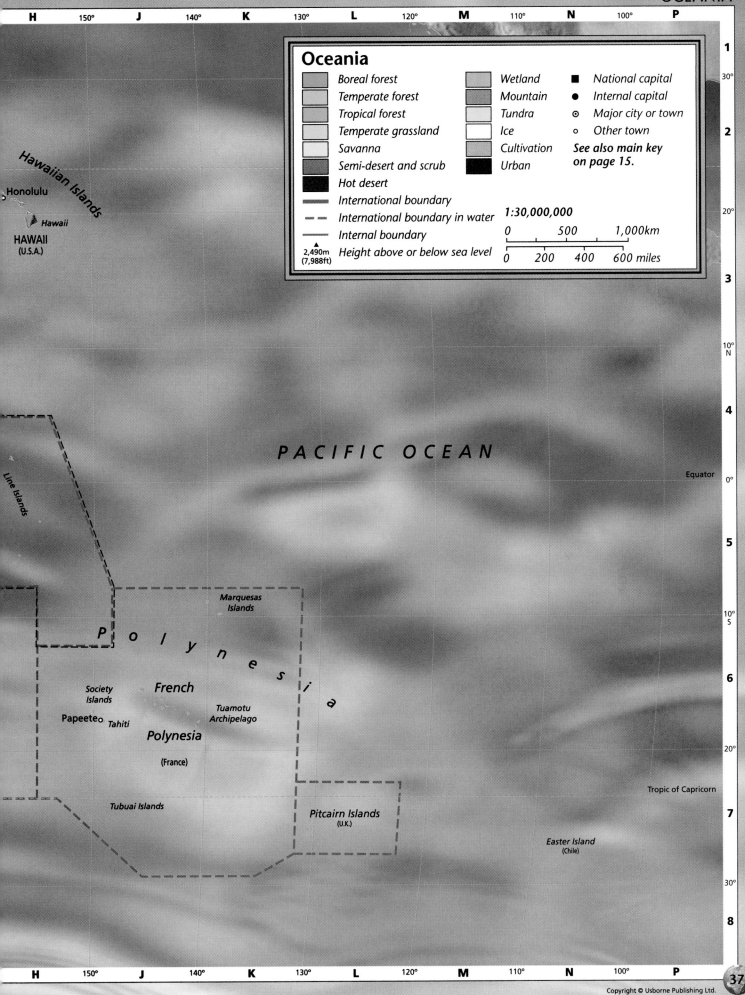

H 150° **J** 140° **K** 130° **L** 120° **M** 110° **N** 100° **P**

Oceania

Boreal forest		Wetland	■	National capital
Temperate forest		Mountain	●	Internal capital
Tropical forest		Tundra	⊙	Major city or town
Temperate grassland		Ice	○	Other town
Savanna		Cultivation		
Semi-desert and scrub		Urban	**See also main key**	
Hot desert			**on page 15.**	

International boundary
- - - International boundary in water
International boundary
▲ 2,490m (7,988ft) Height above or below sea level

1:30,000,000

0   500   1,000km

0   200   400   600 miles

Hawaiian Islands

Honolulu

Hawaii

HAWAII
(U.S.A.)

Line Islands

PACIFIC OCEAN

Equator

Marquesas
Islands

P o l y n e s i a

Society
Islands

French

Tuamotu
Archipelago

Papeete○   Tahiti

Polynesia

(France)

Tubuai Islands

Pitcairn Islands
(U.K.)

Easter Island
(Chile)

Tropic of Capricorn

1   30°

2   20°

3

  10° N

4

  0°

5

  10° S

6

  20°

7

  30°

8

H 150° **J** 140° **K** 130° **L** 120° **M** 110° **N** 100° **P**

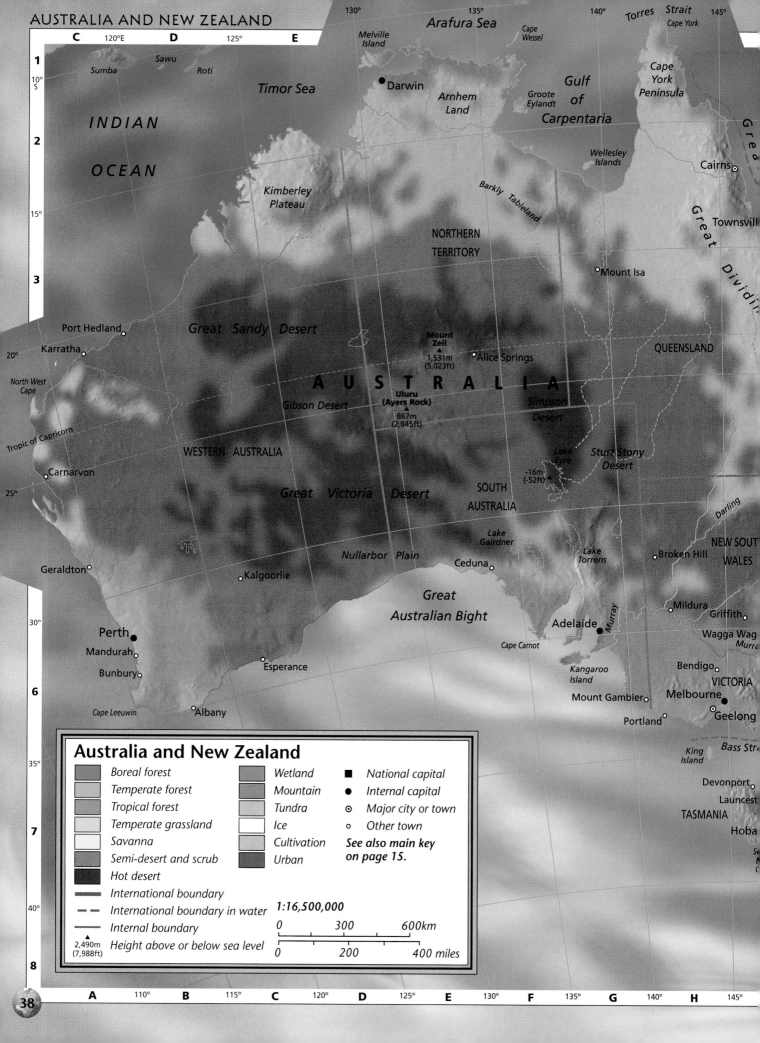

Map labels

Torres Strait
Arafura Sea
Cape York
Cape Wessel
Melville Island
Timor Sea
Darwin
Arnhem Land
Gulf of Carpentaria
Groote Eylandt
Cape York Peninsula
INDIAN OCEAN
Sumba
Sawu
Roti
Wellesley Islands
Cairns
Kimberley Plateau
Barkly Tableland
Townsvill
NORTHERN TERRITORY
Great Dividin
Mount Isa
QUEENSLAND
Great Sandy Desert
Port Hedland
Karratha
Mount Zeil
1,531m
(5,023ft)
Alice Springs
A U S T R A L I A
North West Cape
Gibson Desert
Uluru
(Ayers Rock)
867m
(2,845ft)
Simpson Desert
Tropic of Capricorn
Carnarvon
WESTERN AUSTRALIA
Lake Eyre
-16m
(-52ft)
Sturt Stony Desert
Great Victoria Desert
SOUTH AUSTRALIA
Darling
Geraldton
Great Australian Bight
Nullarbor Plain
Lake Gairdner
Lake Torrens
Broken Hill
NEW SOUT WALES
Kalgoorlie
Ceduna
Mildura
Griffith
Perth
Great Australian Bight
Adelaide
Murray
Wagga Wag
Murra
Mandurah
Esperance
Cape Carnot
Bendigo
Bunbury
Kangaroo Island
VICTORIA
Cape Leeuwin
Albany
Mount Gambier
Melbourne
Portland
Geelong
King Island
Bass Str
Devonport
Launcest
TASMANIA
Hoba

Legend

Australia and New Zealand

- Boreal forest
- Temperate forest
- Tropical forest
- Temperate grassland
- Savanna
- Semi-desert and scrub
- Hot desert

- Wetland
- Mountain
- Tundra
- Ice
- Cultivation
- Urban

- ■ National capital
- ● Internal capital
- ⊙ Major city or town
- ○ Other town

See also main key on page 15.

International boundary
- - - International boundary in water
Internal boundary
▲ 2,490m (7,988ft) Height above or below sea level

1:16,500,000

0   300   600km

0   200   400 miles

1

10°
S

Coral Sea

SOLOMON ISLANDS

*Rennell
Island*

*Santa Cruz
Islands*

TUVALU

2

*Coral Sea
Islands
Territory*

(Australia)

VANUATU

Banks Islands

*Espiritu
Santo*

Luganville

FIJI

15°

Malakula

Efate ■ **Port-Vila**

Vanua Levu

Lautoka

Barrier Reef

*Chesterfield
Islands*

New Caledonia

(France)

Viti Levu ■ **Suva**

Mackay

khampton

Gladstone

Range

Noumea

*Loyalty
Islands*

20°

Bundaberg

Fraser Island

Gympie

Tropic of Capricorn

4

Toowoomba

● Brisbane

○ Gold Coast

PACIFIC OCEAN

Moree

Grafton

Norfolk Island
(Australia)

25°

Armidale

Dubbo

Port Macquarie

*Lord Howe
Island*
(Australia)

5

Great Dividing Range

Newcastle

● Sydney

○ Wollongong

Kermadec Islands
(New Zealand)

30°

■ **Canberra**
AUSTRALIAN CAPITAL
TERRITORY

**Mount
osciuszko**

229m
313ft)

North Cape

6

Tasman Sea

Whangarei

*Flinders
Island*

Auckland

North Island

35°

Hamilton

East Cape

New Plymouth

Rotorua

*Lake
Taupo*

Napier

*Cape
Farewell*

7

Nelson

■ **Wellington**

South Island

**Aoraki
(Mount Cook)**
▲
3,754m
(12,316ft)

○ Christchurch

**NEW
ZEALAND**

Sutherland Falls

40°

Cape Providence

Invercargill

○ Dunedin

Chatham Islands
(New Zealand)

Stewart Island

South West Cape

8

ASIA

Asia is the largest continent and has over 40 countries, including Russia, the biggest country in the world. As well as large land masses, it has thousands of islands and inlets, giving it over 160,000km (100,000 miles) of coastline. Turkey and Russia are partly in Europe and partly in Asia, but both are shown in full on the map on the right.

Internet link

For a link to a website where you can read about the Great Wall of China and see a photo of it taken from space, go to www.usborne-quicklinks.com

This is a type of Chinese boat called a junk, sailing in the sea off Singapore.

The shading on this map is there to help you see clearly the different countries that make up the continent.

ARCTIC OCEAN

Franz Josef Land

Novaya Zemlya

Barents Sea

Kara Sea

Moscow

R U S

Volga

Black Sea

Ankara

TURKEY

GEORGIA

Caspian Sea

Astana

KAZAKHSTAN

Aral Sea

CYPRUS

ARMENIA

AZERBAIJAN

UZBEKISTAN

Bishkek

LEBANON   SYRIA
Beirut   Damascus

TURKMENISTAN

Tashkent

KYRGYZSTAN

Jerusalem   Amman
ISRAEL
JORDAN

Baghdad

Ashgabat

Dushanbe

TAJIKISTAN

IRAQ

Tehran

IRAN

Kabul

AFGHANISTAN

Islamabad

Tropic of Cancer

KUWAIT

SAUDI
ARABIA

BAHRAIN
QATAR

Riyadh   Doha

Abu Dhabi

Muscat

UNITED ARAB
EMIRATES

PAKISTAN

Indus

New Delhi

NEPAL
Kathmandu

Ganges

Thimp

BANGLADES

Sana

YEMEN

OMAN

Arabian Sea

INDIA

Socotra (Yemen)

Bay of Bengal

INDIAN OCEAN

Equator

SRI LANKA

Sri Jayewardenepura Kotte

Colombo

MALDIVES
Male

Wrangel Island
Bering Sea
New Siberia Islands
East Siberian Sea
Severnaya Zemlya
Laptev Sea
Lena
Sea of Okhotsk
A
Lake Baikal
Hokkaido
Ulan Bator ■
MONGOLIA
Sea of Japan
NORTH KOREA
JAPAN
Pyongyang ■
■ **Tokyo**
■ **Seoul**
Beijing ■
Honshu
SOUTH KOREA
Huang He (Yellow)
C H I N A
East China Sea
Chang Jiang (Yangtze)
Tropic of Cancer
■ **Taipei**
TAIWAN
PACIFIC
TAN
Irrawaddy
OCEAN
aka
BURMA (MYANMAR)
LAOS
Hanoi ■
PHILIPPINES
Vientiane ■
Mekong
South China Sea
ngoon
THAILAND
VIETNAM
■ **Manila**
CAMBODIA
Philippine Sea
Bangkok ■
Andaman Islands (India)
Phnom Penh ■
Nicobar Islands (India)
BRUNEI
Equator
MALAYSIA
New Guinea
Kuala Lumpur ■
SINGAPORE
Borneo
Celebes
Sumatra
INDONESIA
Dili
Arafura Sea
■ **Jakarta**
EAST TIMOR
Java

Facts

Total land area 44,537,920 sq km (17,196,090 sq miles)

Total population 3.8 billion (including all of Russia)

Biggest city Tokyo, Japan

Biggest country Russia *Total area: 17,075,200 sq km (6,592,735 sq miles) Area of Asiatic Russia: 12,780,800 sq km (4,934,667 sq miles)*

Smallest country Maldives *300 sq km (116 sq miles)*

Highest mountain Mount Everest, Nepal/China border *8,850m (29,035ft)*

Longest river Chang Jiang (Yangtze), China *6,380km (3,964 miles)*

Biggest lake Caspian Sea, western Asia *370,999 sq km (143,243 sq miles)*

Highest waterfall Jog Falls, on the Sharavati River, India *253m (830ft)*

Biggest desert Arabian Desert, in and around Saudi Arabia *2,230,000 sq km (900,000 sq miles)*

Biggest island Borneo *751,100 sq km (290,000 sq miles)*

Main mineral deposits Zinc, mica, tin, chromium, iron, nickel

Main fuel deposits Oil, coal, uranium, natural gas

These are lotus flowers, a type of water lily. In China they are associated with purity and for Buddhists they are sacred.

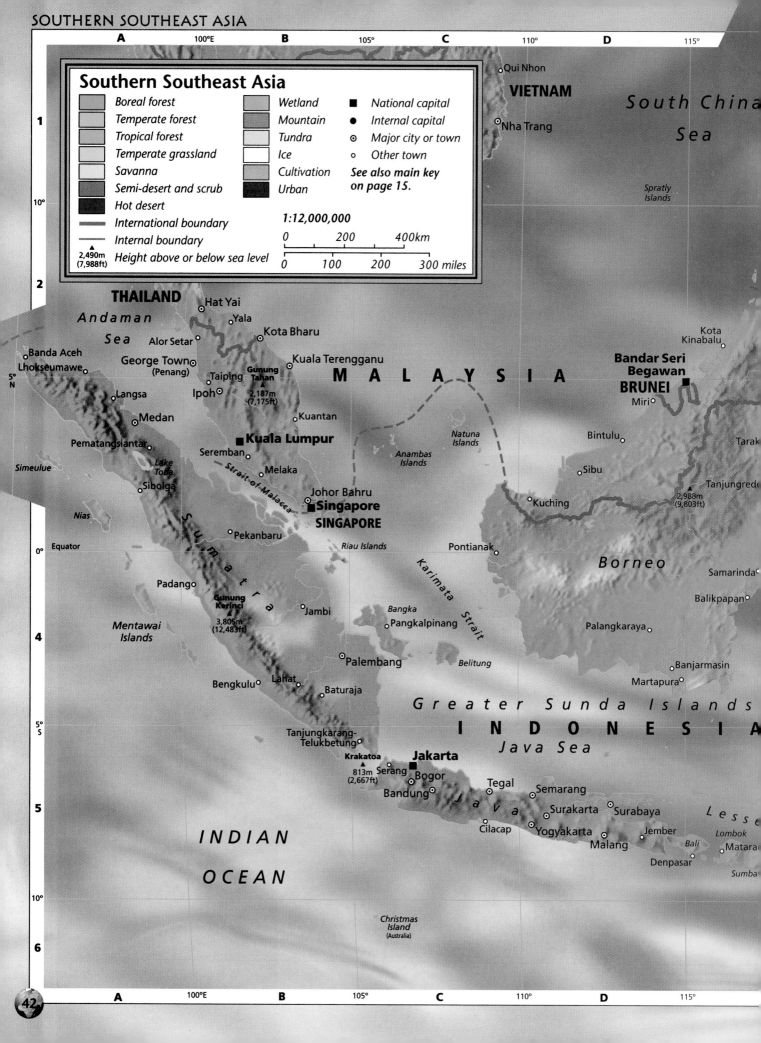

Southern Southeast Asia

Boreal forest		■	National capital
Temperate forest	Wetland	●	Internal capital
Tropical forest	Mountain	◉	Major city or town
Temperate grassland	Tundra	○	Other town
Savanna	Ice		
Semi-desert and scrub	Cultivation	**See also main key**	
Hot desert	Urban	**on page 15.**	

International boundary
Internal boundary

▲ 2,490m (7,988ft) Height above or below sea level

1:12,000,000

0	200	400km
0	100	200	300 miles

Qui Nhon

VIETNAM

South China Sea

Nha Trang

Spratly Islands

THAILAND

Andaman Sea

Hat Yai
Yala
Kota Bharu
Kuala Terengganu

Banda Aceh
Lhokseumawe

George Town (Penang)
Alor Setar

Taiping
Gunung Tahan 2,187m (7,175ft)

Kota Kinabalu

Bandar Seri Begawan
BRUNEI
Miri

M A L A Y S I A

Ipoh
Kuantan

Langsa

Medan

Kuala Lumpur

Seremban

Natuna Islands

Bintulu

Tarak

Pematangsiantar

Lake Toba
Sibolga

Melaka

Simeulue

Anambas Islands

Sibu

Tanjungrede 2,988m (9,803ft)

Johor Bahru

Nias

Singapore
SINGAPORE

Kuching

Borneo

Pekanbaru

Samarinda

Equator 0°

Riau Islands

Pontianak

Padang

Karimata Strait

Balikpapan

Gunung Kerinci 3,805m (12,483ft)

Jambi

Bangka
Pangkalpinang

Palangkaraya

Mentawai Islands

4

S u m a t r a

Banjarmasin
Martapura

Palembang

Belitung

Bengkulu
Lahat
Baturaja

G r e a t e r   S u n d a   I s l a n d s

I N D O N E S I A

5° S

Tanjungkarang-Telukbetung

Java Sea

Krakatoa 813m (2,667ft)

Jakarta
Serang
Bogor

Tegal

Semarang

L e s s e

Bandung

J a v a

Surakarta
Surabaya

INDIAN

Cilacap

Yogyakarta

Jember

Lombok

Malang

Bali

Matara

OCEAN

Denpasar

Sumba

10°

Christmas Island (Australia)

6

A   90°E   B   95°   C   100°   D   105°   E

Brahmaputra

Lhasa

Himalayas

Mount Everest
8,850m
(29,035ft)

2

Thimphu

NEPAL   Darjeeling   BHUTAN

Biratnagar

INDIA

Gongga Shan
7,556m
(24,790m)

Chengdu

Wanxian

Enshi

Chongqing

Neijiang

Luzhou

Yibin

Darbhanga

Rangpur

Dibrugarh

Brahmaputra

Jorhat

Guwahati

Shillong

Xichang

Zhaotong

C   H

Zunyi

Huai

25°
N

Bhagalpur

Ganges

Rajshahi

Sylhet

BANGLADESH

Dhaka

Myitkyina

Baoshan

Dali

Panzhihua

Guiyang

Anshun

Asansol

Jamshedpur

Imphal

Kunming

Liuzhou

3

Kolkata
(Calcutta)

Khulna

Aizawl

Lashio

Kaiyuan

Gejiu

Simao

Ha Giang

Lao Cai

Nanni

Chittagong

Mouths of the Ganges

Monywa

Mount
Victoria
3,053m
(10,016ft)

Mandalay

BURMA
(MYANMAR)

Phongsali

Son La

Thai Nguyen

Qinzhou

20°

Sittwe

Meiktila

Taunggyi

Salween

Hanoi

Hai Phong

Bay of Bengal

Pyinmana

Pye

Irrawaddy

Mekong

Louangphrabang

Thanh Hoa

*Gulf of
Tonkin*

4

Sandoway

Chiang Mai

LAOS

Vinh

Sany

Henzada

Pegu

Vientiane

Udon Thani

Pathein

Thaton

Phitsanulok

Savannakhet

Hue

Rangoon

Moulmein

Khon
Kaen

Da Nar

15°

*Mouths of the
Irrawaddy*

Nakhon Sawan

Ubon
Ratchathani

THAILAND

Nakhon Ratchasima

Pakxe

Attapu

VIETNA

INDIAN

Tavoy

Bangkok

Stoeng Treng

Qui Nhon

OCEAN

Angkor   *Tonle Sap*

CAMBODIA

Buon Me
Thuot

5

Andaman
Islands
(India)

*Andaman

Sea*

Pattaya

Batdambang

Kampong
Cham

Dà Lat

Nh
Tra

Mergui

Kampong
Chhnang

Port Blair

Prachuap
Khiri Khan

Krong
Kaoh Kong

Phnom
Penh

Bien Hoa

Little
Andaman

*Mergui
Archipelago*

Kampong Saom

Mekong

Ho Chi Minh City
(Saigon)

Ten Degree Channel

Chumphon

Long Xuyen

Can Tho

Gulf of Thailand

6

Nicobar Islands
(India)

Nakhon Si
Thammarat

Bac Lieu

Con Son

Hat Yai

5°

Yala

Banda Aceh

Alor Setar

Kota Bharu

Lhokseumawe

George Town
(Penang)   Gunung
Tahan

Kuala Terengganu

*Natuna
Islands*
(Indonesia)

7

Sumatra

Langsa

Taiping   Ipoh

2,187m
(7,175ft)

MALAYSIA

INDONESIA

A   90°E   B   95°   C   100°   D   105°   E

A 80°E B 85° C 90° D 95° E 100° F 105° G 110°

KAZAKHSTAN

Bulgan

2
Almaty
Karamay
Dzungarian Basin
Altay
■ Ulan Bator

Lake Issyk
Yining
Kuytun
Shihezi

KYRGYZSTAN
Urumqi
MONGOLIA

Pik Pobedy
7,439m
(24,406ft)

Tien Shan

Aksu
Turpan

40°N
Korla
Bosten Lake
-154m (-505ft)
Turpan Depression
Hami

Erenho

Tarim Basin
Lop Lake
Gobi Desert
Hohhot

3
Hotan
Taklimakan Desert
Mogao Caves
Baotou

Altun Mountains
Yumen
The Great Wall of China
Wuhai

Yinchuan

35°
Kunlun Mountains
5,547m (18,199ft)

Qaidam Basin
Taiyu

Golmud
Qinghai Lake
Xining
Lanzhou

CHINA
Huang He (Yellow)

4
Plateau of Tibet
Baoji
Mount Li (Terracotta Ar

Siling Lake
Xian

30°
TIBET
Yushu

Nam Lake
Changjiang (Yangtze)
Shiyan

Himalayas
Brahmaputra
Xiangfa

5
NEPAL
Lhasa
Gongga Shan
7,556m (24,790ft)
Chengdu
Yichang

Kathmandu ■
Leshan
Chongqing

Mount Everest
8,850m (29,035ft)
Thimphu ■
Luzhou
Changde

Darbhanga
Darjeeling
BHUTAN
Brahmaputra
Dibrugarh
Chang Jiang (Yangtze)

Patna
Biratnagar
Xichang
Zunyi
Huaihua

25°
Ganges
Guwahati
Panzhihua
Huaihua

Bhagalpur
Rangpur
Shillong
Guiyang
Hengy

INDIA
Irrawaddy
Dali

Ranchi
Asansol
Rajshahi
Sylhet
Imphal
Myitkyina
Kunming

Tropic of Cancer
BANGLADESH
Guilin

6
Dhaka ■
Aizawl

Kolkata (Calcutta)
Khulna
Lashio
Gejiu
Liuzhou

Chittagong
Red
Wuzhou

Cuttack
Mouths of the Ganges
Monywa
Mandalay
Simao
Nanning
Yulin

20°
Mount Victoria
3,053m (10,016ft)
Lao Cai

Bay of Bengal
Phongsali
Son La
Thai Nguyen
Zhanjiang

Sittwe
BURMA (MYANMAR)
Taunggyi
Hanoi ■
Hai Phong
Gulf of Tonkin
Haikou

7
INDIAN
Pyinmana
Mekong
Louangphrabang
Thanh Hoa
Hainan

OCEAN
Sandoway
Pye
Chiang Mai
LAOS
Vinh

Henzada
Irrawaddy
Saltween
THAILAND
Vientiane ■
VIETNAM

15°
Pathein
Pegu
Rangoon ■
Udon Thani
Sanya

C 90°E D Mouths of the Irrawaddy 95° Moulmein F 100° G 105° 110°

Q

115° J 120° K 125° L 130° M 135° N 140° P 145°

45°N

Hailar
Hulun Lake

Yichun
Hegang
Amur
Jiamusi

Greater Khingan Range

RUSSIA

La Perouse Strait

Kuril Islands (Russia)

2

Qiqihar

Daqing

Harbin
Jixi
Mudanjiang

Asahikawa
Hokkaido Kushiro
Sapporo
Tomakomai

Ulanhot

MANCHURIA

Vladivostok
Nakhodka

Hakodate

40°

NNER
ONGOLIA

Xilinhot
Tongliao

Changchun
Jilin
Yanji
Liaoyuan

Lake Khanka

Sikhote Alin Range

Sea of Japan

Aomori

Akita

Chifeng
Fuxin
Fushun
Shenyang
Anshan

Chongjin
Hyesan
Kanggye
Kimchaek

Sendai
Fukushima

Honshu

3

of China

Zhangjiakou
Jinzhou

NORTH KOREA
Dandong
Sinuiju
Hamhung

Niigata

Utsunomiya

Datong
Beijing
Qinhuangdao
Tangshan
Tianjin
Gulf of Chihli
Dalian

Wonsan

Korea Bay
Pyongyang
Nampo

JAPAN

Toyama
Kanazawa

Tokyo

35°

Baoding
Shijiazhuang
Yantai

Seoul
Inchon
Suwon
Chongju

Fukui
Shizuoka
Mount Fuji
3,776m
(12,388ft)

Nagoya
Kyoto
Osaka
Hamamatsu
Wakayama

Handan
Zibo
Weifang

Taejon
Taegu

Huang He (Yellow)
Taian
Qingdao

Yellow
Sea

SOUTH KOREA
Pusan

ngzhi
Jining

Kwangju

Okayama
Hiroshima
Matsuyama
Shikoku

Zhengzhou
Xuzhou
ngdingshan

Grand Canal

Lianyungang

Korea Strait
Fukuoka
Kitakyushu

Cheju
Nagasaki
Kumamoto

4

Yancheng

Cheju
Kyushu
Kagoshima

30°

Nanjing
Hefei

Chang Jiang (Yangtze)
Wuxi
Tai Lake
Shanghai

Amami

Wuhan
Anqing
Hangzhou

Ningbo

East China Sea

Ryukyu Islands (Japan)

Okinawa

5

25°

Poyang Lake
Nanchang
Jinhua

ngting

angsha
Linchuan
Wenzhou

uzhou
Nanping

Sakishima Islands

Tropic of Cancer

Ganzhou
Yongan
Fuzhou

6

zhou

Shaoguan
Quanzhou
Xiamen
Meizhou

Taipei
Chilung

Canton
uangzhou)
Shantou

Taiwan Strait
Taichung
Changhua

Yu Shan
3,997m
(13,113ft)

TAIWAN

20°

Hong Kong
(Xianggang)

Tainan
Kaohsiung

Batan Islands

PACIFIC

OCEAN

7

outh China Sea

Luzon Strait

Babuyan Islands
PHILIPPINES

15°

Laoag
Aparri
Luzon
Tuguegarao

115° J 120° K 125° L 130° M 135° N

China, Korea and Japan

Boreal forest
Temperate forest
Tropical forest
Temperate grassland
Savanna
Semi-desert and scrub
Hot desert
Wetland
Mountain
Tundra
Ice
Cultivation
Urban

■ National capital
● Internal capital
⊙ Major city or town
○ Other town

International boundary
Internal boundary

▲ 2,490m (7,988ft) Height above or below sea level

See also main key on page 15.
1:14,000,000

0   200   400km
0 100 200 300 miles

MONGOLIA

Altai Mountains

Altay

Altay

Hami

Dzungarian Basin

Karamay

Kuytun

Shihezi

Urumqi

Turpan

Turpan Depression

-154m
(-505ft)

Bosten Lake

Korla

Mogao Caves

Lop Lake

Qaidam Basin

Golmud

CHINA

Plateau of Tibet

TIBET

Lhasa

Nam Lake

Salween

Brahmaputra

Siling Lake

Mount Everest
8,850m
(29,035ft)

Thimphu
BHUTAN

Darjeeling

Dibrugarh

Jorhat

Brahmaputra

Guwahati

Rangpur

Kathmandu

NEPAL

Pokhara

Biratnagar

Darbhanga

Patna

Gorakhpur

Ganges

Yining

Altun Mountains

Tarim Basin

Taklimakan Desert

Hotan

Kunlun Mountains

Karakorum Range

Himalayas

Lucknow

Kanpur

Bareilly

Ganges

Saharanpur

Meerut

Aligarh

Agra

Taj Mahal

Gwalior

Lake Balkhash

Balqash

Lake Zaysan

KAZAKHSTAN

Taldyqorghan

Pik Pobedy
7,439m
(24,406ft)

Aksu

Kashi

Kongur Shan
7,719m
(25,325ft)

Karakol

Lake Issyk

Tien Shan

Almaty

Bishkek

KYRGYZSTAN

Kara-Balta

Jalal-Abad

Osh

K2
8,611m
(28,251ft)

Gilgit

JAMMU AND KASHMIR

Srinagar

Indus

Jammu

Sialkot

Gujranwala

Amritsar

Ludhiana

Chandigarh

Delhi

New Delhi

Jaipur

Ajmer

Bikaner

Jodhpur

Taraz

Qyzylorda

Shieli

Turkistan

Shymkent

Namangan

Fargona

Khujand

Communism Peak
7,495m
(24,590ft)

Khorugh

Kulob

Peshawar

Islamabad

Jalalabad

Sargodha

Lahore

Faisalabad

Sahiwal

Multan

Bahawalpur

Thar Desert

Syr Darya

Navoiy

Tashkent

Angren

Jizzax

Samarqand

TAJIKISTAN

Dushanbe

Ourghonteppa

Konduz

Hindu Kush

Kabul

AFGHANISTAN

5,143m
(16,873ft)

Dera Ghazi Khan

Rahimyar Khan

Sukkur

Larkana

PAKISTAN

Indus

UZBEKISTAN

Buxoro

Urganch

Aral Sea

Mazar-e Sharif

Amu Darya

TURKMENISTAN

Turkmenabat

Mary

Herat

Kandahar

Quetta

Nawabshah

Panjgur

India and Central Asia

Legend
- Boreal forest
- Temperate forest
- Tropical forest
- Temperate grassland
- Savanna
- Semi-desert and scrub
- Hot desert
- Wetland
- Mountain
- Tundra
- Ice
- Cultivation
- Urban
- ■ National capital
- ● Internal capital
- ⊙ Major city or town
- ○ Other town
- —— International boundary
- ---- Internal boundary
- ▲ 2,490m (7,988ft) Height above or below sea level

See also main key on page 15.

1:12,000,000

0 100 200 300 400km
0 100 200 300 miles

Labels

BURMA (MYANMAR)
Monywa
Mount Victoria 3,053m (10,016ft)
Pye
Irrawaddy
Pathein
Sandoway
Mouths of the Irrawaddy
Sittwe
Aizawl

Dhaka
Khulna
BANGLADESH
Chittagong
Mouths of the Ganges

Asansol
Kolkata (Calcutta)
Ranchi
Jamshedpur
Sambalpur
Cuttack
Brahmapur
Vishakhapatnam

Bay of Bengal

Andaman Islands (India)
Port Blair
Little Andaman
Ten Degree Channel
Nicobar Islands (India)

INDIAN OCEAN

INDIA

Raipur
Jabalpur
Nagpur
Amravati
Chandrapur
Rajahmundry
Vijayawada
Eastern Ghats
Nellore
Chennai (Madras)

Bhopal
Indore
Akola
Dhule
Malegaon
Nanded
Godavari
Warangal
Hyderabad
Krishna
Deccan Plateau
Bangalore
Salem
Coimbatore
Tiruchchirappalli
Palk Strait
Jaffna
Mannar
Trincomalee

Ahmadabad
Vadodara
Surat
Narmada
Nashik
Mumbai (Bombay)
Pune
Solapur
Gulbarga
Belgaum
Hubli
Davangere
Western Ghats
Mysore
Mangalore
Kozhikode (Calicut)
Kochi (Cochin)
Madurai
Trivandrum

Rajkot
Bhavnagar
Jamnagar
Porbandar
Kutch
Arabian Sea

Aurangabad
Kolhapur

SRI LANKA
Sri Jayewardenepura Kotte
Kandy
Galle
Negombo
Colombo
Gulf of Mannar

MALDIVES
■ Male

Tropic of Cancer

Copyright © Usborne Publishing Ltd.

49

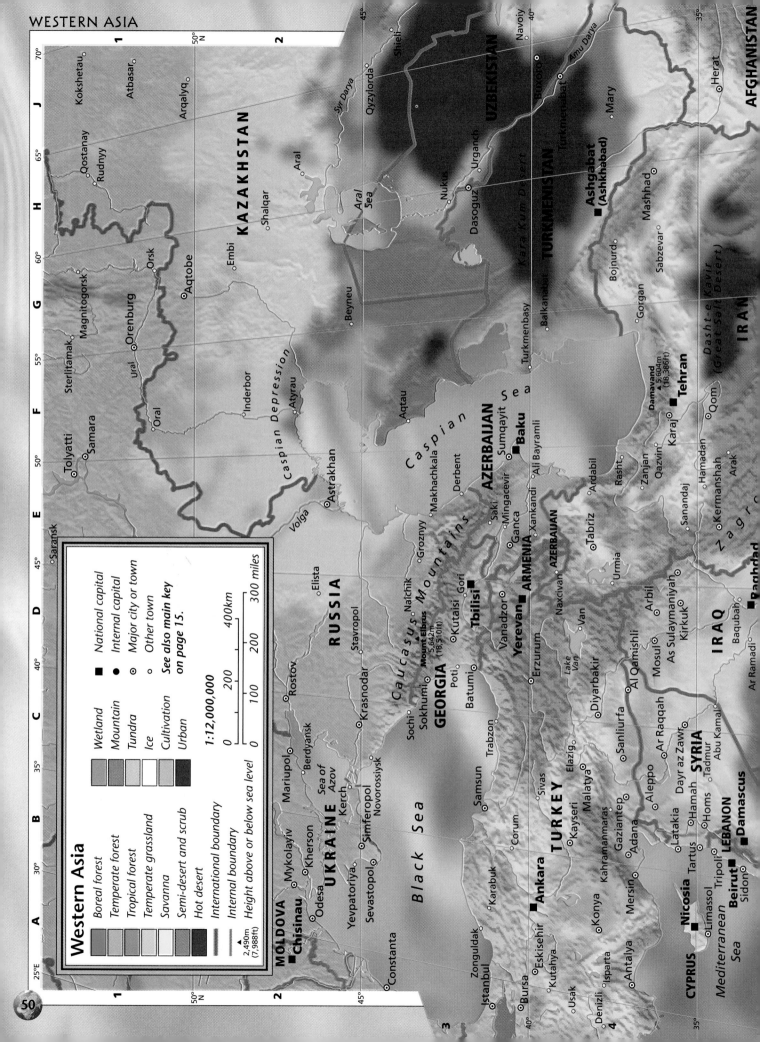

Western Asia

Boreal forest
Temperate forest
Tropical forest
Temperate grassland
Savanna
Semi-desert and scrub
Hot desert

International boundary
Internal boundary

▲ 2,490m
(7,988ft)

Height above or below sea level

Wetland
Mountain
Tundra
Ice
Cultivation
Urban

■ National capital
● Internal capital
◉ Major city or town
○ Other town

See also main key
on page 15.

1:12,000,000

0   100   200   300 miles
0 200 400km
0   200   400km

MOLDOVA
■ Chisinau

Saransk

RUSSIA

Elista

Rostov
Stavropol
Krasnodar

Mykolayiv
Kherson
Odesa
Yevpatoriya
Sevastopol
Simferopol

UKRAINE

Mariupol
Berdyansk
Kerch
Novorossiysk

Sea of
Azov

Black Sea

Constanta

Zonguldak
Istanbul
Bursa
Eskisehir
Kutahya
Usak
Denizli
Isparta
Antalya

Ankara
■

Konya
Mersin
Adana
Kahramanmaras
Gaziantep
Kayseri
Corum
Sivas
Malatya
Elazig
Sanliurfa
Diyarbakir

TURKEY

Samsun
Trabzon
Erzurum

Sochi
Sokhumi
Batumi
Poti

GEORGIA
Kutaisi
▲ Mount Elbrus
5,642m
(18,510ft)

Caucasus Mountains

Nalchik
Grozny

Makhachkala
Derbent

Tbilisi
■

Gori
Vanadzor

ARMENIA
■ Yerevan
Naxcivan

AZERBAIJAN

Saki
Mingacevir
Ganca
Xankandi

Van
Lake
Van

Urmia
Tabriz
Ardabil
Rasht

Al Qamishli
Mosul
Arbil
Kirkuk
As Sulaymaniyah

IRAQ
Baqubah
Baghdad

Ar Ramadi

SYRIA
Aleppo
Ar Raqqah
Dayr az Zawr
Abu Kamal
Tadmur

Hamah
Homs
Latakia
Tartus
LEBANON
Tripoli
■ Beirut
Sidon
DAMASCUS
■ Damascus

CYPRUS
■ Nicosia
Limassol

Mediterranean
Sea

Caspian
Sea

Caspian Depression

AZERBAIJAN
■ Baku
Sumqayit
Ali Bayramli

Balkanabat

Aqtau

Astrakhan

Volga

Atyrau
Inderbor
Oral
Ural

KAZAKHSTAN

Embi
Aqtobe
Orsk
Orenburg
Magnitogorsk
Sterlitamak
Samara
Tolyatti

Beyneu
Shalqar

Aral
Sea

Aral

Shieli
Qyzylorda
Syr Darya

UZBEKISTAN
Navoiy

Nukus
Dasoguz
Urganch
Buxoro

Turkmenbasy
Turkmenabat
TURKMENISTAN
Ashgabat
(Ashkhabad)
■

Mary

Kara Kum Desert

Amu Darya

Bojnurd
Gorgan
Sabzevar
Mashhad
Herat

AFGHANISTAN

Dasht-e Kavir
(Great Salt Desert)

▲ 5,604m
(18,386ft)
Damavand

Tehran
■
Karaj
Qazvin
Zanjan

Qom

Arak
Hamadan
Kermanshah
Sanandaj

Zagros

IRAN

Saransk

Qostanay
Rudnyy
Atbasar
Kokshetau
Arqalyq

Zangilan

50

25°E   30°   35°   40°   45°   50°   55°   60°   65°   70°

51

60°

2

80°

1

UNITED
KINGDOM
London

*North
Sea*

*Norwegian
Sea*

Arctic Circle

Svalbard
(Norway)

20°

A

40°

B

*Franz Josef
Land*

ARCTI

Paris

NETHERLANDS

BELGIUM

LUXEMBOURG

FRANCE

NORWAY

Oslo

DENMARK

SWEDEN

C

60°

D

80°

3

GERMANY

Berlin

*Baltic
Sea*

Stockholm

FINLAND

Helsinki

Murmansk

*Barents
Sea*

*Kola
Peninsula*

North Cape

*Novaya
Zemlya*

*Kara
Sea*

CZECH
REPUBLIC

AUSTRIA

POLAND

Warsaw

LITHUANIA

Vilnius

LATVIA

ESTONIA

*Lake
Ladoga*

St. Petersburg

*Lake
Onega*

Arkhangelsk

Vorkuta

Noril'sk

SLOVAKIA

Budapest

HUNGARY

Minsk

BELARUS

Lviv

Cherepovets

Ukhta

Ural Mountains

Novyy Urengoy

ROMANIA

Kiev

MOLDOVA

Chisinau

UKRAINE

Moscow

Ryazan

Nizhniy Novgorod

Volga

Kazan

Perm

Ob

*West Siberian
Plain*

Surgut

Ob

Yenisey

40°
N

Kharkiv

Odesa

Simferopol

Voronezh

Samara

Yekaterinburg

Chelyabinsk

Omsk

Irtysh

R

U

Tomsk

Krasnoya

*Black
Sea*

Rostov

Volgograd

Krasnodar

Volga

Oral

Orenburg

Novosibirsk

Barnaul

Abal

Ankara

TURKEY

Mount Elbrus
5,642m
(18,510ft)

Astrakhan

Aqtobe

Atyrau

KAZAKHSTAN

Astana

Pavlodar

Uskemen

Kyzy

Adana

GEORGIA

Tbilisi

ARMENIA

Yerevan

Aqtau

Qaraghandy

Balqash

*Lake
Balkhash*

Altay

Aleppo

SYRIA

AZERBAIJAN

Baku

*Caspian
Sea*

*Aral
Sea*

Nukus

Qyzylorda

Mosul

Tabriz

Dasoguz

UZBEKISTAN

Shymkent

Almaty

Urumqi

Baghdad

IRAQ

Tehran

Damavand
5,604m
(18,386ft)

TURKMENISTAN

**Ashgabat
(Ashkhabad)**

Tashkent

Bishkek

KYRGYZSTAN

Osh

Tien Shan

Aksu

4

Ahvaz

Esfahan

Mashhad

Turkmenabat

Samarqand

Dushanbe

TAJIKISTAN

Kuwait City

KUWAIT

IRAN

Shiraz

Herat

Mazar-e Sharif

Taklimakan Desert

Hotan

SAUDI
ARABIA

Riyadh

Manama

*Persian
Gulf
(The Gulf)*

AFGHANISTAN

Kabul

K2
8,611m
(28,251ft)

QATAR

Doha

Bandar-e
Abbas

Zahedan

Kandahar

Islamabad

Srinagar

Abu Dhabi

PAKISTAN

Lahore

INDIA

Plateau of Tibet

C

60°E

D

80°

E

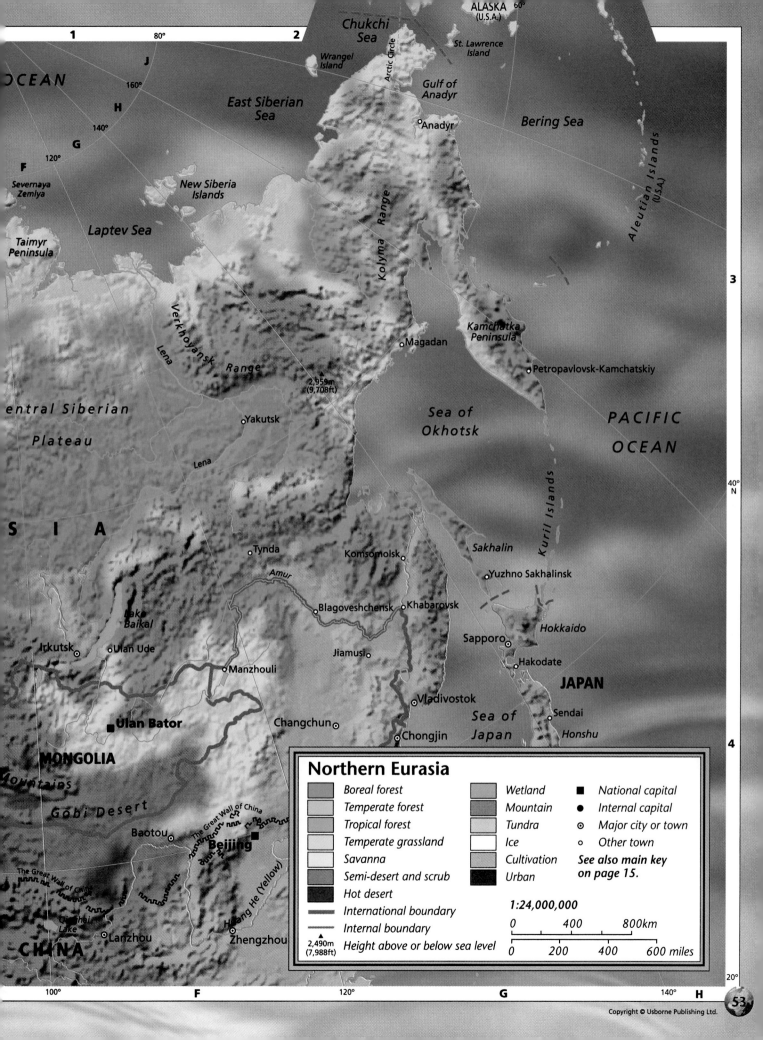

ALASKA
(U.S.A.)

Chukchi
Sea

Wrangel
Island

East Siberian
Sea

St. Lawrence
Island

Gulf of
Anadyr

Bering Sea

Anadyr

Aleutian Islands
(U.S.A.)

OCEAN

Severnaya
Zemlya

New Siberia
Islands

Laptev Sea

Taimyr
Peninsula

Kolyma Range

Kamchatka
Peninsula

Magadan

Petropavlovsk-Kamchatskiy

Verkhoyansk

Lena

Range

2,959m
(9,708ft)

Yakutsk

Sea of
Okhotsk

PACIFIC

OCEAN

entral Siberian

Plateau

Lena

Kuril Islands

S I A

Tynda

Komsomolsk

Sakhalin

Yuzhno Sakhalinsk

Amur

Blagoveshchensk   Khabarovsk

Hokkaido

Lake
Baikal

Irkutsk   Ulan Ude

Jiamusi

Sapporo

Hakodate

Manzhouli

JAPAN

Vladivostok

Sendai

Ulan Bator

Changchun

Chongjin

Sea of
Japan

Honshu

MONGOLIA

Mountains

Gobi Desert

Baotou

The Great Wall of China

Beijing

The Great Wall of China

Lanzhou

Qinghai
Lake

Huang He (Yellow)

Zhengzhou

CHINA

Northern Eurasia

Boreal forest	Wetland	■	National capital
Temperate forest	Mountain	●	Internal capital
Tropical forest	Tundra	◎	Major city or town
Temperate grassland	Ice	○	Other town
Savanna	Cultivation		
Semi-desert and scrub	Urban		**See also main key on page 15.**
Hot desert			

International boundary

Internal boundary

▲ 2,490m
(7,988ft)   Height above or below sea level

1:24,000,000

0   400   800km

0   200   400   600 miles

53

EUROPE

Europe is a small continent, packed with over 40 countries and more than 700 million people. Russia is an enormous country, spanning two continents. Its western part is in Europe, while its eastern part is in Asia. The European part of Russia is larger than any other country in Europe.

The shading on this map is there to help you see clearly the different countries that make up the continent.

Internet link

For a link to a website where you can find out about the European Union and read key facts about each of its member states, go to **www.usborne-quicklinks.com**

Arctic Circle

ARCTIC OCEAN

Reykjavik
ICELAND

Norwegian Sea

Faroe Islands (Denmark)

SWEDEN

Shetland Islands

NORWAY

Oslo

North Sea

Orkney Islands

Stockholm

DENMARK
Copenhagen

Balti Sea

IRELAND
Dublin

UNITED KINGDOM

Amsterdam
The Hague
London
NETHERLANDS

Berlin

POLAN

Brussels
BELGIUM
GERMANY

Prague
CZECH REPUBLIC

LUXEMBOURG
Paris
Luxembourg

Rhine

Vienna
Bratislava

ATLANTIC

Bay of Biscay

FRANCE

Bern
Vaduz
LIECHTENSTEIN
SWITZERLAND

AUSTRIA
Budapest

SLOVENIA
Ljubljana

HUNGA

OCEAN

MONACO

SAN MARINO

Zagreb
CROATIA

BOSNIA AND HERZEGOVINA
Sarajevo

PORTUGAL

Lisbon

ANDORRA
Andorra la Vella

Madrid

SPAIN

Corsica

ITALY

Rome
VATICAN CITY

ALBAN
Tiran

Balearic Islands

Sardinia

Mediterranean Sea

Sicily

MALTA
Valletta

54

Barents Sea

Murmansk

Arctic Circle

Arkhangelsk

FINLAND

R U S S I A

Isinki

⊙ St. Petersburg

Tallinn
ESTONIA

Nizhniy Novgorod ⊙

Kazan ⊙

Riga **LATVIA**

■ **Moscow**

LITHUANIA
Vilnius

SIA

Volga

■ **Minsk**

BELARUS

Warsaw

■ **Kiev**

Dnieper

Volgograd ⊙

UKRAINE

OVAKIA

MOLDOVA

■ **Chisinau**

ROMANIA

Black Sea

grade

■ **Bucharest**

Danube

ERBIA AND
ONTENEGRO

BULGARIA

■**Sofia**

Skopje

TURKEY

ACEDONIA

REECE

■**Athens**

Crete

Facts

Total land area 10,205,720 sq km
(3,940,428 sq miles) (including
European Russia)

Total population 727 million
(including all of Russia)

Biggest city Moscow, Russia

Biggest country Russia *Total area:*
17,075,200 sq km (6,592,735 sq
miles) Area of European Russia:
4,294,400 sq km (1,658,068 sq miles)

Smallest country Vatican City *0.44*
sq km (0.17 sq miles)

Highest mountain Elbrus, Russia
5,642m (18,510ft)

Longest river Volga *3,700km*
(2,298 miles)

Biggest lake Lake Ladoga, Russia
17,700 sq km (6,834 sq miles)

Highest waterfall Utigard, on the
Jostedal Glacier, Norway *800m*
(2,625ft)

Biggest desert No deserts in Europe

Biggest island Great Britain *234,410*
sq km (90,506 sq miles)

Main mineral deposits Bauxite, zinc,
iron, potash, fluorspar

Main fuel deposits Oil, coal, natural
gas, peat, uranium

A cow in Devon, in the
south of England

Copyright © Usborne Publishing Ltd

55

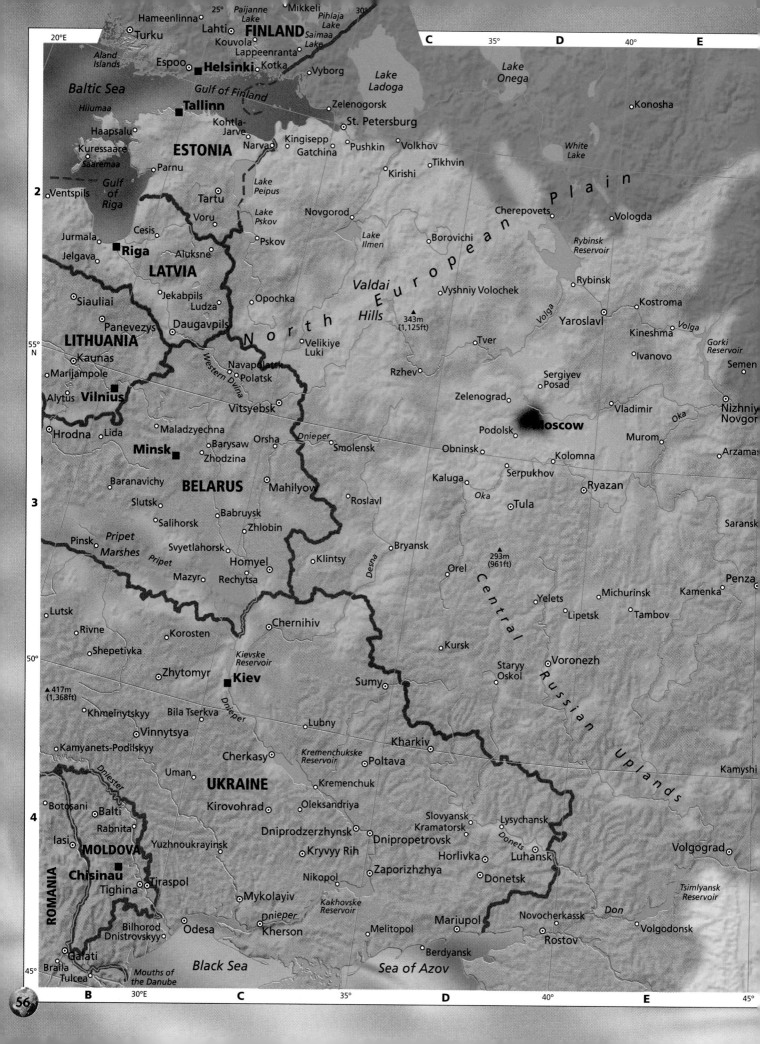

Hameenlinna Lahti Paijanne Lake 25° Mikkeli Pihlaja Lake 30°

Turku Kouvola FINLAND Saimaa Lake

20°E Espoo Lappeenranta Vyborg Lake Ladoga **C** 35° **D** 40° **E**

Helsinki Kotka Zelenogorsk Lake Onega

Baltic Sea Gulf of Finland St. Petersburg Konosha

Hiiumaa **Tallinn** Kohtla-Jarve Volkhov White Lake

Haapsalu Narva Kingisepp Pushkin Tikhvin

Kuressaare ESTONIA Gatchina

Saaremaa Parnu Kirishi

2 Ventspils Gulf of Riga Tartu Lake Peipus Novgorod Cherepovets Vologda

Voru Lake Pskov Rybinsk Reservoir

Jurmala Cesis Pskov Lake Ilmen Borovichi Rybinsk Kostroma

Jelgava **Riga** Aluksne Valdai Hills Vyshniy Volochek Volga Yaroslavl Kineshma Volga

Siauliai LATVIA Jekabpils Opochka 343m (1,125ft) Ivanovo Gorki Reservoir Semen

Panevezys Ludza Tver

55° N LITHUANIA Daugavpils Velikiye Luki Sergiyev Posad Vladimir Nizhniy Novgor

Kaunas Navapolatsk Rzhev Zelenograd **Moscow** Murom Arzam

Marijampole Polatsk Podolsk Oka

Alytus **Vilnius** Vitsyebsk Smolensk Obninsk Kolomna

Hrodna Lida Maladzyechna Orsha Dnieper Kaluga Serpukhov Ryazan

Minsk Barysaw Mahilyow Oka Tula Saransk

3 Baranavichy Zhodzina BELARUS Roslavl

Slutsk Babruysk 293m (961ft)

Salihorsk Zhlobin Bryansk Penza

Pinsk Pripet Marshes Svyetlahorsk Orel Michurinsk Kamenka

Pripet Homyel Klintsy Desna Yelets Tambov

Mazyr Rechytsa Lipetsk

Lutsk Chernihiv Kursk Central Russian Uplands

50° Rivne Korosten Kievske Reservoir Staryy Oskol Voronezh

Shepetivka

417m (1,368ft) Zhytomyr **Kiev** Sumy Kamyshi

Khmelnytskyy Bila Tserkva Dnieper Lubny Kharkiv

Vinnytsya

Kamyanets-Podilskyy Cherkasy Kremenchukske Reservoir Poltava

Uman UKRAINE Kremenchuk Slovyansk Lysychansk Volgograd

4 Botosani Balti Kirovohrad Oleksandriya Kramatorsk Luhansk

Iasi Rabnita Dniester Dniprodzerzhynsk Dnipropetrovsk Horlivka Donets

MOLDOVA Yuzhnoukrayinsk Kryvyy Rih Donetsk

ROMANIA **Chisinau** Tiraspol Zaporizhzhya Tsimlyansk Reservoir

Tighina Nikopol Novocherkassk Don

Bilhorod-Dnistrovskyy Mykolayiv Kakhovske Reservoir Mariupol Volgodonsk

Galati Odesa Kherson Dnieper Melitopol Rostov

Braila Black Sea Berdyansk

45° Tulcea Mouths of the Danube Sea of Azov

B 30°E **C** 35° **D** 40° **E** 45°

North European Plain

56

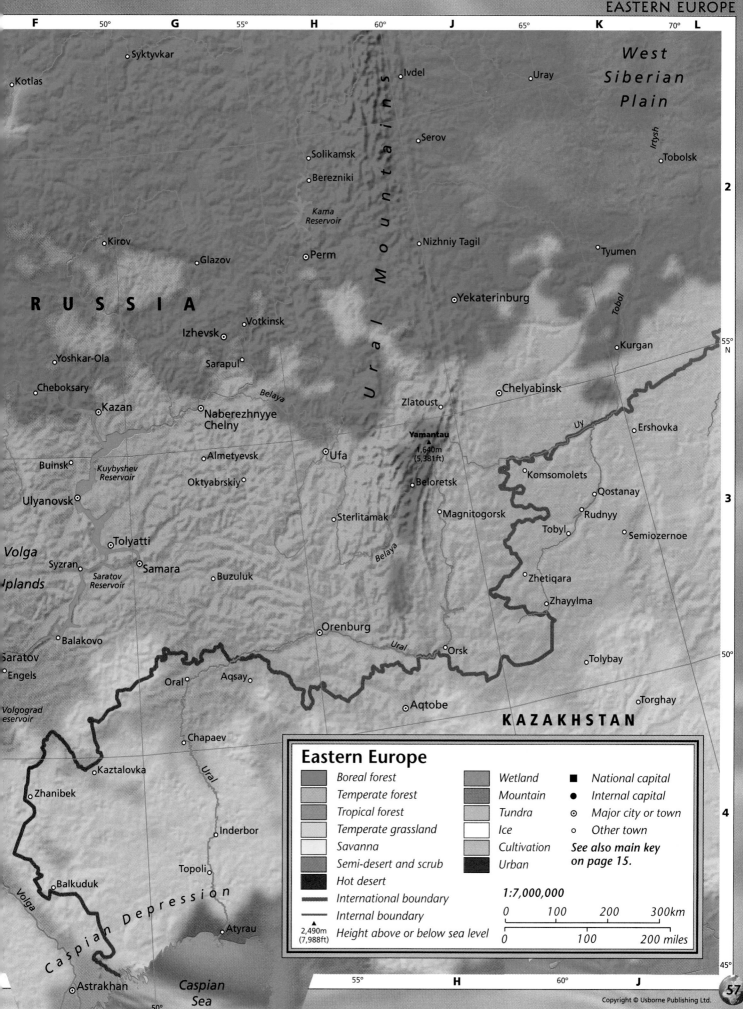

F   50°   G   55°   H   60°   J   65°   K   70°   L

West Siberian Plain

Syktyvkar

Kotlas

Ivdel

Uray

Irtysh

Serov

Solikamsk

Tobolsk

Berezniki

Kama Reservoir

2

Kirov

Perm

Nizhniy Tagil

Tyumen

Glazov

R U S S I A

Yekaterinburg

Tobol

Votkinsk

Izhevsk

Yoshkar-Ola

55° N

Sarapul

Kurgan

Cheboksary

Belaya

Chelyabinsk

Uy

Kazan

Zlatoust

Ershovka

Naberezhnyye Chelny

▲ Yamantau 1,640m (5,381ft)

Buinsk

Almetyevsk

Ufa

Komsomolets

Kuybyshev Reservoir

Beloretsk

Qostanay

Ulyanovsk

Oktyabrskiy

Rudnyy

Semiozernoe

3

Sterlitamak

Magnitogorsk

Tobyl

Volga Uplands

Tolyatti

Belaya

Syzran

Saratov Reservoir

Samara

Zhetiqara

Buzuluk

Zhayylma

Saratov

Balakovo

Orenburg

Tolybay

Engels

Orsk

Ural

50°

Volgograd Reservoir

Oral

Aqsay

Torghay

Aqtobe

K A Z A K H S T A N

Chapaev

Ural

Kaztalovka

4

Zhanibek

Inderbor

Topoli

Balkuduk

Volga

Caspian Depression

Atyrau

Astrakhan

Caspian Sea

50°

45°

55°   H   60°   J

Eastern Europe

■ Boreal forest	■ Wetland
■ Temperate forest	■ Mountain
■ Tropical forest	■ Tundra
■ Temperate grassland	□ Ice
■ Savanna	■ Cultivation
■ Semi-desert and scrub	■ Urban
■ Hot desert	

■ National capital
● Internal capital
◎ Major city or town
○ Other town

See also main key on page 15.

—— International boundary
— Internal boundary
▲ Height above or below sea level

2,490m (7,988ft)

1:7,000,000

0   100   200   300km

0   100   200 miles

Main map labels:

M L K G F E D 1 2 3 4

40° 36° 32° 28° 24° 20° 16° 12° 8° 4°E 0° 4°W

68°N 64° 60°

Barents Sea

Kola Peninsula

Severomorsk
Murmansk
Monchegorsk
▲1,191m 3,907ft
Apatity
Kandalaksha

White Sea

Belomorsk

Lake Top
Lake Pya
Lake Kuyto
Kostomuksha
Lake Vyg
Lake Onega
Lake Seg
Medvezhyegorsk
Lieksa
R U S S I A
Petrozavodsk
Volkhov
Tikhvin
Borovichi
Lake Ilmen
Novgorod

Vadso
Kirkenes
Utsjoki
Sevettijarvi
Kaamanen
Lake Inari
Lokan Reservoir
Sodankyla
Arctic Circle

North Cape
Soroya
Hammerfest
Alta
Tromso

L a p l a n d

Rovaniemi
Kuusamo
Kuhmo
Kajaani
Oulu Lake
Pielis Lake
Kiuruvesi
Kuopio
Varkaus
Hauki Lake
Pihlaja Lake
Lappeenranta
Saimaa Lake
Puula Lake
Mikkeli
Paijanne Lake
Kouvola
Kotka
Lahti
Vyborg
Zelenogorsk
St. Petersburg
Pushkin
Gatchina
Kingisepp
Narva
Lake Peipus

Tornio
Oulu
Raahe

F I N L A N D

Jyvaskyla
Saarijarvi
Alavus
Hameenlinna
Tampere
Helsinki
Espoo
Kohtla-Jarve
Tallinn
ESTONIA
Haapsalu
Hiiumaa

Kiruna
Gallivare
Kebnekaise
2,114m (6,95ft)
Narvik
Svolvaer
Lofoten
Vesteralen
Vestfjorden
Bodo
Mo i Rana

Gulf of Bothnia

Skelleftea
Stora Lule Lake
Boden
Horn Lake
Storavan Lake
Ume
Umea
Vaasa
Kokkola
Kurikka
Pori
Rauma
Turku
Aland Islands
Gulf of Finland

Stockholm
Sodertalje

Sundsvall
Hudiksvall
Gavle
Uppsala
Lake Malar
Eskilstuna
Orebro

S W E D E N

Ostersund
Stor Lake
Indals
Storavan Lake
Borlange
Dal
Karlstad
Lake Vaner
Lidkoping

Namsos
Steinkjer
Vikna
Norwegian Sea
Trondheim
Oppdal
Lillehammer
Klar
Honefoss
Glama
Oslo
Drammen
Fredrikstad
Larvik
Arendal

Froya
Hitra
Smola
Kristiansund
Alesund
Sula
Galdhopiggen
2,469m (8,100ft)
NORWAY
Odda
Bergen
Sotra
Karmoy
Stavanger
Varhaug

Inset map — Iceland:

D C B A N Q P N

2 3 2 3

64°N

Langanes
Seydhisfjordhur
Vatnajokull
Hvannadalshnukur
▲2,119m (6,952ft)
Same scale as main map

Siglufjordhur
ICELAND
Isafjordhur
Arctic Circle
Faxafloi
Keflavik
Reykjavik
ATLANTIC OCEAN

20°W 16° 8° 4°E 0°
24°W 20° 16°
64°N

1 2 3 4
68°N 64° 60°

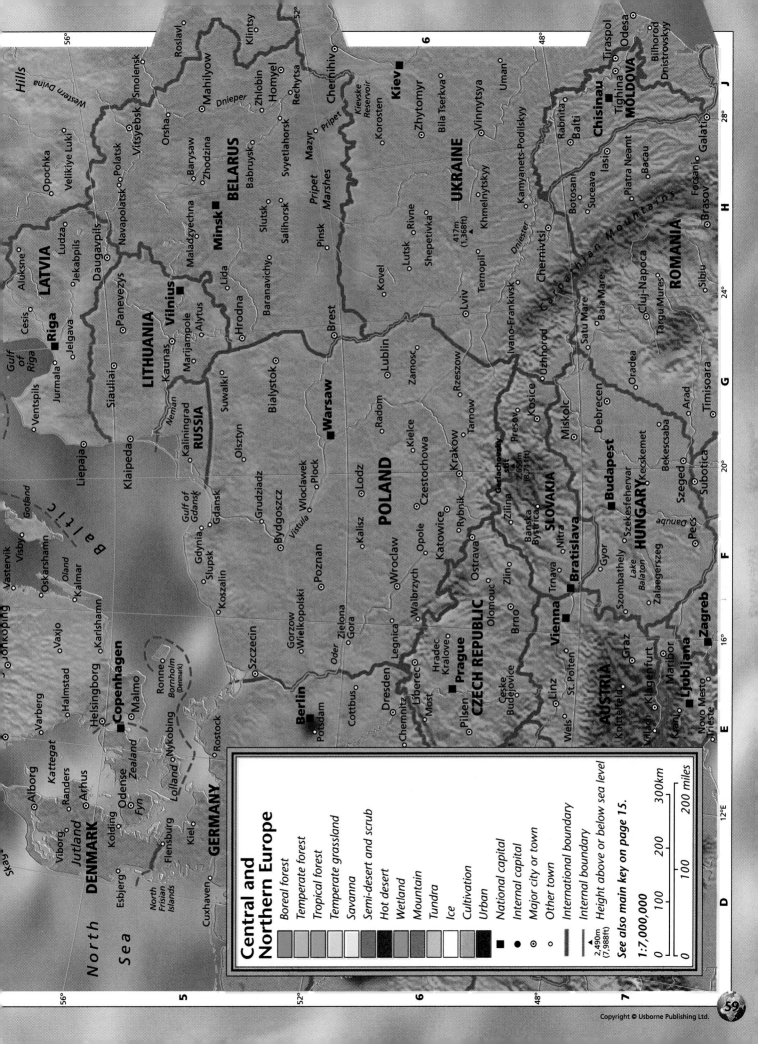

Central and Northern Europe

Boreal forest
Temperate forest
Tropical forest
Temperate grassland
Savanna
Semi-desert and scrub
Hot desert
Wetland
Mountain
Tundra
Ice
Cultivation
Urban

■ National capital
● Internal capital
◉ Major city or town
○ Other town

— International boundary
— Internal boundary

▲ 2,490m (7,988ft) Height above or below sea level

See also main key on page 15.

1:7,000,000

0 100 200 300km
0 100 200 miles

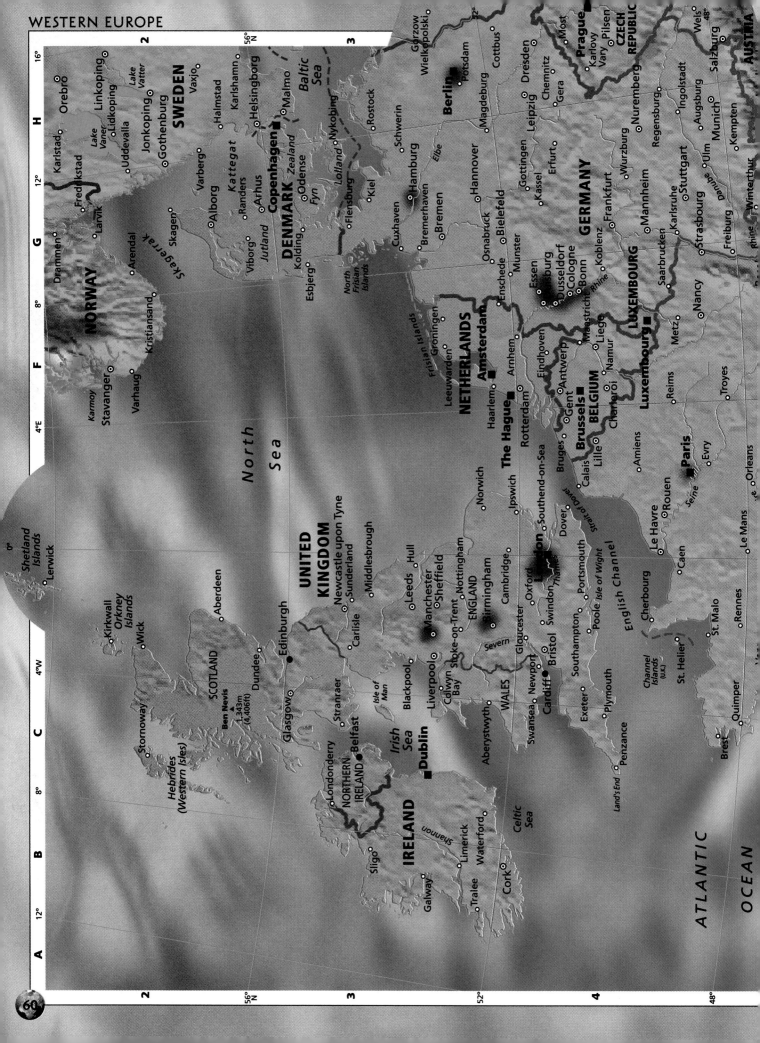

WESTERN EUROPE

NORWAY
Drammen
Larvik
Arendal
Kristiansand
Stavanger
Varhaug
Karmoy

SWEDEN
Orebro
Linkoping
Lidkoping
Uddevalla
Jonkoping
Vaxjo
Gothenburg
Varberg
Halmstad
Karlshamn
Helsingborg
Malmo
Karlstad
Fredrikstad

Lake Vaner
Lake Vatter
Skagen
Alborg
Skagerrak
Kattegat
Randers
Arhus
Viborg
Jutland
Kolding
Esbjerg

DENMARK
Copenhagen
Zealand
Odense
Fyn
Flensburg
Lolland
Nykobing

Baltic Sea
Rostock
Schwerin

Kiel
North Frisian Islands
Cuxhaven
Hamburg
Bremerhaven
Bremen
Elbe
Hannover
Magdeburg

Berlin
Potsdam
Gorzow Wielkopolski
Cottbus
Dresden
Chemnitz
Gera
Leipzig

CZECH REPUBLIC
Prague
Karlovy Vary
Pilsen
Most

AUSTRIA
Wels
Linz
Salzburg

Gottingen
Kassel
Erfurt

GERMANY
Wurzburg
Frankfurt
Nuremberg
Regensburg
Ingolstadt
Augsburg
Munich
Kempten
Winterthur

Essen
Dusseldorf
Cologne
Bonn
Maastricht
Koblenz
Rhine
Mannheim
Karlsruhe
Stuttgart
Ulm
Freiburg
Strasbourg
Danube

LUXEMBOURG
Luxembourg
Saarbrucken
Metz
Nancy
Troyes

Osnabruck
Enschede
Munster
Bielefeld
Groningen
Frisian Islands
Leeuwarden

NETHERLANDS
Amsterdam
Haarlem
Arnhem
Eindhoven
The Hague
Rotterdam
Antwerp
Gent
BELGIUM
Brussels
Charleroi
Namur
Liege
Lille
Bruges
Calais

North Frisian Islands

North Sea

Shetland Islands
Lerwick

Kirkwall
Orkney Islands
Wick
Aberdeen
SCOTLAND
Ben Nevis
1,343m
(4,406ft)
Stornoway
Hebrides
(Western Isles)
Dundee
Edinburgh
Glasgow
Stranraer
Carlisle
Newcastle upon Tyne
Sunderland
Middlesbrough

UNITED KINGDOM
Leeds
Hull
Manchester
Sheffield
Stoke-on-Trent
Nottingham
ENGLAND
Birmingham
Cambridge
Norwich
Ipswich
Southend-on-Sea
London
Thames
Oxford
Swindon
Dover
Strait of Dover
Portsmouth
Isle of Wight
Poole
Southampton
Bristol
Cardiff
WALES
Newport
Swansea
Gloucester
Severn
Colwyn Bay
Aberystwyth
Blackpool
Liverpool
Isle of Man
Belfast
NORTHERN IRELAND
Londonderry

IRELAND
Dublin
Sligo
Galway
Limerick
Waterford
Tralee
Cork
Celtic Sea
Shannon
Irish Sea

Calais
Amiens
Reims
Rouen
Le Havre
Paris
Seine
Evry
Orleans
Le Mans
Caen
Cherbourg
St. Malo
Rennes
Channel Islands (U.K.)
St. Helier
English Channel
Plymouth
Exeter
Land's End
Penzance
Brest
Quimper

ATLANTIC OCEAN

60

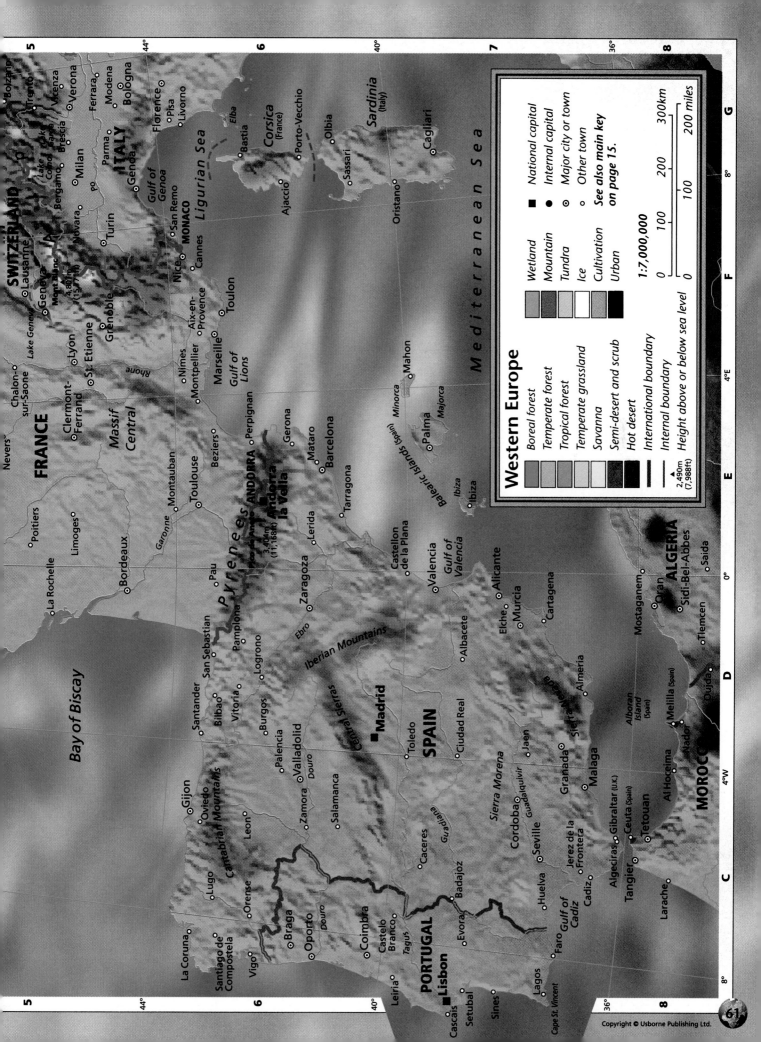

A   0°   B   4°E   C   8°   D   12°   E   16°

Cherbourg
Le Havre
Caen
Rouen
Amiens
Charleroi
Namur
BELGIUM
Koblenz
Frankfurt
Erfurt
Gera
Dresden
Chemnitz
Liberec
Wroclaw
Walbrzyc
Most
LUXEMBOURG
■ **Luxembourg**
Hradec Kralove
Karlovy
Vary
Pilsen
■ **Prague**
CZECH REPUBLIC

1

Paris
Reims
Metz
Mannheim
Saarbrucken
GERMANY
Nuremberg
Wurzburg
Olomouc
Brno
Zli

48°N
Evry
Nancy
Karlsruhe
Regensburg
Ceske
Budejovice

Le Mans
Orleans
Troyes
Strasbourg
Stuttgart
Ingolstadt
Danube
Augsburg
Linz
Wels
St. Polten
Vienna
Trn

Angers
Tours
Rhine
Ulm
Munich
Salzburg
Bratisla

Poitiers
Nevers
Dijon
Besancon
Basel
Zurich
Winterthur
Kempten
Innsbruck
Grossglockner
3,798m
(12,461ft)
AUSTRIA
Knittelfeld
Szombathe

FRANCE
Chalon-
sur-Saone
Biel
Bern ■
Lucerne
Vaduz ■
Villach
Graz
Klagenfurt
Zalaegers

2
Limoges
Geneva
Lausanne
SWITZERLAND
LIECHTENSTEIN
Bolzano
Kranj
Maribor
L
Bala

Clermont-Ferrand
Lyon
Lake Geneva
Mont Blanc
4,807m
(15,771ft)
Lake
Como
Trento
Lake
Garda
Bergamo
Brescia
Vicenza
SLOVENIA
Novo
Mesto
Ljubljana ■
Trieste
Zagreb
CROAT!

St. Etienne
Grenoble
Novara
Milan
Verona
Venice
Rijeka
Karlovac
Slavor

44°
*Massif
Central*
Rhone
Turin
Po
Pula
Zadar
Banja Luka
BOSNIA
AND
Ze

Garonne
Montauban
Parma
Modena
Ferrara
Bologna
Ravenna
HERZEGOVIN

Toulouse
Nimes
Genoa
*Gulf of
Genoa*
ITALY
Rimini
BOSNIA
AND
HERZEGOVI

Montpellier
Aix-en-
Provence
MONACO
San Remo
Pisa
SAN MARINO
Ancona
Split
Mos

Beziers
*Gulf of
Lions*
Nice
Cannes
Livorno
Florence
Perugia

Andorra la Vella ■
Marseille
Toulon
Ligurian Sea
Bastia
Elba
Terni
Pescara

3

Corsica
(France)
Foggia

Southern Europe

Boreal forest
Temperate forest
Tropical forest
Temperate grassland
Savanna
Semi-desert and scrub
Hot desert
Wetland
Mountain
Tundra
Ice
Cultivation
Urban

■ National capital
● Internal capital
◉ Major city or town
○ Other town
━━ International boundary
━━ Internal boundary
▲ 2,490m
(7,988ft) Height above or below sea level

See also main key on page 15.

1:7,000,000

0   100   200   300km

0   100   200 miles

Ajaccio
Porto-Vecchio
VATICAN CITY
■ **Rome**
Bari

Olbia
Naples
Pompeii
Salerno
Taranto

40°
Sassari

Cosenza

4
Oristano
Sardinia
(Italy)
Tyrrhenian
Catanzar

Cagliari
Sea
*Lipari
Islands*

M e d i t e r r a n e a n   S e a
Trapani
Palermo
Messina

Mount Etna
3,323m
(10,902ft)
Catania

Sicily
Bizerte
Agrigento
Syracuse

Annaba
Menzel
Bourguiba
Carthage
Pantelleria
(Italy)
Ragusa

36°
Guelma
Tunis ■
Nabeul

Souk Ahras
Sousse
MALTA

5
TUNISIA
Kairouan
Pelagian Islands
(Italy)
■ **Valletta**

Tebessa
Monastir
Kasserine
El Jem

62

POLAND

Czestochowa
Katowice
Rybnik Krakow Tarnow
strava
Zilina
Banska Presov
Bystrica Kosice
LOVAKIA
a
Miskolc

Budapest
ekesfehervar
HUNGARY
ecskemet
Bekescsaba
Szeged Arad
Subotica Timisoara
CS
Osijek Novi Sad
Tuzla Belgrade
SERBIA AND
MONTENEGRO
Sarajevo Kragujevac
Kraljevo
Niksic Nis
rovnik Leskovac
igorica Pristina
Shkoder Vranje
Tetovo Kumanovo
Durres Skopje
MACEDONIA
Tirana Prilep
Elbasan Bitola
ALBANIA
Korce
ce Vlore

Kielce
Zamosc
Rzeszow
Lutsk Rivne
Shepetivka
Lviv
Ternopil Khmelnytskyy
Ivano-Frankivsk
Uzhhorod
Chernivtsi
Satu Mare Botosani
Baia Mare Suceava
Debrecen
Oradea
Cluj-Napoca
Targu Mures
ROMANIA
Mount
Moldoveanu
2,544m
(8,346ft)
Sibiu Brasov
Transylvanian Alps
Ramnicu Valcea
Pitesti
Drobeta-Turnu Severin
Craiova
Ruse
Vratsa
Pleven
BULGARIA
Sofia Plovdiv
Balkan Mountains
Shumen
Sliven
Stara Zagora
Blagoevgrad
Serres
Kavala
Thessaloniki Thasos

Gerlachovsky
stit
2,655m
(8,711ft)

417m
(1,368ft)

Dniester

Carpathian Mountains

Kamyanets-
Podilskyy

Zhytomyr

Kiev

Lubny
Poltava

Bila Tserkva
Cherkasy

Slovyansk
Kramatorsk

Kremenchukske
Reservoir
Kremenchuk

UKRAINE

Vinnytsya

Uman

Dniprodzerzhynsk
Oleksandriya
Kirovohrad

Dnipropetrovsk

Zaporizhzhya

Kryvyy Rih

Nikopol

Rabnita

Balti
MOLDOVA
Chisinau
Tighina Tiraspol
Bilhorod-
Dnistrovskyy

Iasi
Piatra Neamt
Bacau
Focsani
Galati
Braila
Buzau
Ploiesti
Bucharest
Danube
Dobrich
Varna
Burgas

Tulcea

Yuzhnoukrayinsk

Mykolaiv
Odesa

Kherson

Kakhovske
Reservoir

Dnieper

Berdyansk
Melitopol

Dzhankoy
Kerch

Crimea Feodosiya
Simferopol

Yevpatoriya

Sevastopol

Mouths of
the Danube

Constanta

Black Sea

Sea of
Azov

Zonguldak
Karabuk

Corum

Istanbul
Adapazari
Edirne
Tekirdag Sea of
Marmara
Bursa
Canakkale
Ankara Kirikkale
Eskisehir

Bosporus

TURKEY

Mount Olympus
2,917m
(9,570ft)
Larisa
Ioannina
Corfu
Corfu
GREECE
Preveza Lamia
Vlore
Pindus Mountains
Volos
Limnos
Lesvos
Euboea
Skyros
Chios
Chalkida
Kefallonia
Patra
Peiraias Athens
Pyrgos
Kalamata
Cyclades
nian Sea
Kythira
Aegean
Sea
Balikesir
Akhisar
Manisa
Izmir Odemis
Ephesus
Aydin
Kutahya
Usak
Denizli
Lake Tuz
Aksaray
Konya
Beysehir
Lake
Karaman
Isparta
Antalya
Alanya
Gulf of
Antalya
Taurus Mountains
Dodecanese
Rhodes
Rhodes
Karpathos
Nicosia
CYPRUS
Kyrenia
Larnaca
Paphos Limassol

Chania Crete Irakleio
Ierapetra

1

48°
N

2

44°

3

40°

4

AFRICA

Africa is the second-biggest continent in the world, and has 53 countries. These range from the vast, dry Sudan, to small, tropical islands such as the Seychelles. More than a quarter of Africa's countries are landlocked, with no access to the sea except through other countries.

Here is a group of Masai people from East Africa, silhouetted against a sunset over the flat grasslands of Africa.

Madeira
(Portugal)

Canary Islands
(Spain)

Algiers
Tunis

Rabat

MOROCCO

TUNISIA
Tripoli

Laayoune

ALGERIA

LIBYA

Tropic of Cancer

WESTERN SAHARA
(Morocco)

MAURITANIA
Nouakchott

MALI

Niger

NIGER

CHAD

CAPE VERDE
Praia

Dakar
SENEGAL
THE GAMBIA Banjul
Bissau
GUINEA-BISSAU
GUINEA
Conakry
Freetown
SIERRA LEONE
Monrovia
LIBERIA
Yamoussoukro

Bamako

Ouagadougou
BURKINA FASO

IVORY COAST

GHANA
Accra

Niamey

BENIN
TOGO
Lome

Porto-Novo

NIGERIA
Abuja

Ndjamen

CENTR
AFRICA
REPUB
Bangui

CAMEROON

Malabo
EQUATORIAL
GUINEA

Yaounde

Equator

SAO TOME
AND PRINCIPE

Libreville

GABON

Con

CONGO

Brazzaville

Kinshasa

ATLANTIC

OCEAN

Luanda

ANGOLA

NAMIBIA

Tropic of Capricorn

Windhoek

Orang

64

The shading on this map is there to help you see clearly the different countries that make up the continent.

Cairo■
EGYPT

Tropic of Cancer

Nile

ERITREA
Khartoum■ ■Asmara
SUDAN
■**DJIBOUTI** ■Djibouti
Addis Ababa■ **SOMALIA**
ETHIOPIA

■Mogadishu

UGANDA
Kampala■ **KENYA** Equator
ONGO
Kigali■ ■Nairobi
DEM. ■**RWANDA**
BURUNDI
EP.) Bujumbura
■Dodoma
TANZANIA ■Dar es Salaam

Victoria■
SEYCHELLES

INDIAN

MALAWI ■Moroni
COMOROS
AMBIA ■Lilongwe
OCEAN
Lusaka■
Zambezi
Harare■ **MOZAMBIQUE**
ZIMBABWE
TSWANA ■Antananarivo
MAURITIUS
borone■ **MADAGASCAR** ■Port Louis
Pretoria■ ■Maputo *Reunion*
Mbabane■**SWAZILAND** *(France)* Tropic of Capricorn
emfontein■ Lobamba
■Maseru
LESOTHO
OUTH
RICA

Internet link
For a link to a website where you can find facts, photos and a quiz about Madagascar's amazing wildlife, go to **www.usborne-quicklinks.com**

Facts

Total land area 30,311,690 sq km (11,703,343 sq miles)
Total population 794 million
Biggest city Lagos, Nigeria
Biggest country Sudan *2,505,810 sq km (967,493 sq miles)*
Smallest country Seychelles *455 sq km (176 sq miles)*

Highest mountain Kilimanjaro, Tanzania *5,895m (19,340ft)*
Longest river Nile, running from to Burundi to Egypt *6,671km (4,145 miles)*
Biggest lake Lake Victoria, between Tanzania, Kenya and Uganda *69,215 sq km (26,724 sq miles)*
Highest waterfall Tugela Falls, on the Tugela River, South Africa *610m (2,000ft)*
Biggest desert Sahara, North Africa *9,100,000 sq km (3,500,000 sq miles)*
Biggest island Madagascar *587,040 sq km (226,656 sq miles)*

Main mineral deposits Gold, copper, diamonds, iron ore, manganese, bauxite
Main fuel deposits Coal, uranium, natural gas

This greater flamingo is from the Transvaal National Park, South Africa.

A 0° B 5°E

Saida
Djelfa
Batna
Atlas Mountains
Biskra
Tebessa
El Oued
Touggourt
Ghardaia
Ouargla
Chott
el Jerid
Gafsa
Tozeur
Gabes
Jerba
Tataouine
TUNISIA

Annaba
Menzel
Bourguiba
Bizerte
Carthage
Tunis
Kairouan
Sousse
Monastir
El Jem
Sfax
Kerkenah
Islands
Gulf of Gabes

Sicily
(Italy)
Catania
Syracuse
Pantelleria
(Italy)
Pelagian
Islands
(Italy)

MALTA
Valletta

GREECE Ath

Mediterranea

Tripoli
Al Khums
Leptis Magna
Gharyan
Misratah

Benghazi
Cyrene
Al Bayda
Darnah
Tubruq
Ajdabiya

Surt
Gulf of
Sidra

2

30°
N

Tademait
Plateau

Great
Eastern Erg

Ghadamis

ALGERIA

3

Illizi

Sabha

LIBYA

Liby

25°

Murzuq

Ahaggar
Mountains
Ghat

Mount Tahat
2,918m
(9,573ft)

Tropic of Cancer

Tamanrasset

Al Jaw

4

Djado
Plateau

Tibesti
Mountains

20°

Emi Koussi
3,415m
(11,204ft)

MALI S   A   H   A   R   A

5

Agadez

NIGER

Faya-Largeau

Bodele
Depression

Ennedi
Plateau

Tahoua

15°

CHAD

Dosso
Sokoto
Maradi
Zinder
Mao

Abeche

Mount M

Birnin-Kebbi
Katsina
Gusau
S   A   H   E   L

6

Kandi
Kano
Lake Chad

Ndjamena

3,08
(10,1

Zaria
Potiskum
Maiduguri

Mongo
Am Timan

Ny

Kainji
Reservoir
Kaduna
NIGERIA
Niger
Minna
Jos
Kumo

Saki
Bida

Abuja

Maroua
CAMEROON
Bongor

Birao

7

10°

B 5°E C 10° D 15° E 20° F

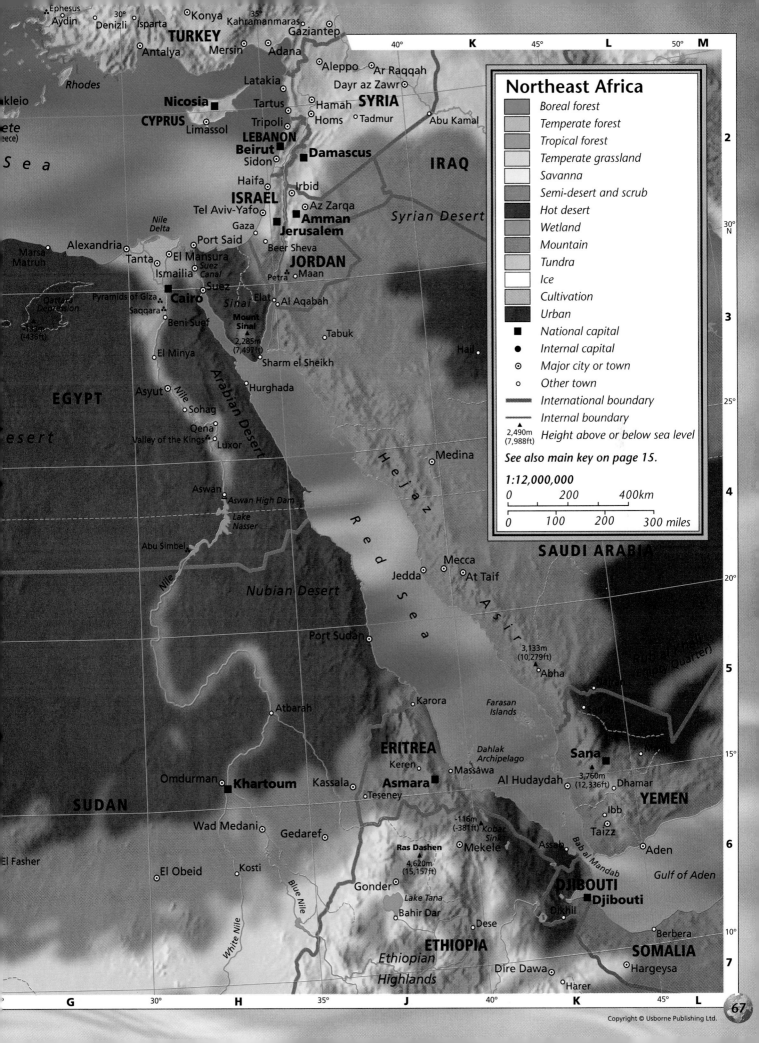

Northeast Africa

Ephesus
Aydin
30°
Denizli
Isparta
Konya
35°
Kahramanmaras
Gaziantep
K
45°
50°
M

TURKEY
Antalya
Mersin
Adana
Aleppo
Ar Raqqah
Dayr az Zawr
2

Rhodes
Latakia
Tartus
Hamah
Homs
SYRIA
Tadmur
Abu Kamal
IRAQ

kleio
(Greece)
Nicosia
CYPRUS
Limassol
Tripoli
Sidon
LEBANON
Beirut
Damascus
Syrian Desert
30°N

Sea
Haifa
Irbid
Az Zarqa
Amman
Jerusalem
Gaza
Beer Sheva
JORDAN
Petra
Maan

Marsa
Matruh
Alexandria
Tanta
El Mansura
Port Said
Ismailia
Suez Canal
Suez
Sinai
Elat
Al Aqabah
Tabuk
Hail
3

Nile
Delta
Pyramids of Giza
Cairo
Saqqara
Beni Suef
Mount
Sinai
2,285m
(7,497ft)
Sharm el Sheikh

Qattara
Depression
(-436ft)
El Minya
Asyut
Nile
Sohag
Qena
Valley of the Kings
Luxor
Hurghada
Medina
4

EGYPT
Desert
Arabian Desert
Aswan
Aswan High Dam
Lake
Nasser
Hejaz
Red
Sea

Abu Simbel
Nubian Desert
Jedda
Mecca
At Taif
SAUDI ARABIA
Rub al Khali
(empty quarter)
20°

Port Sudan
Asir
3,133m
(10,279ft)
Abha
5

Atbarah
Karora
Farasan
Islands

ERITREA
Keren
Dahlak
Archipelago
Sana
3,760m
(12,336ft)
Dhamar
15°

Omdurman
Khartoum
Kassala
Asmara
Massawa
Al Hudaydah
YEMEN

SUDAN
Teseney
Ibb
Taizz

Wad Medani
Gedaref
-116m
(-381ft)
Kobar
Sink
Mekele
Assab
Aden
Gulf of Aden
6

El Fasher
El Obeid
Kosti
Ras Dashen
4,620m
(15,157ft)
Gonder
Lake Tana
Bahir Dar
Dese
DJIBOUTI
Djibouti
Dikhil
Berbera
10°

Blue Nile
White Nile
ETHIOPIA
Ethiopian
Highlands
Dire Dawa
Harer
SOMALIA
Hargeysa
7

G
30°
H
35°
J
40°
K
45°
L

Boreal forest
Temperate forest
Tropical forest
Temperate grassland
Savanna
Semi-desert and scrub
Hot desert
Wetland
Mountain
Tundra
Ice
Cultivation
Urban

■ National capital
● Internal capital
⊙ Major city or town
○ Other town
International boundary
Internal boundary
▲ 2,490m (7,988ft) Height above or below sea level

See also main key on page 15.

1:12,000,000

0   200   400km
0 100 200 300 miles

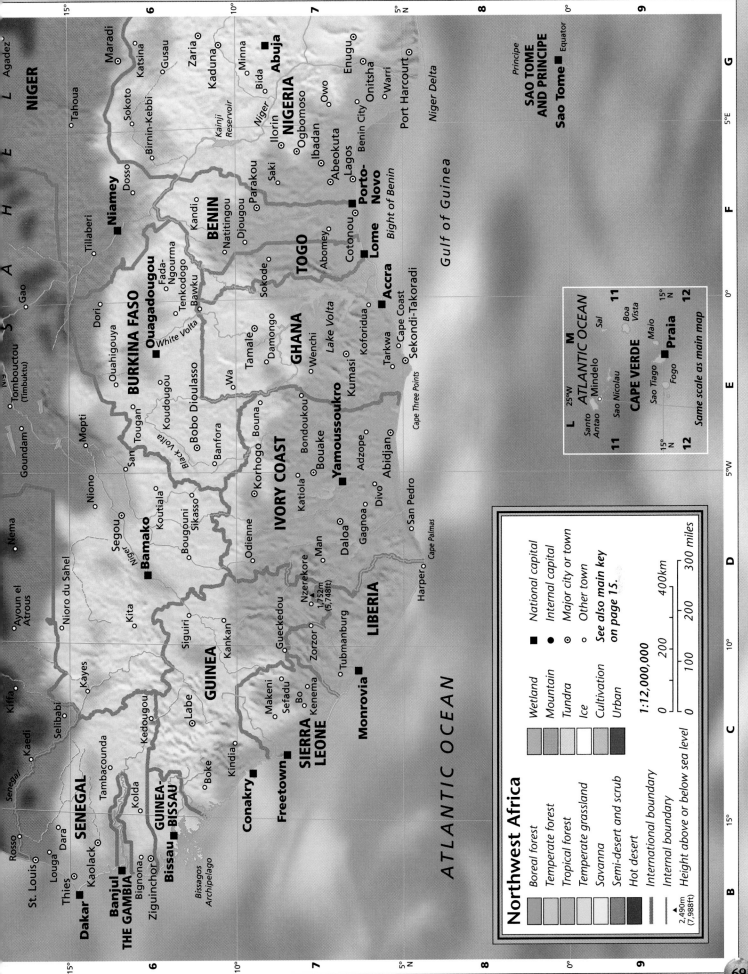

Northwest Africa

Boreal forest
Temperate forest
Tropical forest
Temperate grassland
Savanna
Semi-desert and scrub
Hot desert
International boundary
Internal boundary
Height above or below sea level

▲ 2,490m (7,998ft)

■ National capital
● Internal capital
◉ Major city or town
○ Other town

See also main key on page 15.

1:12,000,000

0	100	200	300 miles
0	200	400km	

Wetland
Mountain
Tundra
Ice
Cultivation
Urban

ATLANTIC OCEAN

L   **M**

25°W

ATLANTIC OCEAN

Santo
Antao
Mindelo
Sao Nicolau
Sal
Boa
Vista

CAPE VERDE
Sao Tiago
Maio
■ **Praia**
Fogo

15°N

11   **11**

12   **12**

Same scale as main map

NIGER

S A H E L

S A H A R A

Agadez
Maradi
Katsina
Gusau
Zaria
Minna
Enugu
Port Harcourt
Tahoua
Sokoto
Birnin-Kebbi
Kaduna
Bida
■ **Abuja**
Ilorin
NIGERIA
Ogbomoso
Ibadan
Abeokuta
Benin City
Onitsha
Warri
Niger Delta
Tombouctou (Timbuktu)
Gao
Dori
Kandi
Nattingou
Djougou
Parakou
Saki
Owo
Port-Novo
Bight of Benin
Niamey
Tillaberi
BURKINA FASO
Ouahigouya
Fada-Ngourma
Tenkodogo
Bawku
BENIN
Sokode
Cotonou
Abomey
Lome
TOGO
Gulf of Guinea
Dosso
Goundam
Mopti
Niono
Ouagadougou
Dori
White Volta
Tamale
Damongo
Wenchi
Lake Volta
Accra
Cape Coast
Sekondi-Takoradi
Koforidua
Tarkwa
Cape Three Points

SAO TOME AND PRINCIPE
Principe
■ **Sao Tome**   *Equator*

5°E

G

F

E

D

C

B

Nema
Ayoun el Atrous
Nioro du Sahel
Kiffa
Selibabi
Kaedi
Rosso
St. Louis
Louga
Dara
Thies
■ **Dakar**
Kaolack
SENEGAL
Tambacounda
Kolda
Bignona
■ **Banjul**
THE GAMBIA
Ziguinchor
GUINEA-BISSAU
■ **Bissau**
Bissagos Archipelago
Boke
Kindia
■ **Conakry**
GUINEA
Labe
Siguiri
Kankan
Kedougou
Kayes
Kita
Segou
SENEGAL
Senegal
San
Tougan
Koudougou
Bobo Dioulasso
Banfora
Sikasso
Koutiala
■ **Bamako**
Niger
Bougouni
Odienne
Bouna
Korhogo
Katiola
Bouake
Man
IVORY COAST
Daloa
Gagnoa
Divo
Abidjan
Adzope
Yamoussoukro
San Pedro
Nzerekore
▲ 1,752m (5,748ft)
Zorzor
Gueckedou
Kenema
Bo
Makeni
Sefadu
SIERRA LEONE
■ **Freetown**
Kindia
Tubmanburg
■ **Monrovia**
LIBERIA
Harper
Cape Palmas
Black Volta
Wa
Bondoukou
Kumasi
GHANA
ATLANTIC OCEAN

6   **7**   **8**   **9**

15°   *10°*   *5°N*   *0°*   *5°E*

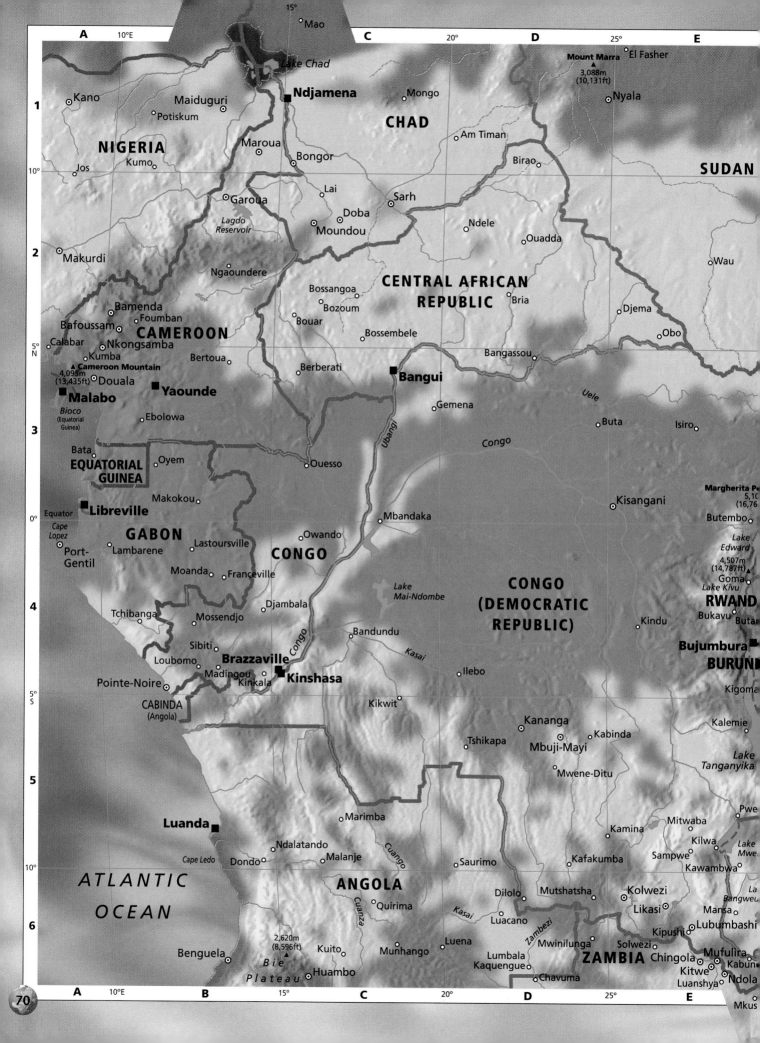

F 35° G 40° H 45° J 50° K

Obeid

Kosti

Ras Dashen
4,620m
(15,157ft)

Gonder

Mekele

Assab

Bab al Mandab

Taizz

YEMEN

Aden

Gulf of Aden

Cape
Guardafui

Lake Tana

Bahir Dar

DJIBOUTI

Dikhil ■ Djibouti

Boosaaso

1

Malakal

Blue Nile

White Nile

*Ethiopian
Highlands*

Dese

Berbera

10°

Dire Dawa

Hargeysa

SOMALIA

Gambela

Nekemte

Addis Ababa

Harer

Debre Zeyit Nazret

Eyl

White Nile

Jima

ETHIOPIA

2

Juba

Awasa

Gode

*Lake
Abaya*

5°
N

Beledweyne

Gulu

Moyale

Mandera

Juba

Baydhabo

UGANDA

Soroti

Mount Elgon
4,321m
(14,176ft)

Baardheere

Mogadishu

3

Lake
Albert

Lake
Kyoga

Mbale

Kitale

KENYA

Marka

Kampala ■

Jinja

Eldoret

Meru

Entebbe

Nakuru

Kirinyaga
(Mount Kenya)
5,199m
(17,057ft)

Garissa

Kismaayo

Masaka

Kisumu

Mbarara

Kisii

Nyeri

0°

igali

Lake Victoria

Nairobi ■

Thika

Machakos

Mwanza

Kilimanjaro
5,895m
(19,340ft)

Malindi

4

Great Rift Valley

Moshi

Arusha

Mombasa

Tabora

Tanga

Pemba Island

INDIAN

5°
S

Dodoma ■

Zanzibar

Zanzibar Island

OCEAN

TANZANIA

Morogoro

Dar es Salaam ■

Lake Rukwa

Iringa

*Mafia
Island*

5

Mbeya

Makumbako

Ilonga

Njinjo

Great Rift Valley

bala

Tunduma

Liwale

Lindi

10°

Kasama

Karonga

Songea

Masasi

Mtwara

Isoka

Mzuzu

Lake Nyasa
(Lake Malawi)

Tunduru

Palma

Cape Delgado

COMOROS

Grand Comoro
(Njazidja)

ZAMBIA

Mpika

Lupilichi

Ruvuma

Mueda

Moroni ■

Anjouan
Island
(Nzwani)

6

Lundazi

Kasungu

Lichinga

Mecula

Pemba

Mutsamudu

Mamoudzou

Chipata

MALAWI

MOZAMBIQUE

Nungo

Fomboni

Mohilla Island
(Mwali)

Mayotte
(France)

Petauke

Lilongwe ■

Cuamba

35°

G 40° H 45° J 50° K

Central Africa

- Boreal forest
- Temperate forest
- Tropical forest
- Temperate grassland
- Savanna
- Semi-desert and scrub
- Hot desert
- Wetland
- Mountain
- Tundra
- Ice
- Cultivation
- Urban
- ■ National capital
- ● Internal capital
- ⊙ Major city or town
- ○ Other town
- ─── International boundary
- ─ ─ ─ Internal boundary
- ▲ 2,490m (7,988ft) Height above or below sea level

See also main key on page 15.

1:12,000,000

0 200 400km

0 100 200 300 miles

ATLANTIC OCEAN

ANGOLA

CONGO (DEMOCRATIC REPUBLIC)

ZAMBIA

ZIMBABWE

NAMIBIA

BOTSWANA

SOUTH AFRICA

LESOTHO

SWAZILAND

Luanda
Marimba
Ndalatando
Dondo
Cape Ledo
Malanje
Saurimo
Kamina
Kafakumba
Dilolo
Mutshatsha
Kolwezi
Likasi
Mitwaba
Kilwa
Sampwe
Pweto
Kawambwa
Mbala
Kasa
Lake Mweru
Lake Bangweulu
Mansa
Mpika
Lubumbashi
Kipushi
Mufulira
Kabunda
Chingola
Kitwe
Ndola
Luanshya
Mkushi
Kabwe
Petau
Solwezi
Mwinilunga
Luacano
Quirima
Cuanza
Kasai
Zambezi
Luena
Munhango
Lumbala Kaquengue
Chavuma
Zambezi
Kuito
Cangombe
Lumbala Nguimbo
Lukulu
Mongu
Rufunsa
Lusaka
Zumbo
Cabora B Reservo
Mo Dar
Mute
Bindura
Harare
Kadoma
Benguela
Huambo
2,620m (8,596ft)
Bie Plateau
Mumbue
Menongue
Caiundo
Mavinga
Kataba
Ngoma
Kafue
Zambezi
Lake Kariba
Kariba
Chinhoyi
Binga
Lucira
Cape St. Martha
Matala
Lubango
Namibe
Albino Point
Xangongo
Cunene
Luiana
Sesheke
Zimba
Livingstone
Victoria Falls
Kamativi
Gweru
Masvir
Zvishavane
Chiredzi
Foz do Cunene
Opuwo
Ondangwa
Cuangar
Rundu
Andara
Caprivi Strip
Okavango Swamp
Hwange
Kamanjab
Okaukuejo
Etosha Pan
Tsumeb
Otavi
Kaukau Veld
Okavango
Nokaneng
Maun
Tsau
Makgadikgadi Pans (Makarikari)
Bulawayo
Plumtree
Messina
Pa Lir
Otjiwarongo
Lake Ngami
Rakops
Francistown
Orapa
Selebi-Phikwe
Serowe
Sukses
NAMIBIA
Karibib
Okahandja
Gobabis
Mamuno
Tshwane
Mahalapye
Swakopmund
Walvis Bay
Windhoek
Leonardville
Kang
Molepolole
Mochudi
Warmbad
Grasko
Tropic of Capricorn
Rehoboth
Pietersburg
Nelspruit
Kalkrand
Mariental
Gochas
Kalahari Desert
Tshane
Gaborone
Kanye
Werda
Pretoria
Krugersdorp
Benoni
Mbaban
Johannesburg
Springs
Lobamba
Terra Firma
Mmabatho
Tses
Keetmanshoop
Seeheim
Grunau
Molopo
Tshabong
Orkneyo
Standerton
Kroonstad
Maseru
Richar
Ladysmith
Pietermaritzbur
Luderitz
Hotazel
Welkom
Bethlehem
Harrismith
Tugela Falls
Upington
Kimberley
Douglas
Bloemfontein
Mafeteng
LESOTHO
Durba
Alexander Bay
Orange
Kenhardt
Prieska
Orange
2,770m (9,088ft)
Drakensberg
Umtata
Bitterfontein
Carnarvon
De Aar
Beaufort West
Graaff-Reinet
Cradock
Bisho
East London
Grahamstown
Cape Columbine
Great Karoo
Groot
Uitenhage
Port Elizabeth
Paarl
Worcester
Oudtshoorn
Cape Town
Stellenbosch
Cape of Good Hope
Cape Agulhas
Cape St. Francis

72

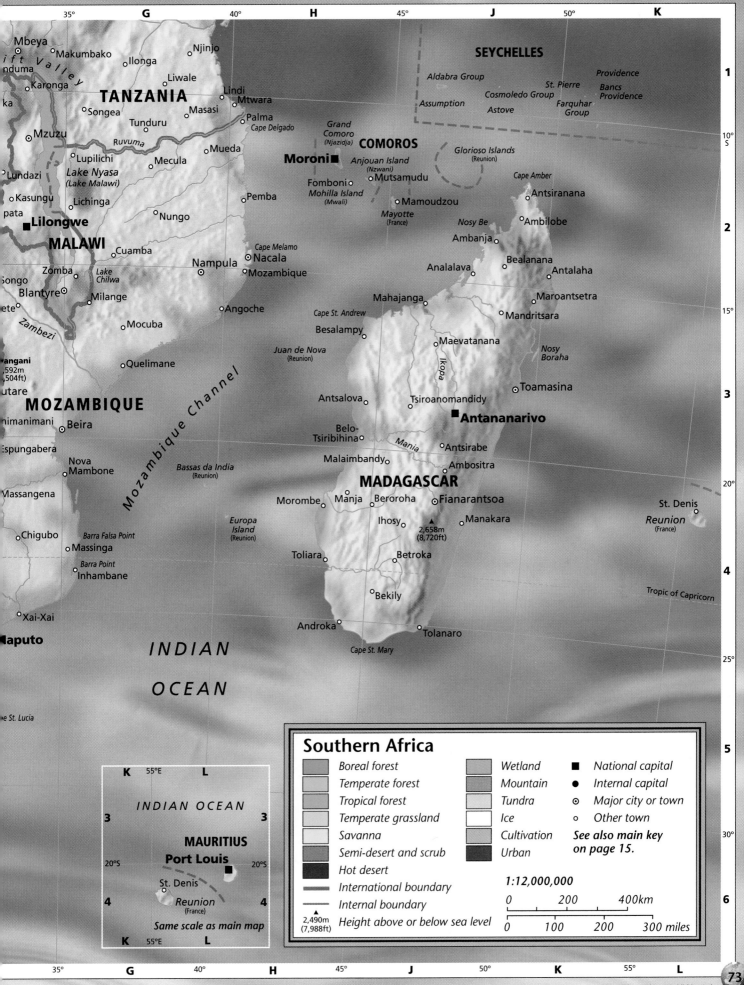

SEYCHELLES

Aldabra Group
Assumption
Cosmoledo Group
Astove
St. Pierre
Farquhar Group
Providence
Bancs Providence

Mbeya
Makumbako
Ilonga
Njinjo
nduma
Karonga
Liwale
TANZANIA
Lindi
Mtwara
Songea
Masasi
Tunduru
Palma
Cape Delgado
Mueda
Grand Comoro
(Njazidja)
COMOROS
Glorioso Islands
(Reunion)
Cape Amber
Mzuzu
Lupilichi
Mecula
Pemba
Moroni
Anjouan Island
(Nzwani)
Mutsamudu
Antsiranana
Lundazi
Kasungu
Lichinga
Nungo
Fomboni
Mohilla Island
(Mwali)
Mamoudzou
Ambilobe
pata
Lilongwe
MALAWI
Cuamba
*Lake Nyasa
(Lake Malawi)*
Nampula
Cape Melamo
Nacala
Mozambique
Mayotte
(France)
Nosy Be
Ambanja
Analalava
Bealanana
Antalaha
Zomba
*Lake
Chilwa*
Milange
Angoche
Cape St. Andrew
Besalampy
Mahajanga
Mandritsara
Maroantsetra
Songo
Blantyre
Maevatanana
*Nosy
Boraha*
Zambezi
Mocuba
Juan de Nova
(Reunion)
Ikopa
angani
,592m
,504ft)
Quelimane
Antsalova
Tsiroanomandidy
Toamasina
utare
MOZAMBIQUE
Beira
Mozambique Channel
Belo-
Tsiribihina
Mania
Antananarivo
imanimani
Espungabera
Antsirabe
Nova
Mambone
Malaimbandy
Ambositra
Massangena
MADAGASCAR
Europa
Island
(Reunion)
Morombe
Manja
Beroroha
Fianarantsoa
St. Denis
Reunion
(France)
Chigubo
Barra Falsa Point
Ihosy
2,658m
(8,720ft)
Manakara
Massinga
Barra Point
Inhambane
Toliara
Betroka
Bekily
Xai-Xai
Androka
Tolanaro
laputo
Cape St. Mary

INDIAN

OCEAN

e St. Lucia

Tropic of Capricorn

Southern Africa

Boreal forest	Wetland	■ National capital
Temperate forest	Mountain	● Internal capital
Tropical forest	Tundra	◉ Major city or town
Temperate grassland	Ice	○ Other town
Savanna	Cultivation	*See also main key*
Semi-desert and scrub	Urban	*on page 15.*
Hot desert		

International boundary
Internal boundary
▲ 2,490m
(7,988ft) Height above or below sea level

1:12,000,000

0   200   400km
0 100 200 300 miles

Inset map

K 55°E L

INDIAN OCEAN

MAURITIUS
Port Louis

St. Denis
Reunion
(France)

Same scale as main map

K 55°E L

THE ARCTIC

The Arctic is not a continent. It is a region north of the Arctic Circle line of latitude, around the North Pole. The Arctic consists of the Arctic Ocean, islands such as Greenland and the most northerly parts of mainland Europe, North America and Asia. The Arctic region is covered in ice and snow almost all year round.

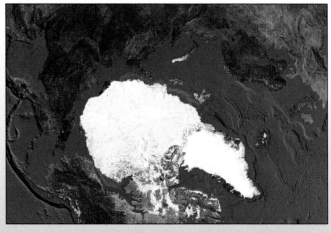

The large white area in this satellite image is ice covering the Arctic Ocean and Greenland. At the top left of the image is the edge of Russia and at the top right is part of Europe.

These Inuit people are wearing thick, animal-skin coats, boots and gloves to keep warm.

Internet link

For a link to a website where you can discover more about the Arctic, including its wildlife, climate and native peoples, go to **www.usborne-quicklinks.com**

Facts

Size of Arctic Ocean
14,056,000 sq km (5,426,000 sq miles)

Highest point Gunnbjorns Mountain, Greenland *3,700m (12,139ft)*

Lowest point Fram Basin, Arctic Ocean *-4,665m (-15,305ft)*

Lowest recorded temperature -67.8°C (-90°F)

Main mineral deposits Diamonds, gold

Main fuel deposits Oil, natural gas

Seals living in Arctic regions have a thick layer of fat under their skin to keep them warm in the freezing weather.

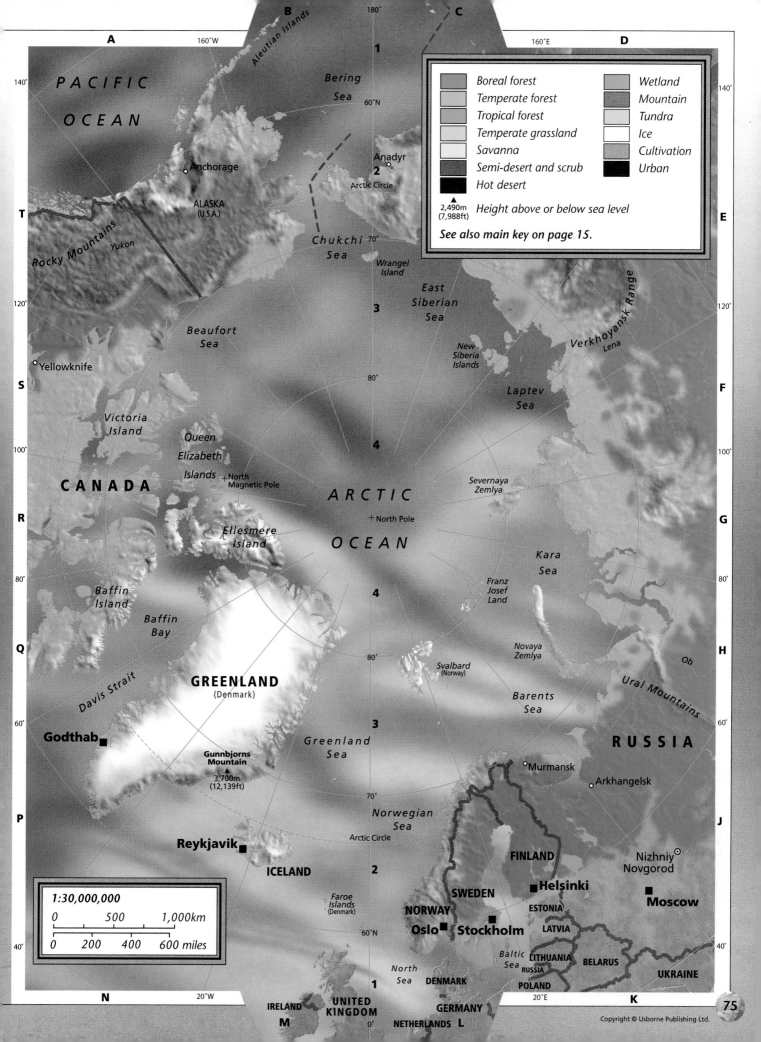

PACIFIC OCEAN

A · 160°W · 140° · B · 180° · C · 160°E · D

Aleutian Islands

Bering Sea

60°N

Anadyr

Arctic Circle

ALASKA (U.S.A.)

Rocky Mountains · Yukon

Chukchi Sea · 70°

Wrangel Island

East Siberian Sea

Anchorage

Beaufort Sea

New Siberia Islands

Verkhoyansk Range · Lena

Yellowknife

80°

Laptev Sea

Victoria Island

Queen Elizabeth Islands

North Magnetic Pole

Severnaya Zemlya

ARCTIC OCEAN

North Pole

CANADA

Ellesmere Island

Kara Sea

Baffin Island

Franz Josef Land

Baffin Bay

80°

Novaya Zemlya

Svalbard (Norway)

Ob

Ural Mountains

Davis Strait

GREENLAND (Denmark)

Barents Sea

RUSSIA

60°

Godthab

Gunnbjorns Mountain
▲
3,700m (12,139ft)

Greenland Sea

Murmansk

Arkhangelsk

70°

Norwegian Sea

Arctic Circle

Reykjavik

FINLAND

Nizhniy Novgorod

ICELAND

Faroe Islands (Denmark)

SWEDEN

Helsinki

Moscow

ESTONIA

NORWAY

Oslo · Stockholm

LATVIA

North Sea

Baltic Sea

LITHUANIA

RUSSIA

BELARUS

60°N

DENMARK

40°

POLAND

20°E

UKRAINE

N · 20°W · M · 0° · L · 20°E · K

IRELAND · UNITED KINGDOM · GERMANY · NETHERLANDS

Key

	Boreal forest		Wetland
	Temperate forest		Mountain
	Tropical forest		Tundra
	Temperate grassland		Ice
	Savanna		Cultivation
	Semi-desert and scrub		Urban
	Hot desert		

▲ 2,490m (7,988ft) Height above or below sea level

See also main key on page 15.

1:30,000,000

0 · 500 · 1,000km

0 · 200 · 400 · 600 miles

ANTARCTICA

Antarctica is a huge, frozen continent within the Antarctic Circle. It is almost completely covered by an enormous ice sheet, which is more than 3km (2 miles) deep in some places. Nobody lives permanently in Antarctica, though many scientists visit to study the area. No plants grow in the ice, and the only land animals are tiny mites. But many animals, including penguins, seals, whales and fish, live in the seas around Antarctica.

This ship takes tourists on Antarctic expeditions. Visitors can see animals such as these gentoo penguins, which come onto land to breed.

Internet link

For a link to a website where you can find out more about Antarctica and the creatures that live in the seas around it, go to **www.usborne-quicklinks.com**

Facts

Total land area 14,000,000 sq km (5,405,442 sq miles), of which 13,720,000 sq km (5,297,333 sq miles) are covered in ice

Highest point Vinson Massif *5,140m (16,863ft)*

Lowest point Bentley Subglacial Trench *-2,555m (-8,382ft)*

Lowest recorded temperature -89.2°C (-128.6°F)

Main mineral deposits Iron ore, chromium, copper, gold, nickel, platinum

The green area in this satellite photograph is a hole in the ozone layer over Antarctica. The hole is caused by atmospheric pollution.

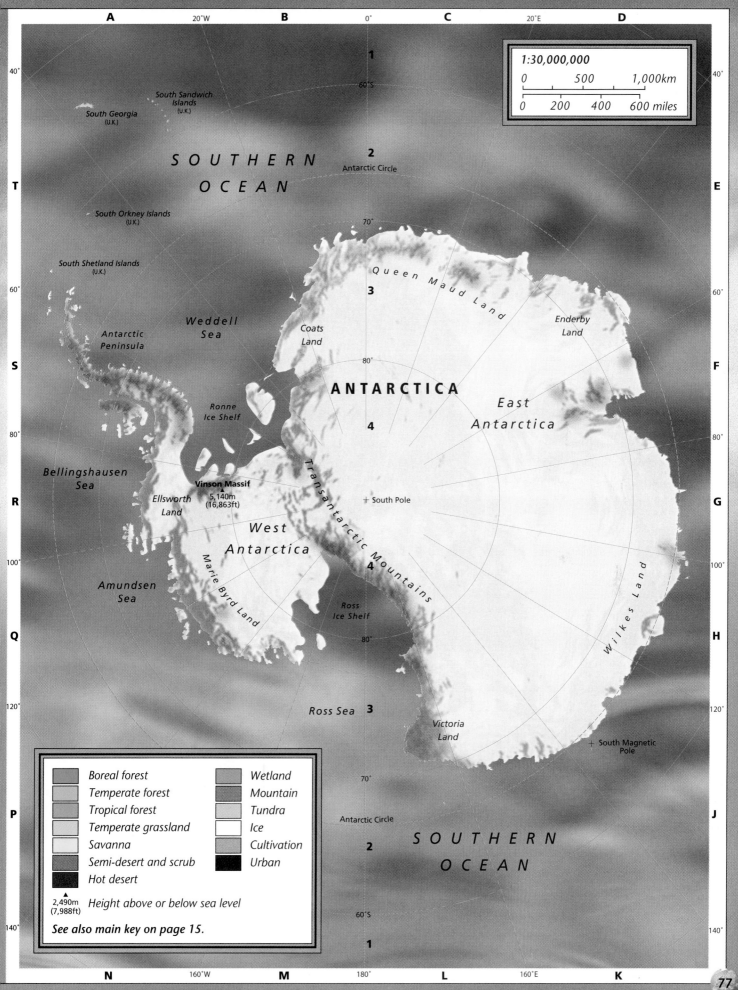

A 20°W B 0° C 20°E D

1

60°S

40°

1:30,000,000

| 0 | 500 | 1,000km |
| 0 | 200 | 400 | 600 miles |

T E

S O U T H E R N

2

Antarctic Circle

O C E A N

70°

South Georgia
(U.K.)

South Sandwich
Islands
(U.K.)

South Orkney Islands
(U.K.)

South Shetland Islands
(U.K.)

60°

*Weddell
Sea*

3

Q u e e n   M a u d   L a n d

Coats
Land

*Enderby
Land*

60°

80°

*Antarctic
Peninsula*

S F

80°

ANTARCTICA

*East
Antarctica*

Ronne
Ice Shelf

*Bellingshausen
Sea*

Vinson Massif
▲
5,140m
(16,863ft)

4

+ South Pole

80°

R G

*Ellsworth
Land*

T r a n s a n t a r c t i c   M o u n t a i n s

*West
Antarctica*

4

100°

*Amundsen
Sea*

Marie Byrd Land

W i l k e s   L a n d

100°

Ross
Ice Shelf

Q H

80°

Ross Sea

3

*Victoria
Land*

+ South Magnetic
Pole

120° 120°

70°

P J

Antarctic Circle

S O U T H E R N

2

O C E A N

60°S

1

140° 140°

N 160°W M 180° L 160°E K

Key

Boreal forest		Wetland	
Temperate forest		Mountain	
Tropical forest		Tundra	
Temperate grassland		Ice	
Savanna		Cultivation	
Semi-desert and scrub		Urban	
Hot desert			

▲
2,490m
(7,988ft)   Height above or below sea level

See also main key on page 15.

WORLD RECORDS

Here are some of the Earth's longest rivers, highest mountains and other amazing world records. But the world is always changing; mountains wear down, rivers change shape, and new buildings are constructed. Ways of measuring things can also change. That's why you may find slightly different figures in different books.

Highest mountains	
Everest, Nepal/China	8,850m (29,035ft)
K2, Pakistan/China	8,611m (28,251ft)
Kanchenjunga, India/Nepal	8,597m (28,208ft)
Lhotse I, Nepal/China	8,511m (27,923ft)
Makalu I, Nepal/China	8,481m (27,824ft)
Lhotse II, Nepal/China	8,400m (27,560ft)
Dhaulagiri, Nepal	8,172m (26,810ft)
Manaslu I, Nepal	8,156m (26,760ft)
Cho Oyu, Nepal/China	8,153m (26,750ft)
Nanga Parbat, Pakistan	8,126m (26,660ft)

Longest rivers	
Nile, Africa	6,671km (4,145 miles)
Amazon, South America	6,440km (4,000 miles)
Chang Jiang (Yangtze), China	6,380km (3,964 miles)
Mississippi/Missouri, U.S.A.	6,019km (3,741 miles)
Yenisey/Angara, Russia	5,540km (3,442 miles)
Huang He (Yellow), China	5,464km (3,395 miles)
Ob/Irtysh/Black Irtysh, Asia	5,411km (3,362 miles)
Amur/Shilka/Onon, Asia	4,416km (2,744 miles)
Lena, Russia	4,400km (2,734 miles)
Congo, Africa	4,374km (2,718 miles)

Biggest natural lakes	
Caspian Sea	370,999 sq km (143,243 sq miles)
Lake Superior	82,414 sq km (31,820 sq miles)
Lake Victoria	69,215 sq km (26,724 sq miles)
Lake Huron	59,596 sq km (23,010 sq miles)
Lake Michigan	58,016 sq km (22,400 sq miles)
Lake Tanganyika	32,764 sq km (12,650 sq miles)
Lake Baikal	31,500 sq km (12,162 sq miles)
Great Bear Lake	31,328 sq km (12,096 sq miles)
Lake Nyasa	29,928 sq km (11,555 sq miles)
Aral Sea	28,600 sq km (11,042 sq miles)

Deepest ocean
The Mariana Trench, part of the Pacific Ocean, is the deepest part of the sea at 10,911m (35,797ft) deep.

Deepest lake
Lake Baikal in Russia is the deepest lake in the world. At its deepest point it is 1,637m (5,370ft) deep.

Biggest islands	
Greenland	2,175,600 sq km (840,000 sq miles)
New Guinea	800,000 sq km (309,000 sq miles)
Borneo	751,100 sq km (290,000 sq miles)
Madagascar	587,040 sq km (226,656 sq miles)
Baffin Island	507,451 sq km (195,928 sq miles)
Sumatra	437,607 sq km (184,706 sq miles)
Great Britain	234,410 sq km (90,506 sq miles)
Honshu	227,920 sq km (88,000 sq miles)
Victoria Island	217,290 sq km (83,896 sq miles)
Ellesmere Island	196,236 sq km (75,767 sq miles)

Tallest inhabited buildings	
Petronas Towers, Malaysia	452m (1,483ft)
Sears Tower, U.S.A.	443m (1,454ft)
Jin Mao Building, China	420m (1,378ft)
CITIC Plaza, China	391m (1,283ft)
Shun Hing Square, China	384m (1,260ft)
Plaza Rakyat, Malaysia	382m (1,254ft)
Empire State Building, U.S.A.	381m (1,250ft)
Central Plaza, China	373m (1,227ft)
Bank of China, China	368m (1,209ft)
Emirates Tower, U.A.E.	350m (1,148ft)

Biggest cities/urban areas	
Tokyo, Japan	26.4 million
Mexico City, Mexico	18.1 million
Bombay, India	18.1 million
Sao Paulo, Brazil	17.8 million
New York, U.S.A.	16.6 million
Lagos, Nigeria	13.4 million
Los Angeles, U.S.A.	13.1 million
Calcutta, India	12.9 million
Shanghai, China	12.9 million
Buenos Aires, Argentina	12.6 million

Famous waterfalls	Height
Angel Falls, Venezuela	979m (3,212ft)
Sutherland Falls, New Zealand	580m (1,904ft)
Mardalfossen, Norway	517m (1,696ft)
Jog Falls, India	253m (830ft)
Victoria Falls, Zimbabwe/Zambia	108m (355ft)
Iguacu Falls, Brazil/Argentina	82m (269ft)
Niagara Falls, Canada/U.S.A.	57m (187ft)

Natural disasters

Natural disasters can be measured in different ways. For example, some earthquakes score highly on the Richter scale, while others cause more destruction. The earthquakes, volcanic eruptions, floods, hurricanes and tornadoes listed here are among the most famous and destructive disasters in history.

Earthquakes	Richter scale	Disastrous effects
San Francisco, U.S.A., 1906	7.9	3,000 died in resulting fire
Messina, Italy, 1908	7.5	More than 70,000 people died
Tokyo-Kanto, Japan, 1923	8.3	Great Tokyo Fire; 142,807 died
Quetta, Pakistan, 1935	7.5	30–60,000 died; city destroyed
Concepcion, Chile, 1960	8.7	2,000 died; strongest quake ever
Alaska, U.S.A., 1964	8.6	125 died; strongest U.S. quake ever
Tangshan, China, 1976	7.9	More than 655,000 people died
Manjil-Rudbar, Iran, 1990	7.7	50,000 died; cities destroyed
Kobe, Japan, 1995	6.8	6,400 died; over $147bn damage
Gujarat, India, 2001	8.0	20,085 died; 2nd strongest Indian quake

Volcanic eruptions	Disastrous effects
Mount Vesuvius, Italy, AD79	Pompeii flattened; up to 20,000 died
Tambora, Indonesia, 1815	92,000 people starved to death
Krakatau, Indonesia, 1883	36,500 drowned in resulting tsunami
Mount Pelee, Martinique, 1902	Nearly 30,000 people buried in ash flows
Kelut, Indonesia, 1919	Over 5,000 people drowned in mud
Agung, Indonesia, 1963	1,200 people suffocated in hot ash
Mount St. Helens, U.S.A., 1980	Only 61 died but a large area was destroyed
Ruiz, Colombia, 1985	25,000 people died in giant mud flows
Mt. Pinatubo, Philippines, 1991	800 killed by collapsing roofs and disease
Island of Montserrat, 1995	Volcano left most of the island uninhabitable

Floods	Disastrous effects
Holland, 1228	100,000 drowned by a sea flood
Kaifeng, China, 1642	300,000 died after rebels destroyed a dyke
Johnstown, U.S.A., 1889	2,200 killed in a flood caused by rain
Italy, 1963	Vaoint Dam overflowed; 2–3,000 killed
East Pakistan, 1970	Giant wave caused by cyclone killed 250,000
Bangladesh, 1988	1,300 died, 30m homeless in monsoon flood
Southern U.S.A., 1993	$12bn of damage after Mississippi flooded
China, 1998	Chang Jiang overflow left 14m homeless
Papua New Guinea, 1998	Tsunamis killed 2,000 people
Venezuela, 1999	Floods and mudslides killed 5,000–20,000

Storms	Disastrous effects
Caribbean "Great Hurricane", 1780	Biggest ever hurricane killed over 20,000
Hong Kong typhoon, China, 1906	10,000 people died in this giant hurricane
Killer tornado, U.S.A., 1925	Up to 700 people died in Ellington, Missouri
Tropical Storm Agnes, U.S.A., 1972	$3.5bn damage, 129 dead
Hurricane Fifi, Honduras, 1974	8,000 people died and 100,000 left homeless
Hurricane Georges, U.S.A., 1998	Caribbean and U.S.A. hit; $5bn of damage
Hurricane Mitch, C. America, 1998	Over 9,000 killed across Central America

Amazing Earth facts

The Earth is 12,103km (7,520 miles) across. Its circumference (the distance around the Equator) is 38,022km (23,627 miles) and it is 149,503,000 km (92,897,000 miles) away from the Sun.

To make one complete orbit around the Sun, the Earth has to travel 938,900,000km (583,400,000 miles). To do this in just a year, it has to travel very fast. Because of the atmosphere surrounding the Earth, you can't feel it moving. But in fact you are zooming through space faster than any rocket.

• **Orbit speed** The Earth travels around the Sun at a speed of about 106,000kph (65,868mph).

• **Spinning speed** The Earth also spins around an axis, but the speed you are spinning at depends on where you live. Places on the Equator move at 1,600kph (995mph). New York moves at around 1,100kph (684mph). Near the poles, the spinning is not very fast at all. (You can see how this works by looking at a spinning globe.)

• **Solar System speed** The whole Solar System, including the Sun, the Earth and its moon, and the other planets and their moons, is moving at 72,400kph (45,000 mph) through the galaxy.

• **Galaxy speed** Our galaxy, the Milky Way, whizzes through the universe at a speed of 2,172,150kph (1,350,000mph).

TIME ZONES

The Earth is divided into different time zones. Within each zone, people usually set their clocks to the same time. If you fly between two zones, you change your watch to the time in the new zone.

Dividing up time

There are 25 time zones. They are separated by one-hour intervals and there is a time zone every 15 degrees of longitude. There are 12 one-hour zones both ahead of and behind Greenwich Mean Time (GMT), the time at the Prime Meridian Line.

For convenience, whole countries usually keep the same local time instead of sticking to the zones exactly. For example, China could be divided into several time zones, but instead the whole country has the same time. A few places, such as India, use non-standard half hour deviations.

Summer time

Some places adjust their clocks in summer. For example, in the U.K. all clocks go forward one hour. It is a way of getting more out of the days by having an extra hour of light.

Changing dates

The International Date Line runs mostly through the Pacific Ocean and bends to avoid the land. Places to the west of it are 24 hours ahead of places to the east. This means that if you travel east across it you lose a day and if you travel west across it you gain a day.

This map shows the time zones. The times at the top of the map tell you the time in the different zones when it is noon at the Prime Meridian Line. There are two midnight zones, one for each day on either side of the International Date Line. The numbers in circles tell you how many hours ahead of or behind Greenwich Mean Time an area is.

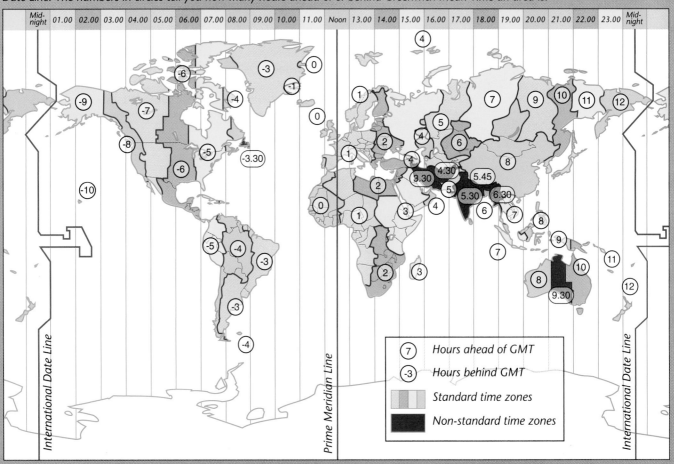

TYPES OF GOVERNMENTS

Most states have one main leader along with a parliament or assembly of politicians. The main types of governments are listed and explained below. A state can have a combination of more than one of these types of governments. For example, the United States of America is a federal republic.

Anarchy
Anarchy means a situation where there is no government. This can happen after a civil war, when a government has been destroyed and rival groups are battling to take its place.

Capitalist state
In a Capitalist or free-market state, people can own their own businesses and property, and buy services such as healthcare privately. However, most Capitalist governments also provide national health, education and welfare services.

Commonwealth
This word is sometimes used to mean a democratic republic, in which all the state's citizens are seen as having an equal interest in the functioning of the state.

Communist state
Under Communism, the state owns things like factories, farms and businesses, and provides healthcare, welfare and education for its people.

Democracy
In a democracy, the government is elected by the people, using a voting system.

Dictatorship
This is a state run by a single, unelected leader, who may use force to keep control. In a military dictatorship, the army is in power.

Federal government
In a federal system, such as that of the U.S.A., a central government shares power with a number of smaller regional governments.

Monarchy
A monarchy is a state with a king or queen. In some traditional monarchies, the monarch has complete power. A constitutional monarchy, however, also has a separate, usually democratic, government and the monarch's powers are limited.

Regional or local government
A government that controls a smaller area within a state. Some regional governments have very limited powers, and are largely directed by the central government. Others, such as the regional governments in the U.S.A., have much more power and can make their own laws.

Republic
A republic is a state with no monarch. The head of state is usually an elected president.

Revolutionary government
After a revolution, when a government is overthrown by force, the new regime is sometimes called a revolutionary government.

Totalitarian state
This is a state with only one political party, in which individuals are forced to obey the government and may also be prevented from leaving the country.

Transitional government
A government that is changing from one system to another is known as a transitional government. For example, a dictatorship may become a democracy after the dictator dies, but the transition between the systems can take several years.

GAZETTEER OF STATES

Afghanistan

Albania

Algeria

Andorra

Angola

Antigua and Barbuda

• **Argentina**

This gazetteer lists the world's 193 independent states, along with key facts about each one. In the lists of languages, the language that is most widely spoken is given first, even if it is not the official language. In the lists of religions, the one followed by the most people is also placed first. Every state has a national flag, which is usually used to represent the country abroad. A few states also have a state flag which they prefer to use instead. The state flags appear here with a dot • beside them.

AFGHANISTAN (Asia)
Area: 647,500 sq km (249,935 sq miles)
Population: 27,755,775
Capital city: Kabul
Main languages: Dari, Pashto
Main religion: Muslim
Government: transitional
Currency: 1 afghani = 100 puls

ALBANIA (Europe)
Area: 28,750 sq km (11,100 sq miles)
Population: 3,544,841
Capital city: Tirana
Main language: Albanian
Main religions: Muslim, Albanian Orthodox
Government: emerging democracy
Currency: 1 lek = 100 qintars

ALGERIA (Africa)
Area: 2,381,740 sq km (919,589 sq miles)
Population: 32,277,942
Capital city: Algiers
Main languages: Arabic, French, Berber dialects
Main religion: Sunni Muslim
Government: republic
Currency: 1 Algerian dinar = 100 centimes

ANDORRA (Europe)
Area: 468 sq km (181 sq miles)
Population: 68,403
Capital city: Andorra la Vella
Main languages: Catalan, Spanish
Main religion: Roman Catholic
Government: parliamentary democracy
Currency: 1 euro = 100 cents

ANGOLA (Africa)
Area: 1,246,700 sq km (481,351 sq miles)
Population: 10,593,171
Capital city: Luanda
Main languages: Kilongo, Kimbundu, other Bantu languages, Portuguese
Main religions: indigenous, Roman Catholic, Protestant
Government: transitional
Currency: 1 kwanza = 100 lwei

ANTIGUA AND BARBUDA (North America)
Area: 442 sq km (171 sq miles)
Population: 67,448
Capital city: Saint John's
Main languages: Caribbean Creole, English
Main religion: Protestant
Government: constitutional monarchy
Currency: 1 East Caribbean dollar = 100 cents

ARGENTINA (South America)
Area: 2,766,890 sq km (1,068,305 sq miles)
Population: 37,812,817
Capital city: Buenos Aires
Main language: Spanish
Main religion: Roman Catholic
Government: republic
Currency: 1 peso = 100 centavos

ARMENIA (Asia)
Area: 29,800 sq km (11,506 sq miles)
Population: 3,336,100
Capital city: Yerevan
Main language: Armenian
Main religion: Armenian Orthodox
Government: republic
Currency: 1 dram = 100 luma

AUSTRALIA (Australasia/Oceania)
Area: 7,686,850 sq km (2,967,124 sq miles)
Population: 19,546,792
Capital city: Canberra
Main language: English
Main religion: Christian
Government: federal democratic monarchy
Currency: 1 Australian dollar = 100 cents

AUSTRIA (Europe)
Area: 83,858 sq km (32,378 sq miles)
Population: 8,169,929
Capital city: Vienna
Main language: German
Main religion: Roman Catholic
Government: federal republic
Currency: 1 euro = 100 cents

Armenia

Australia

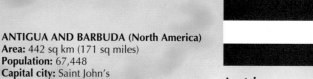

Austria

Azerbaijan

Bahamas, The

Bahrain

Bangladesh

Barbados

Belarus

Belgium

Belize

Benin

Bhutan

• **Bolivia**

AZERBAIJAN (Asia)
Area: 86,600 sq km (33,436 sq miles)
Population: 7,798,497
Capital city: Baku
Main language: Azeri
Main religion: Muslim
Government: republic
Currency: 1 manat = 100 gopiks

BAHAMAS, THE (North America)
Area: 13,940 sq km (5,382 sq miles)
Population: 300,529
Capital city: Nassau
Main languages: Bahamian Creole, English
Main religion: Christian
Government: parliamentary democracy
Currency: 1 Bahamian dollar = 100 cents

BAHRAIN (Asia)
Area: 665 sq km (257 sq miles)
Population: 656,397
Capital city: Manama
Main languages: Arabic, English
Main religion: Muslim
Government: traditional monarchy
Currency: 1 Bahraini dinar = 1,000 fils

BANGLADESH (Asia)
Area: 144,000 sq km (55,598 sq miles)
Population: 133,376,684
Capital city: Dhaka
Main languages: Bengali, English
Main religions: Muslim, Hindu
Government: republic
Currency: 1 taka = 100 poisha

BARBADOS (North America)
Area: 430 sq km (166 sq miles)
Population: 276,607
Capital city: Bridgetown
Main languages: Bajan, English
Main religion: Christian
Government: parliamentary democracy
Currency: 1 Barbadian dollar = 100 cents

BELARUS (Europe)
Area: 207,600 sq km (80,154 sq miles)
Population: 10,335,382
Capital city: Minsk
Main language: Belarusian
Main religion: Eastern Orthodox
Government: republic
Currency: 1 Belarusian ruble = 100 kopecks

BELGIUM (Europe)
Area: 30,510 sq km (11,780 sq miles)
Population: 10,274,595
Capital city: Brussels
Main languages: Dutch, French
Main religions: Roman Catholic, Protestant
Government: constitutional monarchy
Currency: 1 euro = 100 cents

BELIZE (North America)
Area: 22,960 sq km (8,865 sq miles)
Population: 262,999
Capital city: Belmopan
Main languages: Spanish, Belize Creole, English, Garifuna, Maya

Main religions: Roman Catholic, Protestant
Government: parliamentary democracy
Currency: 1 Belizean dollar = 100 cents

BENIN (Africa)
Area: 112,620 sq km (43,483 sq miles)
Population: 6,787,625
Capital city: Porto-Novo
Main languages: Fon, French, Yoruba
Main religions: indigenous, Christian, Muslim
Government: republic
Currency: 1 CFA* franc = 100 centimes

BHUTAN (Asia)
Area: 47,000 sq km (18,146 sq miles)
Population: 2,094,176
Capital city: Thimphu
Main languages: Dzongkha, Nepali
Main religions: Buddhist, Hindu
Government: monarchy
Currency: 1 ngultrum = 100 chetrum

BOLIVIA (South America)
Area: 1,098,580 sq km (424,162 sq miles)
Population: 8,445,134
Capital cities: La Paz, Sucre
Main languages: Spanish, Quechua, Aymara
Main religion: Roman Catholic
Government: republic
Currency: 1 boliviano = 100 centavos

BOSNIA AND HERZEGOVINA (Europe)
Area: 51,129 sq km (19,741 sq miles)
Population: 3,964,388
Capital city: Sarajevo
Main languages: Bosnian, Serbian, Croatian
Main religions: Muslim, Orthodox, Roman Catholic
Government: emerging federal democracy
Currency: 1 marka = 100 pfenninga

BOTSWANA (Africa)
Area: 600,372 sq km (231,743 sq miles)
Population: 1,591,232
Capital city: Gaborone
Main languages: Setswana, Kalanga, English
Main religions: indigenous, Christian
Government: parliamentary republic
Currency: 1 pula = 100 thebe

BRAZIL (South America)
Area: 8,547,400 sq km (3,300,151 sq miles)
Population: 176,029,560
Capital city: Brasilia
Main language: Portuguese
Main religion: Roman Catholic
Government: federal republic
Currency: 1 real = 100 centavos

BRUNEI (Asia)
Area: 5,770 sq km (2,228 sq miles)
Population: 350,898
Capital city: Bandar Seri Begawan
Main languages: Malay, English, Chinese
Main religions: Muslim, Buddhist
Government: constitutional sultanate (a type of monarchy)
Currency: 1 Bruneian dollar = 100 cents

Bosnia and Herzegovina

Botswana

Brazil

Brunei

Bulgaria

Burkina Faso

Burma (Myanmar)

*CFA = Communaute Financiere Africaine

Burundi

Cambodia

Cameroon

Canada

Cape Verde

Central African Republic

Chad

BULGARIA (Europe)
Area: 110,910 sq km (42,822 sq miles)
Population: 7,621,337
Capital city: Sofia
Main language: Bulgarian
Main religions: Bulgarian Orthodox, Muslim
Government: parliamentary democracy
Currency: 1 lev = 100 stotinki

BURKINA FASO (Africa)
Area: 274,200 sq km (105,869 sq miles)
Population: 12,603,185
Capital city: Ouagadougou
Main languages: Moore, Jula, French
Main religions: Muslim, indigenous
Government: republic
Currency: 1 CFA* franc = 100 centimes

BURMA (MYANMAR) (Asia)
Area: 678,500 sq km (261,969 sq miles)
Population: 42,238,224
Capital city: Rangoon
Main language: Burmese
Main religion: Buddhist
Government: military dictatorship
Currency: 1 kyat = 100 pyas

BURUNDI (Africa)
Area: 27,830 sq km (10,745 sq miles)
Population: 6,373,002
Capital city: Bujumbura
Main languages: Kirundi, French, Swahili
Main religions: Christian, indigenous
Government: republic
Currency: 1 Burundi franc = 100 centimes

CAMBODIA (Asia)
Area: 181,040 sq km (69,900 sq miles)
Population: 12,775,324
Capital city: Phnom Penh
Main language: Khmer
Main religion: Buddhist
Government: constitutional monarchy
Currency: 1 new riel = 100 sen

CAMEROON (Africa)
Area: 475,440 sq km (183,567 sq miles)
Population: 16,184,748
Capital city: Yaounde
Main languages: Cameroon Pidgin English, Ewondo, Fula, French, English
Main religions: indigenous, Christian, Muslim
Government: republic
Currency: 1 CFA* franc = 100 centimes

CANADA (North America)
Area: 9,970,610 sq km (3,849,653 sq miles)
Population: 31,902,268
Capital city: Ottawa
Main languages: English, French
Main religions: Roman Catholic, Protestant
Government: federal democracy
Currency: 1 Canadian dollar = 100 cents

CAPE VERDE (Africa)
Area: 4,033 sq km (1,557 sq miles)
Population: 408,760
Capital city: Praia
Main languages: Crioulo*, Portuguese

Main religions: Roman Catholic, Protestant
Government: republic
Currency: 1 Cape Verdean escudo = 100 centavos

CENTRAL AFRICAN REPUBLIC (Africa)
Area: 622,984 sq km (240,536 sq miles)
Population: 3,642,739
Capital city: Bangui
Main languages: Sangho, French
Main religions: indigenous, Christian, Muslim
Government: republic
Currency: 1 CFA* franc = 100 centimes

CHAD (Africa)
Area: 1,284,000 sq km (495,752 sq miles)
Population: 8,997,237
Capital city: Ndjamena
Main languages: Arabic, Sara, French
Main religions: Muslim, Christian, indigenous
Government: republic
Currency: 1 CFA* franc = 100 centimes

CHILE (South America)
Area: 756,626 sq km (292,133 sq miles)
Population: 15,498,930
Capital city: Santiago
Main language: Spanish
Main religions: Roman Catholic, Protestant
Government: republic
Currency: 1 Chilean peso = 100 centavos

CHINA (Asia)
Area: 9,596,960 sq km (3,705,386 sq miles)
Population: 1,284,303,705
Capital city: Beijing
Main languages: Mandarin Chinese, Yue, Wu
Main religions: Taoist, Buddhist
Government: Communist state
Currency: 1 yuan = 10 jiao

COLOMBIA (South America)
Area: 1,138,910 sq km (439,733 sq miles)
Population: 41,008,227
Capital city: Bogota
Main language: Spanish
Main religion: Roman Catholic
Government: republic
Currency: 1 Colombian peso = 100 centavos

COMOROS (Africa)
Area: 2,170 sq km (838 sq miles)
Population: 614,382
Capital city: Moroni
Main languages: Comorian*, French, Arabic
Main religion: Sunni Muslim
Government: republic
Currency: 1 Comoran franc = 100 centimes

CONGO (Africa)
Area: 342,000 sq km (132,046 sq miles)
Population: 2,958,448
Capital city: Brazzaville
Main languages: Munukutuba, Lingala, French
Main religions: Christian, animist
Government: republic
Currency: 1 CFA* franc = 100 centimes

Chile

China

Colombia

Comoros

Congo

Congo (Democratic Republic)

Costa Rica

*CFA = Communaute Financiere Africaine; Comorian = a blend of Swahili and Arabic; Crioulo = a blend of Portuguese and West African

Croatia

Cuba

Cyprus

Czech Republic

Denmark

Djibouti

Dominica

CONGO (DEMOCRATIC REPUBLIC) (Africa)
Area: 2,345,410 sq km (905,563 sq miles)
Population: 55,225,478
Capital city: Kinshasa
Main languages: Lingala, Swahili, Kikongo, Tshiluba, French
Main religions: Roman Catholic, Protestant, Kimbanguist, Muslim
Government: transitional
Currency: 1 Congolese franc = 100 centimes

COSTA RICA (North America)
Area: 51,100 sq km (19,730 sq miles)
Population: 3,834,934
Capital city: San Jose
Main language: Spanish
Main religions: Roman Catholic, Evangelical
Government: democratic republic
Currency: 1 Costa Rican colon = 100 centimos

CROATIA (Europe)
Area: 56,538 sq km (21,829 sq miles)
Population: 4,390,751
Capital city: Zagreb
Main language: Croatian
Main religions: Roman Catholic, Orthodox
Government: parliamentary democracy
Currency: 1 kuna = 100 lipas

CUBA (North America)
Area: 110,860 sq km (42,803 sq miles)
Population: 11,224,321
Capital city: Havana
Main language: Spanish
Main religion: Roman Catholic
Government: Communist state
Currency: 1 Cuban peso = 100 centavos

CYPRUS (Europe)
Area: 9,250 sq km (3,571 sq miles)
Population: 767,314
Capital city: Nicosia
Main languages: Greek, Turkish
Main religions: Greek Orthodox, Muslim
Government: republic with a self-proclaimed independent Turkish area
Currency: Greek Cypriot area: 1 Cypriot pound = 100 cents; Turkish Cypriot area: 1 Turkish lira = 100 kurus

CZECH REPUBLIC (Europe)
Area: 78,866 sq km (30,450 sq miles)
Population: 10,256,760
Capital city: Prague
Main language: Czech
Main religion: Roman Catholic
Government: parliamentary democracy
Currency: 1 koruna = 100 haleru

DENMARK (Europe)
Area: 43,094 sq km (16,639 sq miles)
Population: 5,368,854
Capital city: Copenhagen
Main language: Danish
Main religion: Evangelical Lutheran
Government: constitutional monarchy
Currency: 1 Danish krone = 100 oere

DJIBOUTI (Africa)
Area: 23,200 sq km (8,957 sq miles)
Population: 472,810
Capital city: Djibouti
Main languages: Afar, Somali, Arabic, French
Main religion: Muslim
Government: republic
Currency: 1 Djiboutian franc = 100 centimes

DOMINICA (North America)
Area: 751 sq km (290 sq miles)
Population: 70,158
Capital city: Roseau
Main languages: English, French patois
Main religions: Roman Catholic, Protestant
Government: democratic republic
Currency: 1 East Caribbean dollar = 100 cents

DOMINICAN REPUBLIC (North America)
Area: 48,730 sq km (18,815 sq miles)
Population: 8,721,594
Capital city: Santo Domingo
Main language: Spanish
Main religion: Roman Catholic
Government: democratic republic
Currency: 1 Dominican peso = 100 centavos

EAST TIMOR (Asia)
Area: 15,007 sq km (5,794 sq miles)
Population: 952,618
Capital city: Dili
Main languages: Tetum, Portuguese, Indonesian
Main religions: Roman Catholic, animist
Government: republic
Currency: 1 U.S. dollar = 100 cents

ECUADOR (South America)
Area: 283,560 sq km (109,483 sq miles)
Population: 13,447,494
Capital city: Quito
Main languages: Spanish, Quechua
Main religion: Roman Catholic
Government: republic
Currency: 1 sucre = 100 centavos

EGYPT (Africa)
Area: 1,001,450 sq km (386,660 sq miles)
Population: 70,712,345
Capital city: Cairo
Main language: Arabic
Main religion: Sunni Muslim
Government: republic
Currency: 1 Egyptian pound = 100 piasters

EL SALVADOR (North America)
Area: 21,040 sq km (8,124 sq miles)
Population: 6,353,681
Capital city: San Salvador
Main language: Spanish
Main religion: Roman Catholic
Government: republic
Currency: 1 Salvadoran colon = 100 centavos

EQUATORIAL GUINEA (Africa)
Area: 28,050 sq km (10,830 sq miles)
Population: 498,144
Capital city: Malabo

• **Dominican Republic**

East Timor

• **Ecuador**

Egypt

• **El Salvador**

Equatorial Guinea

Eritrea

Estonia

Main languages: Fang, Bubi, other Bantu languages, Spanish, French, Pidgin English
Main religion: Christian
Government: republic
Currency: 1 CFA* franc = 100 centimes

ERITREA (Africa)
Area: 121,320 sq km (46,842 sq miles)
Population: 4,465,651
Capital city: Asmara
Main languages: Tigrinya, Afar, Arabic
Main religions: Muslim, Coptic Christian, Roman Catholic, Protestant
Government: transitional
Currency: 1 nafka = 100 cents

Ethiopia

ESTONIA (Europe)
Area: 45,226 sq km (17,462 sq miles)
Population: 1,415,681
Capital city: Tallinn
Main languages: Estonian, Russian
Main religions: Evangelical Lutheran, Russian and Estonian Orthodox, other Christian
Government: parliamentary democracy
Currency: 1 Estonian kroon = 100 senti

Federated States of Micronesia

ETHIOPIA (Africa)
Area: 1,127,127 sq km (435,184 sq miles)
Population: 67,673,031
Capital city: Addis Ababa
Main languages: Amharic, Tigrinya, Arabic
Main religions: Muslim, Ethiopian Orthodox, animist
Government: federal republic
Currency: 1 birr = 100 cents

FEDERATED STATES OF MICRONESIA (Australasia/Oceania)
Area: 702 sq km (271 sq miles)
Population: 135,869
Capital city: Palikir
Main languages: Chuuk, Ponapean, English
Main religions: Roman Catholic, Protestant
Government: democracy
Currency: 1 U.S. dollar = 100 cents

Fiji

FIJI (Australasia/Oceania)
Area: 18,270 sq km (7,054 sq miles)
Population: 856,346
Capital city: Suva
Main languages: Fijian, Hindustani, English
Main religions: Christian, Hindu
Government: republic
Currency: 1 Fijian dollar = 100 cents

Finland

FINLAND (Europe)
Area: 337,030 sq km (130,127 sq miles)
Population: 5,183,545
Capital city: Helsinki
Main language: Finnish
Main religion: Evangelical Lutheran
Government: republic
Currency: 1 euro = 100 cents

France

FRANCE (Europe)
Area: 547,030 sq km (211,208 sq miles)
Population: 59,765,983
Capital city: Paris
Main language: French

Gabon

Main religion: Roman Catholic
Government: republic
Currency: 1 euro = 100 cents

GABON (Africa)
Area: 267,670 sq km (103,347 sq miles)
Population: 1,233,353
Capital city: Libreville
Main languages: Fang, Myene, French
Main religions: Christian, animist
Government: republic
Currency: 1 CFA* franc = 100 centimes

GAMBIA, THE (Africa)
Area: 11,300 sq km (4,363 sq miles)
Population: 1,455,842
Capital city: Banjul
Main languages: Mandinka, Fula, Wolof, English
Main religion: Muslim
Government: democratic republic
Currency: 1 dalasi = 100 butut

GEORGIA (Asia)
Area: 69,700 sq km (26,911 sq miles)
Population: 4,960,951
Capital city: Tbilisi
Main languages: Georgian, Russian
Main religions: Georgian Orthodox, Muslim, Russian Orthodox
Government: republic
Currency: 1 lari = 100 tetri

GERMANY (Europe)
Area: 357,021 sq km (137,846 sq miles)
Population: 83,251,851
Capital city: Berlin
Main language: German
Main religions: Protestant, Roman Catholic
Government: federal republic
Currency: 1 euro = 100 cents

GHANA (Africa)
Area: 239,460 sq km (92,456 sq miles)
Population: 20,244,154
Capital city: Accra
Main languages: Twi, Fante, Ga, Hausa, Dagbani, Ewe, Nzemi, English
Main religions: indigenous, Muslim, Christian
Government: democratic republic
Currency: 1 new cedi = 100 pesewas

GREECE (Europe)
Area: 131,940 sq km (50,942 sq miles)
Population: 10,645,343
Capital city: Athens
Main language: Greek
Main religion: Greek Orthodox
Government: parliamentary republic
Currency: 1 euro = 100 cents

GRENADA (North America)
Area: 340 sq km (131 sq miles)
Population: 89,211
Capital city: Saint George's
Main languages: English, French patois
Main religions: Roman Catholic, Protestant
Government: constitutional monarchy
Currency: 1 East Caribbean dollar = 100 cents

Gambia, The

Georgia

Germany

Ghana

Greece

Grenada

Guatemala

*CFA = Communaute Financiere Africaine

Guinea

Guinea-Bissau

Guyana

• Haiti

Honduras

Hungary

Iceland

GUATEMALA (North America)
Area: 108,890 sq km (42,042 sq miles)
Population: 13,314,079
Capital city: Guatemala City
Main languages: Spanish, Amerindian languages including Quiche, Kekchi, Cakchiquel, Mam
Main religions: Roman Catholic, Protestant, indigenous Mayan beliefs
Government: democratic republic
Currency: 1 quetzal = 100 centavos

GUINEA (Africa)
Area: 245,860 sq km (94,927 sq miles)
Population: 7,775,065
Capital city: Conakry
Main languages: Fuuta Jalon, Mallinke, Susu, French
Main religion: Muslim
Government: republic
Currency: 1 Guinean franc = 100 centimes

GUINEA-BISSAU (Africa)
Area: 36,120 sq km (13,946 sq miles)
Population: 1,345,479
Capital city: Bissau
Main languages: Crioulo*, Balante, Pulaar, Mandjak, Mandinka, Portuguese
Main religions: indigenous, Muslim
Government: republic
Currency: 1 CFA* franc = 100 centimes

GUYANA (South America)
Area: 214,970 sq km (83,000 sq miles)
Population: 698,209
Capital city: Georgetown
Main languages: Guyanese Creole, English, Amerindian languages, Caribbean Hindi
Main religions: Christian, Hindu
Government: republic
Currency: 1 Guyanese dollar = 100 cents

HAITI (North America)
Area: 27,750 sq km (10,714 sq miles)
Population: 7,063,722
Capital city: Port-au-Prince
Main languages: Haitian Creole, French
Main religions: Roman Catholic, Protestant, Voodoo
Government: republic
Currency: 1 gourde = 100 centimes

HONDURAS (North America)
Area: 112,090 sq km (43,278 sq miles)
Population: 6,560,608
Capital city: Tegucigalpa
Main language: Spanish
Main religion: Roman Catholic
Government: republic
Currency: 1 lempira = 100 centavos

HUNGARY (Europe)
Area: 93,030 sq km (35,919 sq miles)
Population: 10,075,034
Capital city: Budapest
Main language: Hungarian
Main religions: Roman Catholic, Calvinist
Government: parliamentary democracy
Currency: 1 forint = 100 filler

ICELAND (Europe)
Area: 103,000 sq km (39,768 sq miles)
Population: 279,384
Capital city: Reykjavik
Main language: Icelandic
Main religion: Evangelical Lutheran
Government: republic
Currency: 1 Icelandic krona = 100 aurar

INDIA (Asia)
Area: 3,287,590 sq km (1,269,339 sq miles)
Population: 1,045,845,226
Capital city: New Delhi
Main languages: Hindi, English, Bengali, Urdu, over 1,600 other languages and dialects
Main religions: Hindu, Muslim
Government: federal republic
Currency: 1 Indian rupee = 100 paise

INDONESIA (Asia)
Area: 1,919,440 sq km (741,096 sq miles)
Population: 231,328,092
Capital city: Jakarta
Main languages: Bahasa Indonesia, English, Dutch, Javanese
Main religion: Muslim
Government: republic
Currency: 1 Indonesian rupiah = 100 sen

IRAN (Asia)
Area: 1,648,000 sq km (636,293 sq miles)
Population: 66,622,704
Capital city: Tehran
Main languages: Farsi and other Persian dialects, Azeri
Main religions: Shi'a Muslim, Sunni Muslim
Government: Islamic republic
Currency: 10 Iranian rials = 1 toman

IRAQ (Asia)
Area: 437,072 sq km (168,754 sq miles)
Population: 24,001,816
Capital city: Baghdad
Main languages: Arabic, Kurdish
Main religion: Muslim
Government: republic under a military regime
Currency: 1 Iraqi dinar = 1,000 fils

IRELAND (Europe)
Area: 70,280 sq km (27,135 sq miles)
Population: 3,883,159
Capital city: Dublin
Main languages: English, Irish (Gaelic)
Main religion: Roman Catholic
Government: republic
Currency: 1 euro = 100 cents

ISRAEL (Asia)
Area: 20,770 sq km (8,019 sq miles)
Population: 6,029,529
Capital city: Jerusalem
Main languages: Hebrew, Arabic
Main religions: Jewish, Muslim
Government: parliamentary democracy
Currency: 1 Israeli shekel = 100 agorot

India

Indonesia

Iran

Iraq

Ireland

Israel

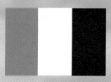

Italy

*CFA = Communaute Financiere Africaine;
Crioulo = a blend of Portuguese and West African

Ivory Coast

ITALY (Europe)
Area: 301,230 sq km (116,305 sq miles)
Population: 57,715,625
Capital city: Rome
Main language: Italian
Main religion: Roman Catholic
Government: republic
Currency: 1 euro = 100 cents

Jamaica

IVORY COAST (Africa)
Area: 322,460 sq km (124,502 sq miles)
Population: 16,804,784
Capital city: Yamoussoukro
Main languages: Baoule, Dioula, French
Main religions: Christian, Muslim, animist
Government: republic
Currency: 1 CFA* = 100 centimes

Japan

JAMAICA (North America)
Area: 10,990 sq km (4,243 sq miles)
Population: 2,680,029
Capital city: Kingston
Main languages: Southwestern Caribbean Creole, English
Main religion: Protestant
Government: parliamentary democracy
Currency: 1 Jamaican dollar = 100 cents

JAPAN (Asia)
Area: 377,835 sq km (145,882 sq miles)
Population: 126,974,628
Capital city: Tokyo
Main language: Japanese
Main religions: Shinto, Buddhist
Government: constitutional monarchy
Currency: 1 yen = 100 sen

Jordan

JORDAN (Asia)
Area: 92,300 sq km (35,637 sq miles)
Population: 5,307,470
Capital city: Amman
Main languages: Arabic, English
Main religion: Sunni Muslim
Government: constitutional monarchy
Currency: 1 Jordanian dinar = 1,000 fils

Kazakhstan

KAZAKHSTAN (Asia)
Area: 2,717,300 sq km (1,049,150 sq miles)
Population: 16,741,519
Capital city: Astana
Main languages: Kazakh, Russian
Main religions: Muslim, Russian Orthodox
Government: republic
Currency: 1 Kazakhstani tenge = 100 tiyn

Kenya

KENYA (Africa)
Area: 582,650 sq km (224,961 sq miles)
Population: 31,138,735
Capital city: Nairobi
Main languages: Swahili, English, Bantu languages
Main religions: Christian, indigenous
Government: republic
Currency: 1 Kenyan shilling = 100 cents

Kiribati

KIRIBATI (Australasia/Oceania)
Area: 811 sq km (313 sq miles)
Population: 96,335
Capital city: Bairiki (on Tarawa island)

Main languages: Gilbertese, English
Main religions: Roman Catholic, Protestant
Government: republic
Currency: 1 Australian dollar = 100 cents

KUWAIT (Asia)
Area: 17,820 sq km (6,880 sq miles)
Population: 2,111,561
Capital city: Kuwait City
Main languages: Arabic, English
Main religion: Muslim
Government: monarchy
Currency: 1 Kuwaiti dinar = 1,000 fils

KYRGYZSTAN (Asia)
Area: 198,500 sq km (76,641 sq miles)
Population: 4,822,166
Capital city: Bishkek
Main languages: Kyrgyz, Russian
Main religions: Muslim, Russian Orthodox
Government: republic
Currency: 1 Kyrgyzstani som = 100 tyiyn

LAOS (Asia)
Area: 236,800 sq km (91,428 sq miles)
Population: 5,777,180
Capital city: Vientiane
Main languages: Lao, French, English
Main religions: Buddhist, animist
Government: Communist state
Currency: 1 new kip = 100 at

LATVIA (Europe)
Area: 64,589 sq km (24,938 sq miles)
Population: 2,366,515
Capital city: Riga
Main languages: Latvian, Russian
Main religions: Lutheran, Roman Catholic, Russian Orthodox
Government: parliamentary democracy
Currency: 1 Latvian lat = 100 santims

LEBANON (Asia)
Area: 10,400 sq km (4,015 sq miles)
Population: 3,677,780
Capital city: Beirut
Main languages: Arabic, French, English
Main religions: Muslim, Christian
Government: republic
Currency: 1 Lebanese pound = 100 piasters

LESOTHO (Africa)
Area: 30,350 sq km (11,718 sq miles)
Population: 2,207,954
Capital cities: Maseru, Lobamba
Main languages: Sesotho, English, Zulu, Xhosa
Main religions: Christian, indigenous
Government: constitutional monarchy
Currency: 1 loti = 100 lisente

LIBERIA (Africa)
Area: 111,370 sq km (43,000 sq miles)
Population: 3,288,198
Capital city: Monrovia
Main languages: Kpelle, English, Bassa
Main religions: indigenous, Christian, Muslim
Government: republic
Currency: 1 Liberian dollar = 100 cents

Kuwait

Kyrgyzstan

Laos

Latvia

Lebanon

Lesotho

Liberia

*CFA = Communaute Financiere Africaine

LIBYA (Africa)
Area: 1,759,540 sq km (679,358 sq miles)
Population: 5,368,585
Capital city: Tripoli
Main languages: Arabic, Italian, English
Main religion: Sunni Muslim
Government: military rule
Currency: 1 Libyan dinar = 1,000 dirhams

LIECHTENSTEIN (Europe)
Area: 160 sq km (62 sq miles)
Population: 32,842
Capital city: Vaduz
Main languages: German, Alemannic
Main religion: Roman Catholic
Government: constitutional monarchy
Currency: 1 Swiss franc = 100 centimes

LITHUANIA (Europe)
Area: 65,200 sq km (25,174 sq miles)
Population: 3,601,138
Capital city: Vilnius
Main languages: Lithuanian, Polish, Russian
Main religions: Roman Catholic, Lutheran, Russian Orthodox
Government: democracy
Currency: 1 Lithuanian litas = 100 centas

LUXEMBOURG (Europe)
Area: 2,586 sq km (998 sq miles)
Population: 448,569
Capital city: Luxembourg
Main languages: Luxemburgish, German, French
Main religion: Roman Catholic
Government: constitutional monarchy
Currency: 1 euro = 100 cents

MACEDONIA (Europe)
Area: 25,333 sq km (9,781 sq miles)
Population: 2,054,800
Capital city: Skopje
Main languages: Macedonian, Albanian
Main religions: Macedonian Orthodox, Muslim
Government: emerging democracy
Currency: 1 Macedonian denar = 100 deni

MADAGASCAR (Africa)
Area: 587,040 sq km (226,656 sq miles)
Population: 16,473,477
Capital city: Antananarivo
Main languages: Malagasy, French
Main religions: indigenous beliefs, Christian
Government: republic
Currency: 1 Malagasy franc = 100 centimes

MALAWI (Africa)
Area: 118,480 sq km (45,745 sq miles)
Population: 10,701,824
Capital city: Lilongwe
Main languages: Chichewa, English
Main religions: Protestant, Roman Catholic, Muslim
Government: parliamentary democracy
Currency: 1 Malawian kwacha = 100 tambala

MALAYSIA (Asia)
Area: 329,750 sq km (127,316 sq miles)
Population: 22,662,365
Capital city: Kuala Lumpur
Main languages: Bahasa Melayu, English, Chinese dialects, Tamil
Main religions: Muslim, Buddhist, Daoist
Government: constitutional monarchy
Currency: 1 ringgit = 100 sen

MALDIVES (Asia)
Area: 300 sq km (116 sq miles)
Population: 320,165
Capital city: Male
Main languages: Maldivian, English
Main religion: Sunni Muslim
Government: republic
Currency: 1 rufiyaa = 100 laari

MALI (Africa)
Area: 1,240,000 sq km (478,764 sq miles)
Population: 11,340,480
Capital city: Bamako
Main languages: Bambara, Fulani, Songhai, French
Main religion: Muslim
Government: republic
Currency: 1 CFA* franc = 100 centimes

MALTA (Europe)
Area: 316 sq km (122 sq miles)
Population: 397,499
Capital city: Valletta
Main languages: Maltese, English
Main religion: Roman Catholic
Government: republic
Currency: 1 Maltese lira = 100 cents

MARSHALL ISLANDS (Australasia/Oceania)
Area: 181 sq km (70 sq miles)
Population: 73,630
Capital city: Majuro
Main languages: Marshallese, English
Main religion: Protestant
Government: republic
Currency: 1 U.S. dollar = 100 cents

MAURITANIA (Africa)
Area: 1,030,700 sq km (397,953 sq miles)
Population: 2,828,858
Capital city: Nouakchott
Main languages: Arabic, Wolof, French
Main religion: Muslim
Government: republic
Currency: 1 ouguiya = 5 khoums

MAURITIUS (Africa)
Area: 2,040 sq km (788 sq miles)
Population: 1,200,206
Capital city: Port Louis
Main languages: Mauritius Creole French, French, Hindi, Bhojpuri, Urdu, Tamil, English
Main religions: Hindu, Christian, Muslim
Government: parliamentary democracy
Currency: 1 Mauritian rupee = 100 cents

MEXICO (North America)
Area: 1,972,550 sq km (761,602 sq miles)
Population: 103,400,165
Capital city: Mexico City
Main languages: Spanish, Mayan, Nahuatl

Libya

Liechtenstein

Lithuania

Luxembourg

Macedonia

Madagascar

Malawi

Malaysia

Maldives

Mali

Malta

Marshall Islands

Mauritania

Mauritius

*CFA = Communaute Financiere Africaine

Mexico

Main religion: Roman Catholic
Government: federal republic
Currency: 1 Mexican peso = 100 centavos

MOLDOVA (Europe)
Area: 33,843 sq km (13,067 sq miles)
Population: 4,434,547
Capital city: Chisinau
Main languages: Moldovan, Russian, Gagauz
Main religion: Eastern Orthodox
Government: republic
Currency: 1 Moldovan leu = 100 bani

Moldova

MONACO (Europe)
Area: 1.95 sq km (0.75 sq miles)
Population: 31,987
Capital city: Monaco
Main languages: French, Monegasque, Italian
Main religion: Roman Catholic
Government: constitutional monarchy
Currency: 1 euro = 100 cents

Monaco

MONGOLIA (Asia)
Area: 1,565,000 sq km (604,247 sq miles)
Population: 2,694,432
Capital city: Ulan Bator
Main language: Khalkha Mongol
Main religion: Tibetan Buddist Lamaist
Government: republic
Currency: 1 tugrik = 100 mongos

Mongolia

MOROCCO (Africa)
Area: 446,550 sq km (172,413 sq miles)
Population: 31,167,783
Capital city: Rabat
Main languages: Arabic, Berber, French
Main religion: Muslim
Government: constitutional monarchy
Currency: 1 Moroccan dirham = 100 centimes

Morocco

MOZAMBIQUE (Africa)
Area: 801,590 sq km (309,494 sq miles)
Population: 19,607,519
Capital city: Maputo
Main languages: Makua, Tsonga, Portuguese
Main religions: indigenous, Christian, Muslim
Government: republic
Currency: 1 metical = 100 centavos

Mozambique

NAMIBIA (Africa)
Area: 825,418 sq km (318,694 sq miles)
Population: 1,820,916
Capital city: Windhoek
Main languages: Afrikaans, German, English
Main religions: Christian, indigenous
Government: republic
Currency: 1 Namibian dollar = 100 cents

Namibia

NAURU (Australasia/Oceania)
Area: 21 sq km (8 sq miles)
Population: 12,329
Capital city: Yaren
Main languages: Nauruan, English
Main religion: Christian
Government: republic
Currency: 1 Australian dollar = 100 cents

NEPAL (Asia)
Area: 140,800 sq km (54,363 sq miles)
Population: 25,873,917
Capital city: Kathmandu
Main languages: Nepali, Maithili
Main religions: Hindu, Buddhist
Government: constitutional monarchy
Currency: 1 Nepalese rupee = 100 paisa

NETHERLANDS (Europe)
Area: 41,532 sq km (16,036 sq miles)
Population: 16,067,754
Capital cities: Amsterdam, The Hague
Main language: Dutch
Main religion: Christian
Government: constitutional monarchy
Currency: 1 euro = 100 cents

NEW ZEALAND (Australasia/Oceania)
Area: 268,680 sq km (103,737 sq miles)
Population: 3,908,037
Capital city: Wellington
Main languages: English, Maori
Main religion: Christian
Government: parliamentary democracy
Currency: 1 New Zealand dollar = 100 cents

NICARAGUA (North America)
Area: 129,494 sq km (49,998 sq miles)
Population: 5,023,818
Capital city: Managua
Main language: Spanish
Main religion: Roman Catholic
Government: republic
Currency: 1 gold cordoba = 100 centavos

NIGER (Africa)
Area: 1,267,000 sq km (489,189 sq miles)
Population: 10,639,744
Capital city: Niamey
Main languages: Hausa, Djerma, French
Main religion: Muslim
Government: republic
Currency: 1 CFA* franc = 100 centimes

NIGERIA (Africa)
Area: 923,768 sq km (356,667 sq miles)
Population: 129,934,911
Capital city: Abuja
Main languages: Hausa, Yoruba, Igbo, English
Main religions: Muslim, Christian, indigenous
Government: republic
Currency: 1 naira = 100 kobo

NORTH KOREA (Asia)
Area: 120,540 sq km (46,540 sq miles)
Population: 22,224,195
Capital city: Pyongyang
Main language: Korean
Main religions: Buddhist, Confucianist
Government: authoritarian socialist
Currency: 1 North Korean won = 100 chon

NORWAY (Europe)
Area: 324,220 sq km (125,181 sq miles)
Population: 4,525,116
Capital city: Oslo
Main language: Norwegian

Nauru

Nepal

Netherlands

New Zealand

Nicaragua

Niger

Nigeria

*CFA = Communaute Financiere Africaine

North Korea

Norway

Oman

Pakistan

Palau

Panama

**Papua
New Guinea**

Main religion: Evangelical Lutheran
Government: constitutional monarchy
Currency: 1 Norwegian krone = 100 oere

OMAN (Asia)
Area: 212,460 sq km (82,031 sq miles)
Population: 2,713,462
Capital city: Muscat
Main languages: Arabic, English, Baluchi
Main religion: Muslim
Government: monarchy
Currency: 1 Omani rial = 1,000 baiza

PAKISTAN (Asia)
Area: 803,940 sq km (310,401 sq miles)
Population: 147,663,429
Capital city: Islamabad
Main languages: Punjabi, Sindhi, Urdu,
English
Main religion: Muslim
Government: federal republic
Currency: 1 Pakistani rupee = 100 paisa

PALAU (Australasia/Oceania)
Area: 459 sq km (177 sq miles)
Population: 19,409
Capital city: Koror
Main languages: Palauan, English
Main religions: Christian, Modekngei
Government: democratic republic
Currency: 1 U.S. dollar = 100 cents

PANAMA (North America)
Area: 78,200 sq km (30,193 sq miles)
Population: 2,882,329
Capital city: Panama City
Main languages: Spanish, English
Main religions: Roman Catholic, Protestant
Government: democracy
Currency: 1 balboa = 100 centesimos

PAPUA NEW GUINEA
(Australasia/Oceania)
Area: 462,840 sq km (178,703 sq miles)
Population: 5,172,033
Capital city: Port Moresby
Main languages: Tok Pisin, Hiri Motu, English
Main religions: Christian, indigenous
Government: parliamentary democracy
Currency: 1 kina = 100 toea

PARAGUAY (South America)
Area: 406,750 sq km (157,046 sq miles)
Population: 5,884,491
Capital city: Asuncion
Main languages: Guarani, Spanish
Main religion: Roman Catholic
Government: republic
Currency: 1 guarani = 100 centimos

PERU (South America)
Area: 1,285,220 sq km (496,223 sq miles)
Population: 27,949,639
Capital city: Lima
Main languages: Spanish, Quechua,
Aymara
Main religion: Roman Catholic
Government: republic
Currency: 1 nuevo sol = 100 centimos

PHILIPPINES (Asia)
Area: 300,000 sq km (115,830 sq miles)
Population: 84,525,639
Capital city: Manila
Main languages: Tagalog, English, Ilocano
Main religion: Roman Catholic
Government: republic
Currency: 1 Philippine peso = 100 centavos

POLAND (Europe)
Area: 312,685 sq km (120,727 sq miles)
Population: 38,625,478
Capital city: Warsaw
Main language: Polish
Main religion: Roman Catholic
Government: democratic republic
Currency: 1 zloty = 100 groszy

PORTUGAL (Europe)
Area: 92,391 sq km (35,672 sq miles)
Population: 10,084,245
Capital city: Lisbon
Main language: Portuguese
Main religion: Roman Catholic
Government: parliamentary democracy
Currency: 1 euro = 100 cents

QATAR (Asia)
Area: 11,437 sq km (4,416 sq miles)
Population: 793,341
Capital city: Doha
Main languages: Arabic, English
Main religion: Muslim
Government: monarchy
Currency: 1 Qatari riyal = 100 dirhams

ROMANIA (Europe)
Area: 237,500 sq km (91,699 sq miles)
Population: 22,317,730
Capital city: Bucharest
Main languages: Romanian, Hungarian, German
Main religion: Romanian Orthodox
Government: republic
Currency: 1 leu = 100 bani

RUSSIA (Europe and Asia)
Area: 17,075,200 sq km (6,592,735 sq miles)
Population: 144,978,573
Capital city: Moscow
Main language: Russian
Main religions: Russian Orthodox, Muslim
Government: federal government
Currency: 1 ruble = 100 kopeks

RWANDA (Africa)
Area: 26,338 sq km (10,169 sq miles)
Population: 7,398,074
Capital city: Kigali
Main languages: Kinyarwanda, French,
English, Swahili
Main religions: Roman Catholic, Protestant,
Adventist
Government: republic
Currency: 1 Rwandan franc = 100 centimes

SAINT KITTS AND NEVIS
(North America)
Area: 261 sq km (101 sq miles)
Population: 38,736

Paraguay

• Peru

Philippines

Poland

Portugal

Qatar

Romania

Russia

Rwanda

Saint Kitts and Nevis

Saint Lucia

Saint Vincent and the Grenadines

Samoa

• **San Marino**

Capital city: Basseterre
Main language: English
Main religions: Protestant, Roman Catholic
Government: constitutional monarchy
Currency: 1 East Caribbean dollar = 100 cents

SAINT LUCIA (North America)
Area: 620 sq km (239 sq miles)
Population: 160,145
Capital city: Castries
Main languages: French patois, English
Main religion: Roman Catholic
Government: parliamentary democracy
Currency: 1 East Caribbean dollar = 100 cents

SAINT VINCENT AND THE GRENADINES (North America)
Area: 389 sq km (150 sq miles)
Population: 116,394
Capital city: Kingstown
Main languages: English, French patois
Main religions: Protestant, Roman Catholic
Government: parliamentary democracy
Currency: 1 East Caribbean dollar = 100 cents

SAMOA (Australasia/Oceania)
Area: 2,860 sq km (1,104 sq miles)
Population: 178,631
Capital city: Apia
Main languages: Samoan, English
Main religion: Christian
Government: constitutional monarchy
Currency: 1 tala = 100 sene

SAN MARINO (Europe)
Area: 61 sq km (24 sq miles)
Population: 27,730
Capital city: San Marino
Main language: Italian
Main religion: Roman Catholic
Government: republic
Currency: 1 euro = 100 cents

SAO TOME AND PRINCIPE (Africa)
Area: 1,001 sq km (386 sq miles)
Population: 170,372
Capital city: Sao Tome
Main languages: Crioulo* dialects, Portuguese
Main religion: Christian
Government: republic
Currency: 1 dobra = 100 centimos

SAUDI ARABIA (Asia)
Area: 1,960,582 sq km (756,987 sq miles)
Population: 23,513,330
Capital city: Riyadh
Main language: Arabic
Main religion: Muslim
Government: monarchy
Currency: 1 Saudi riyal = 100 halalah

SENEGAL (Africa)
Area: 196,190 sq km (75,749 sq miles)
Population: 10,589,571
Capital city: Dakar
Main languages: Wolof, French, Pulaar
Main religion: Muslim
Government: democratic republic
Currency: 1 CFA* franc = 100 centimes

SERBIA AND MONTENEGRO (Europe)
Area: 102,350 sq km (39,517 sq miles)
Population: 10,656,929
Capital city: Belgrade
Main language: Serbian
Main religions: Orthodox, Muslim
Government: republic
Currency: 1 Yugoslavian new dinar = 100 paras

SEYCHELLES (Africa)
Area: 455 sq km (176 sq miles)
Population: 80,098
Capital city: Victoria
Main languages: Seselwa, English, French
Main religion: Roman Catholic
Government: republic
Currency: 1 Seychelles rupee = 100 cents

SIERRA LEONE (Africa)
Area: 71,740 sq km (27,699 sq miles)
Population: 5,614,743
Capital city: Freetown
Main languages: Mende, Temne, Krio, English
Main religions: Muslim, indigenous, Christian
Government: constitutional democracy
Currency: 1 leone = 100 cents

SINGAPORE (Asia)
Area: 692 sq km (267 sq miles)
Population: 4,452,732
Capital city: Singapore
Main languages: Chinese, Malay, English, Tamil
Main religions: Buddhist, Muslim
Government: parliamentary republic
Currency: 1 Singapore dollar = 100 cents

SLOVAKIA (Europe)
Area: 48,845 sq km (18,859 sq miles)
Population: 5,422,366
Capital city: Bratislava
Main languages: Slovak, Hungarian
Main religion: Roman Catholic
Government: parliamentary democracy
Currency: 1 koruna = 100 halierov

SLOVENIA (Europe)
Area: 20,273 sq km (7,827 sq miles)
Population: 1,932,917
Capital city: Ljubljana
Main language: Slovenian
Main religion: Roman Catholic
Government: democratic republic
Currency: 1 tolar = 100 stotins

SOLOMON ISLANDS (Australasia/Oceania)
Area: 28,450 sq km (10,985 sq miles)
Population: 494,786
Capital city: Honiara
Main languages: Solomon pidgin, Kwara'ae, To'abaita, English
Main religion: Christian
Government: parliamentary democracy
Currency: 1 Solomon Islands dollar = 100 cents

SOMALIA (Africa)
Area: 637,657 sq km (246,199 sq miles)
Population: 7,753,310
Capital city: Mogadishu
Main languages: Somali, Arabic, Oromo

Sao Tome and Principe

Saudi Arabia

Senegal

Serbia and Montenegro

Seychelles

Sierra Leone

Singapore

CFA = Communaute Financiere Africaine; Crioulo = a blend of Portuguese and West African

Slovakia

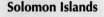

• **Slovenia**

Solomon Islands

Somalia

South Africa

South Korea

• **Spain**

Main religion: Sunni Muslim
Government: currently has no government
Currency: 1 Somali shilling = 100 cents

SOUTH AFRICA (Africa)
Area: 1,219,912 sq km (471,008 sq miles)
Population: 43,647,658
Capital cities: Pretoria, Cape Town, Bloemfontein
Main languages: Zulu, Xhosa, Afrikaans, Pedi, English, Tswana, Sotho, Tsonga, Swati, Venda, Ndebele
Main religions: Christian, indigenous
Government: republic
Currency: 1 rand = 100 cents

SOUTH KOREA (Asia)
Area: 98,480 sq km (38,023 sq miles)
Population: 48,324,000
Capital city: Seoul
Main language: Korean
Main religions: Christian, Buddhist
Government: republic
Currency: 1 South Korean won = 100 chun

SPAIN (Europe)
Area: 504,782 sq km (194,898 sq miles)
Population: 40,077,100
Capital city: Madrid
Main languages: Castilian Spanish, Catalan
Main religion: Roman Catholic
Government: constitutional monarchy
Currency: 1 euro = 100 cents

SRI LANKA (Asia)
Area: 65,610 sq km (25,332 sq miles)
Population: 19,576,783
Capital cities: Colombo, Sri Jayewardenepura Kotte
Main languages: Sinhala, Tamil, English
Main religions: Buddhist, Hindu
Government: republic
Currency: 1 Sri Lankan rupee = 100 cents

SUDAN (Africa)
Area: 2,505,810 sq km (967,493 sq miles)
Population: 37,090,298
Capital city: Khartoum
Main languages: Arabic, English
Main religions: Sunni Muslim, indigenous
Government: Islamic republic
Currency: 1 Sudanese dinar = 100 piastres

SURINAM (South America)
Area: 163,270 sq km (63,039 sq miles)
Population: 436,494
Capital city: Paramaribo
Main languages: Sranang Tongo, Dutch, English
Main religions: Christian, Hindu, Muslim
Government: constitutional democracy
Currency: 1 Surinamese guilder = 100 cents

SWAZILAND (Africa)
Area: 17,363 sq km (6,704 sq miles)
Population: 1,123,605
Capital cities: Mbabane, Lobamba

Main languages: Swati, English
Main religions: Christian, indigenous, Muslim
Government: monarchy
Currency: 1 lilangeni = 100 cents

SWEDEN (Europe)
Area: 449,964 sq km (173,731 sq miles)
Population: 8,876,744
Capital city: Stockholm
Main language: Swedish
Main religion: Lutheran
Government: constitutional monarchy
Currency: 1 Swedish krona = 100 oere

SWITZERLAND (Europe)
Area: 41,290 sq km (15,942 sq miles)
Population: 7,301,994
Capital city: Bern
Main languages: German, French, Italian
Main religions: Roman Catholic, Protestant
Government: federal republic
Currency: 1 Swiss franc = 100 centimes

SYRIA (Asia)
Area: 185,180 sq km (71,498 sq miles)
Population: 17,155,814
Capital city: Damascus
Main languages: Arabic, Kurdish
Main religions: Muslim, Christian
Government: republic under military regime
Currency: 1 Syrian pound = 100 piastres

TAIWAN (Asia)
Area: 35,980 sq km (13,892 sq miles)
Population: 22,548,009
Capital city: Taipei
Main languages: Taiwanese, Mandarin Chinese, Hakka Chinese
Main religions: Buddhist, Confucian, Daoist
Government: democracy
Currency: 1 New Taiwan dollar = 100 cents

TAJIKISTAN (Asia)
Area: 143,100 sq km (55,251 sq miles)
Population: 6,719,567
Capital city: Dushanbe
Main languages: Tajik, Russian
Main religion: Sunni Muslim
Government: republic
Currency: 1 somoni = 100 dirams

TANZANIA (Africa)
Area: 945,087 sq km (364,898 sq miles)
Population: 37,187,939
Capital cities: Dar es Salaam, Dodoma
Main languages: Swahili, English, Sukuma
Main religions: Christian, Muslim, indigenous
Government: republic
Currency: 1 Tanzanian shilling = 100 cents

THAILAND (Asia)
Area: 514,000 sq km (198,455 sq miles)
Population: 62,354,402
Capital city: Bangkok
Main languages: Thai, English, Chaochow
Main religion: Buddhist
Government: constitutional monarchy
Currency: 1 baht = 100 satang

Sri Lanka

Sudan

Surinam

Swaziland

Sweden

Switzerland

Syria

Taiwan

TOGO (Africa)
Area: 56,785 sq km (21,925 sq miles)
Population: 5,285,501
Capital city: Lome
Main languages: Mina, Ewe, Kabye, French
Main religions: indigenous, Christian, Muslim
Government: republic
Currency: 1 CFA* franc = 100 centimes

TONGA (Australasia/Oceania)
Area: 748 sq km (289 sq miles)
Population: 106,137
Capital city: Nukualofa
Main languages: Tongan, English
Main religion: Christian
Government: constitutional monarchy
Currency: 1 pa'anga = 100 seniti

Tajikistan

TRINIDAD AND TOBAGO (North America)
Area: 5,128 sq km (1,980 sq miles)
Population: 1,163,724
Capital city: Port-of-Spain
Main languages: English, French, Spanish, Hindi
Main religions: Christian, Hindu
Government: parliamentary democracy
Currency: 1 Trinidad and Tobago dollar = 100 cents

Tanzania

TUNISIA (Africa)
Area: 163,610 sq km (63,170 sq miles)
Population: 9,815,644
Capital city: Tunis
Main languages: Arabic, French
Main religion: Muslim
Government: republic
Currency: 1 Tunisian dinar = 1,000 millimes

Thailand

TURKEY (Europe and Asia)
Area: 780,580 sq km (301,382 sq miles)
Population: 67,308,928
Capital city: Ankara
Main language: Turkish
Main religion: Muslim
Government: democratic republic
Currency: 1 Turkish lira = 100 kurus

Togo

TURKMENISTAN (Asia)
Area: 488,100 sq km (188,455 sq miles)
Population: 4,688,963
Capital city: Ashgabat (Ashkhabad)
Main languages: Turkmen, Russian
Main religion: Muslim
Government: republic
Currency: 1 Turkmen manat = 100 tenesi

TUVALU (Australasia/Oceania)
Area: 26 sq km (10 sq miles)
Population: 11,146
Capital city: Funafuti
Main languages: Tuvaluan, English
Main religion: Congregationalist
Government: constitutional monarchy
Currency: 1 Tuvaluan dollar or 1 Australian dollar = 100 cents

Tonga

UGANDA (Africa)
Area: 236,040 sq km (91,135 sq miles)
Population: 24,699,073

Capital city: Kampala
Main languages: Luganda, English, Swahili
Main religion: Christian, Muslim, indigenous
Government: republic
Currency: 1 Ugandan shilling = 100 cents

UKRAINE (Europe)
Area: 603,700 sq km (233,089 sq miles)
Population: 48,396,470
Capital city: Kiev
Main languages: Ukrainian, Russian
Main religion: Ukrainian Orthodox
Government: republic
Currency: 1 hryvnia = 100 kopiykas

UNITED ARAB EMIRATES (Asia)
Area: 82,880 sq km (32,000 sq miles)
Population: 2,445,989
Capital city: Abu Dhabi
Main languages: Arabic, English
Main religion: Muslim
Government: federation
Currency: 1 Emirati dirham = 100 fils

UNITED KINGDOM (Europe)
Area: 244,820 sq km (94,525 sq miles)
Population: 59,778,002
Capital city: London
Main language: English
Main religions: Anglican, Roman Catholic
Government: constitutional monarchy
Currency: 1 British pound = 100 pence

UNITED STATES OF AMERICA (North America)
Area: 9,629,091 sq km (3,717,792 sq miles)
Population: 280,562,489
Capital city: Washington D.C.
Main language: English
Main religions: Protestant, Roman Catholic
Government: federal republic
Currency: 1 U.S. dollar = 100 cents

URUGUAY (South America)
Area: 176,220 sq km (68,039 sq miles)
Population: 3,386,575
Capital city: Montevideo
Main language: Spanish
Main religion: Roman Catholic
Government: republic
Currency: 1 Uruguayan peso = 100 centesimos

UZBEKISTAN (Asia)
Area: 447,400 sq km (172,741 sq miles)
Population: 25,563,441
Capital city: Tashkent
Main languages: Uzbek, Russian
Main religions: Muslim, Eastern Orthodox
Government: republic
Currency: 1 Uzbekistani sum = 100 tyyn

VANUATU (Australasia/Oceania)
Area: 12,189 sq km (4,706 sq miles)
Population: 196,178
Capital city: Port-Vila
Main languages: Bislama, French, English
Main religion: Christian
Government: republic
Currency: 1 vatu = 100 centimes

Trinidad and Tobago

Tunisia

Turkey

Turkmenistan

Tuvalu

Uganda

CFA = Communaute Financiere Africaine

Ukraine

United Arab Emirates

United Kingdom

United States of America

Uruguay

Uzbekistan

VATICAN CITY (Europe)
Area: 0.44 sq km (0.17 sq miles)
Population: 900
Capital city: Vatican City
Main languages: Italian, Latin
Main religion: Roman Catholic
Government: led by the Pope
Currency: 1 euro = 100 cents

VENEZUELA (South America)
Area: 912,050 sq km (352,143 sq miles)
Population: 24,287,670
Capital city: Caracas
Main language: Spanish
Main religion: Roman Catholic
Government: federal republic
Currency: 1 bolivar = 100 centimos

VIETNAM (Asia)
Area: 329,560 sq km (127,243 sq miles)
Population: 81,098,416
Capital city: Hanoi
Main languages: Vietnamese, French, English, Khmer, Chinese
Main religion: Buddhist
Government: Communist state
Currency: 1 new dong = 100 xu

YEMEN (Asia)
Area: 527,970 sq km (203,849 sq miles)
Population: 18,701,257
Capital city: Sana
Main language: Arabic
Main religion: Muslim
Government: republic
Currency: 1 Yemeni rial = 100 fils

ZAMBIA (Africa)
Area: 752,614 sq km (290,584 sq miles)
Population: 9,959,037
Capital city: Lusaka
Main languages: Bemba, Tonga, Nyanja, English
Main religions: Christian, Muslim, Hindu
Government: republic
Currency: 1 Zambian kwacha = 100 ngwee

ZIMBABWE (Africa)
Area: 390,580 sq km (150,803 sq miles)
Population: 11,376,676
Capital city: Harare
Main languages: Shona, Ndebele, English
Main religions: Christian, indigenous
Government: republic
Currency: 1 Zimbabwean dollar = 100 cents

Vanuatu

Vatican City

Venezuela

Vietnam

Yemen

Zambia

Zimbabwe

The United Nations

The United Nations (U.N.) is an organization which aims to bring countries together to work for peace and development. Of the world's 193 states, 191 belong to the U.N. Those that don't belong are Taiwan and the Vatican City.

Internet link

For a link to a website where you can match countries and their flags in a great game, go to **www.usborne-quicklinks.com**

Kofi Annan, the Secretary-General of the U.N., with U.N. ambassador Pele

USEFUL WEBSITES

On these pages, there are descriptions of websites that have information, photographs and games on the theme of maps and geography. For links to these sites, go to the Usborne Quicklinks website at **www.usborne-quicklinks.com** and enter the keywords "essential atlas". There you will find links to take you to all the sites.

Map resources

Website 1
Find street maps of any town or city in the world.

Website 2
See maps that show which parts of the Earth are in daylight or darkness at this very moment, plus up-to-date weather conditions across the globe.

Website 3
Download clip art of world, continent, country and state maps, as well as flags and globes.

Website 4
Find maps of any country in the world, plus information about their geography, people, government, economy and more.

This is part of Kluane National Park, in Yukon Territory, Canada. A huge mass of ice known as a glacier flows slowly downhill, cutting valleys through the mountains.

World wildlife

Website 1
Discover some of the weird and wonderful creatures that live in the world's oceans and seas.

Website 2
Learn about the world's endangered animals and find out what can be done to stop them from becoming extinct.

Website 3
Find out about amazing animals and watch videos of them in the wild.

Website 4
Learn about the unusual animals that live in the Galapagos Islands, including iguanas and giant tortoises.

Website 5
Read about animals that live in the Arctic, such as walruses, snowy owls, polar bears and arctic foxes.

Amazing Earth

Website 1
Read fascinating facts about some of the world's most interesting locations, including the Amazon Rainforest, Greenland and Madagascar. This site also has short films to watch and quiz questions to answer.

Website 2
Find out about natural disasters such as earthquakes and tsunamis and see animated diagrams of how each forms.

Website 3
Take an interactive tour of Everest, the highest mountain in the world.

Website 4
Read up-to-date information about all the current volcanic eruptions around the world.

Website 5
Explore the vast Sahara Desert and learn about its landscape and peoples.

Website 6
Discover all kinds of underground caves and find out how they were formed.

A birdwing butterfly feeds from a tropical flower. Birdwings are the world's largest butterflies and live in the rainforests of Asia and Australasia.

Quizzes and games

Website 1
See if you can identify and name countries and capital cities.

Website 2
Try all kinds of geography quizzes and have a go at some online crosswords.

Website 3
Take a safari quiz and find out if you have what it takes to survive in the wild.

Website 4
Test your knowledge of the world's deserts.

MAP INDEX

This is an index of the places and features named on the maps. Each entry consists of the following parts: the name (given in bold type), the country or region within which it is located (given in italics), the page on which the name can be found (given in bold type), and the grid reference (also given in bold type). For some names, there is also a description explaining what kind of place it is – for example a country, internal administrative area (state or province), national capital or internal capital. To find a place on a map, first find the map indicated by the page reference. Then use the grid reference to find the square containing the name or town symbol. See page 9 for help with using the grid.

Atalaia do Norte, *Brazil*, 30 D4
Atar, *Mauritania*, 68 C4
Atbarah, *Sudan*, 67 H5
Atbasar, *Kazakhstan*, 50 J1
Athabasca, *Canada*, 22 H3
Athabasca, Lake, *Canada*, 22 J3
Athens, *Greece, national capital*, 63 G4
Atka Island, *U.S.A.*, 23 B3
Atlanta, *U.S.A., internal capital*, 25 K4
Atlantic City, *U.S.A.*, 25 M3
Atlantic Ocean, 18
Atlas Mountains, *Africa*, 68 D2
At Taif, *Saudi Arabia*, 51 D7
Attapu, *Laos*, 44 E5
Attu Island, *U.S.A.*, 23 A3
Atyrau, *Kazakhstan*, 57 G4
Auckland, *New Zealand*, 39 P7
Augsburg, *Germany*, 60 G4
Augusta, *U.S.A., internal capital*, 25 N2
Aurangabad, *India*, 49 D7
Austin, *U.S.A., internal capital*, 24 G4
Australasia and Oceania, 19
Australia, *Australasia, country*, 38 E4
Australian Capital Territory, *Australia, internal admin. area*, 39 J6
Austria, *Europe, country*, 62 E2
Awasa, *Ethiopia*, 71 G2
Ayacucho, *Peru*, 30 D6
Aydin, *Turkey*, 63 H4
Ayers Rock, *Australia*, 38 F5
Ayoun el Atrous, *Mauritania*, 69 D5
Azerbaijan, *Asia, country*, 50 E3
Azores, *Atlantic Ocean*, 68 K10
Azov, Sea of, *Europe*, 63 K2
Az Zarqa, *Jordan*, 51 C5

b

Baardheere, *Somalia*, 71 H3
Babahoyo, *Ecuador*, 30 C4
Bab al Mandab, *Africa/Asia*, 67 K6
Babruysk, *Belarus*, 59 J5
Babuyan Islands, *Philippines*, 45 H4
Babylon, *Iraq*, 50 D5
Bacabal, *Brazil*, 31 K4
Bacau, *Romania*, 63 H2
Bac Lieu, *Vietnam*, 44 E6
Bacolod, *Philippines*, 45 H5
Badajoz, *Spain*, 61 C7
Baffin Bay, *Canada*, 23 N1
Baffin Island, *Canada*, 23 M2
Bafoussam, *Cameroon*, 70 B2
Bage, *Brazil*, 32 H6
Baghdad, *Iraq, national capital*, 50 D5
Bahamas, The, *North America, country*, 25 L5
Bahawalpur, *Pakistan*, 48 C5
Bahia, *Brazil*, 31 L6
Bahia Blanca, *Argentina*, 33 F7
Bahir Dar, *Ethiopia*, 71 G1
Bahrain, *Asia, country*, 51 F6
Baia Mare, *Romania*, 63 G2
Baie-Comeau, *Canada*, 23 N4
Baikal, Lake, *Russia*, 53 F3
Bairiki, *Kiribati, national capital*, 36 E4
Bakersfield, *U.S.A.*, 24 C3
Baku, *Azerbaijan, national capital*, 50 E3
Balakovo, *Russia*, 57 F3
Balaton, Lake, *Hungary*, 59 F7
Balbina Reservoir, *Brazil*, 31 G4
Baldy Peak, *U.S.A.*, 24 E4
Balearic Islands, *Spain*, 61 E7
Bali, *Indonesia*, 42 E5
Balikesir, *Turkey*, 63 H4
Balikpapan, *Indonesia*, 42 E4
Balkanabat, *Turkmenistan*, 50 F4
Balkan Mountains, *Europe*, 63 G3
Balkhash, Lake, *Kazakhstan*, 48 D1
Balkuduk, *Kazakhstan*, 57 F3
Balqash, *Kazakhstan*, 48 D1
Balti, *Moldova*, 63 H2
Baltic Sea, *Europe*, 59 F4
Baltimore, *U.S.A.*, 25 L3
Bamako, *Mali, national capital*, 69 D6
Bamenda, *Cameroon*, 70 B2
Bancs Providence, *Seychelles*, 73 K1
Banda Aceh, *Indonesia*, 42 A2

Bandar-e Abbas, *Iran*, 51 G6
Bandar Seri Begawan, *Brunei, national capital*, 42 D2
Banda Sea, *Indonesia*, 43 G5
Bandundu, *Democratic Republic of Congo*, 70 C4
Bandung, *Indonesia*, 42 C5
Banfora, *Burkina Faso*, 69 E6
Bangalore, *India*, 49 D8
Bangassou, *Central African Republic*, 70 D3
Bangka, *Indonesia*, 42 C4
Bangkok, *Thailand, national capital*, 44 D5
Bangladesh, *Asia, country*, 49 F6
Bangor, *U.S.A.*, 25 N2
Bangui, *Central African Republic, national capital*, 70 C3
Bangweulu, Lake, *Zambia*, 72 E2
Banja Luka, *Bosnia and Herzegovina*, 62 F2
Banjarmasin, *Indonesia*, 42 D4
Banjul, *The Gambia, national capital*, 69 B6
Banks Island, *Canada*, 22 G1
Banks Islands, *Vanuatu*, 39 N2
Banska Bystrica, *Slovakia*, 59 F6
Baoding, *China*, 47 J3
Baoji, *China*, 46 G4
Baotou, *China*, 46 G2
Baqubah, *Iraq*, 50 D5
Baranavichy, *Belarus*, 59 H5
Barbacena, *Brazil*, 32 K4
Barbados, *North America, country*, 26 N5
Barcelona, *Spain*, 61 E6
Barcelona, *Venezuela*, 30 F1
Bareilly, *India*, 48 D5
Barents Sea, *Europe*, 52 B2
Bari, *Italy*, 62 F3
Barinas, *Venezuela*, 30 D2
Barkly Tableland, *Australia*, 38 G3
Barnaul, *Russia*, 52 E3
Barquisimeto, *Venezuela*, 30 E1
Barra Falsa Point, *Mozambique*, 73 G4
Barranquilla, *Colombia*, 30 D1
Barra Point, *Mozambique*, 73 G4
Barreiras, *Brazil*, 32 J2
Barrow, Point, *U.S.A.*, 22 D1
Barysaw, *Belarus*, 59 J5
Basel, *Switzerland*, 62 C2
Basra, *Iraq*, 51 E5
Bassas da India, *Africa*, 73 G4
Basse-Terre, *Guadeloupe*, 26 M4
Basseterre, *St. Kitts and Nevis, national capital*, 26 M4
Bass Strait, *Australia*, 38 J7
Bastia, *France*, 61 G6
Bata, *Equatorial Guinea*, 70 A3
Batan Islands, *Philippines*, 45 H3
Batdambang, *Cambodia*, 44 D5
Bathurst, *Canada*, 23 N4
Bathurst, *U.S.A.*, 25 N1
Bathurst Island, *Canada*, 23 K1
Batna, *Algeria*, 68 G1
Baton Rouge, *U.S.A., internal capital*, 25 H4
Batumi, *Georgia*, 50 D3
Baturaja, *Indonesia*, 42 B4
Bawku, *Ghana*, 69 E6
Bayamo, *Cuba*, 27 J3
Baydhabo, *Somalia*, 71 H3
Bealanana, *Madagascar*, 73 J2
Beaufort Sea, *North America*, 22 F1
Beaufort West, *South Africa*, 72 D6
Beaumont, *U.S.A.*, 25 H4
Bechar, *Algeria*, 68 E2
Beer Sheva, *Israel*, 51 B5
Beijing, *China, national capital*, 47 J3
Beira, *Mozambique*, 73 G3
Beirut, *Lebanon, national capital*, 50 C5
Bejaia, *Algeria*, 68 F1
Bekescsaba, *Hungary*, 59 G7
Bekily, *Madagascar*, 73 J4
Belarus, *Europe, country*, 59 J5
Belaya, *Russia*, 57 G2
Belcher Islands, *Canada*, 23 L3
Beledweyne, *Somalia*, 71 J3

Belem, *Brazil*, 31 J4
Belfast, *United Kingdom, internal capital*, 60 C3
Belgaum, *India*, 49 C7
Belgium, *Europe, country*, 60 E4
Belgrade, *Serbia and Montenegro, national capital*, 63 G2
Belitung, *Indonesia*, 42 C4
Belize, *North America, country*, 26 G4
Bellingham, *U.S.A.*, 24 B1
Bellingshausen Sea, *Antarctica*, 77 R2
Belmopan, *Belize, national capital*, 26 G4
Belo Horizonte, *Brazil*, 32 K3
Belomorsk, *Russia*, 58 K2
Beloretsk, *Russia*, 57 H3
Belo-Tsiribihina, *Madagascar*, 73 H3
Bendigo, *Australia*, 38 H7
Bengal, Bay of, *Asia*, 49 F7
Benghazi, *Libya*, 66 F2
Bengkulu, *Indonesia*, 42 B4
Benguela, *Angola*, 72 B2
Beni Mellal, *Morocco*, 68 D2
Benin, *Africa, country*, 69 F6
Benin, Bight of, *Africa*, 69 F7
Benin City, *Nigeria*, 69 G7
Beni Suef, *Egypt*, 67 H3
Ben Nevis, *United Kingdom*, 60 C2
Benoni, *South Africa*, 72 E5
Berbera, *Somalia*, 71 J1
Berberati, *Central African Republic*, 70 C3
Berdyansk, *Ukraine*, 56 D4
Berezniki, *Russia*, 57 H2
Bergamo, *Italy*, 62 D2
Bergen, *Norway*, 58 C3
Bering Sea, *North America*, 22 C2
Bering Strait, *U.S.A.*, 22 B2
Berlin, *Germany, national capital*, 60 H3
Bern, *Switzerland, national capital*, 62 C2
Beroroha, *Madagascar*, 73 J4
Bertoua, *Cameroon*, 70 B3
Besalampy, *Madagascar*, 73 H3
Besancon, *France*, 61 F5
Bethel, *U.S.A.*, 22 C2
Bethlehem, *South Africa*, 72 E5
Betroka, *Madagascar*, 73 J4
Beyneu, *Kazakhstan*, 50 G2
Beysehir Lake, *Turkey*, 63 J4
Beziers, *France*, 61 F6
Bhagalpur, *India*, 48 F5
Bhavnagar, *India*, 49 C6
Bhopal, *India*, 49 D6
Bhutan, *Asia, country*, 48 G5
Biak, *Indonesia*, 43 J4
Bialystok, *Poland*, 59 G5
Bida, *Nigeria*, 69 G7
Biel, *Switzerland*, 62 C2
Bielefeld, *Germany*, 60 G3
Bien Hoa, *Vietnam*, 44 E5
Bie Plateau, *Angola*, 72 B2
Bignona, *Senegal*, 69 B6
Bikaner, *India*, 48 C5
Bila Tserkva, *Ukraine*, 59 J6
Bilhorod Dnistrovskyy, *Ukraine*, 56 C4
Billings, *U.S.A.*, 24 E1
Bilbao, *Spain*, 61 D6
Bindura, *Zimbabwe*, 72 F3
Binga, *Zimbabwe*, 72 E3
Bintulu, *Malaysia*, 42 D3
Bioco, *Equatorial Guinea*, 70 A3
Birao, *Central African Republic*, 70 D1
Biratnagar, *Nepal*, 48 F5
Birjand, *Iran*, 50 G5
Birmingham, *United Kingdom*, 60 D3
Birmingham, *U.S.A.*, 25 J4
Birnin-Kebbi, *Nigeria*, 69 F6
Biscay, Bay of, *Europe*, 61 C5
Bishkek, *Kyrgyzstan, national capital*, 48 C2
Bisho, *South Africa*, 72 E6
Biskra, *Algeria*, 68 G2
Bismarck, *U.S.A., internal capital*, 24 F1
Bismarck Sea, *Papua New Guinea*, 43 L4
Bissagos Archipelago, *Guinea-Bissau*, 69 B6
Bissau, *Guinea-Bissau, national capital*, 69 B6

Bitola, *Macedonia*, 63 G3
Bitterfontein, *South Africa*, 72 C6
Bizerte, *Tunisia*, 66 C1
Blackpool, *United Kingdom*, 60 D3
Black Sea, *Asia/Europe*, 52 B3
Black Volta, *Africa*, 69 E6
Blagoevgrad, *Bulgaria*, 63 G3
Blagoveshchensk, *Russia*, 53 G3
Blanca Bay, *Argentina*, 33 F7
Blanc, Cape, *Africa*, 68 B4
Blanc, Mont, *Europe*, 61 F5
Blantyre, *Malawi*, 73 F3
Blida, *Algeria*, 68 F1
Bloemfontein, *South Africa, national capital*, 72 E5
Blue Nile, *Africa*, 67 H6
Bo, *Sierra Leone*, 69 C7
Boa Vista, *Brazil*, 30 F3
Boa Vista, *Cape Verde*, 69 M11
Bobo Dioulasso, *Burkina Faso*, 69 E6
Bodele Depression, *Africa*, 66 E5
Boden, *Sweden*, 58 G2
Bodo, *Norway*, 58 E2
Bogor, *Indonesia*, 42 C5
Bogota, *Colombia, national capital*, 30 D3
Bohol, *Philippines*, 45 H6
Boise, *U.S.A., internal capital*, 24 C2
Bojnurd, *Iran*, 50 G4
Boke, *Guinea*, 69 C6
Bolivar Peak, *Venezuela*, 30 D2
Bolivia, *South America, country*, 32 E3
Bologna, *Italy*, 62 D2
Bolzano, *Italy*, 62 D2
Bombay, *India*, 49 C7
Bondoukou, *Ivory Coast*, 69 E7
Bongor, *Chad*, 70 C1
Bonin Islands, *Japan*, 36 B2
Bonn, *Germany*, 60 F4
Boosaaso, *Somalia*, 71 J1
Boothia, Gulf of, *Canada*, 23 K1
Boothia Peninsula, *Canada*, 23 K1
Bordeaux, *France*, 61 D5
Bordj Bou Arreridj, *Algeria*, 68 F1
Borlange, *Sweden*, 58 E3
Borneo, *Asia*, 42 D4
Bornholm, *Denmark*, 59 E5
Borovichi, *Russia*, 58 K4
Bosnia and Herzegovina, *Europe, country*, 62 F2
Bosporus, *Turkey*, 63 J3
Bossangoa, *Central African Republic*, 70 C2
Bossembele, *Central African Republic*, 70 C2
Bosten Lake, *China*, 48 F2
Boston, *U.S.A., internal capital*, 25 M2
Bothnia, Gulf of, *Europe*, 58 F3
Botosani, *Romania*, 63 H2
Botswana, *Africa, country*, 72 D4
Bouake, *Ivory Coast*, 69 E7
Bouar, *Central African Republic*, 70 C2
Bougouni, *Mali*, 69 D6
Boujdour, *Western Sahara*, 68 C3
Bouna, *Ivory Coast*, 69 E7
Bozoum, *Central African Republic*, 70 C2
Braga, *Portugal*, 61 B6
Braganca, *Brazil*, 31 J4
Brahmapur, *India*, 49 E7
Brahmaputra, *Asia*, 48 G5
Braila, *Romania*, 63 H2
Brandon, *Canada*, 23 K4
Brandon, *U.S.A.*, 24 G1
Brasilia, *Brazil, national capital*, 32 J3
Brasov, *Romania*, 63 H2
Bratislava, *Slovakia, national capital*, 59 F6
Brazil, *South America, country*, 31 H5
Brazilian Highlands, *Brazil*, 32 K2
Brazzaville, *Congo, national capital*, 70 C4
Bremen, *Germany*, 60 G3
Bremerhaven, *Germany*, 60 G3
Brescia, *Italy*, 62 D2
Brest, *Belarus*, 59 G5
Brest, *France*, 60 C4
Bria, *Central African Republic*, 70 D2
Bridgetown, *Barbados, national capital*, 26 N5

Coquimbo, *Chile*, 32 D5
Coral Sea, *Oceania*, 39 K2
Coral Sea Islands Territory, *Oceania, dependency*, 39 K3
Cordoba, *Argentina*, 32 F6
Cordoba, *Spain*, 61 C7
Corfu, *Greece*, 63 F4
Cork, *Ireland*, 60 B4
Corner Brook, *Canada*, 23 P4
Coro, *Venezuela*, 30 E1
Coropuna, Mount, *Peru*, 30 D6
Corpus Christi, *U.S.A.*, 24 G5
Corrientes, *Argentina*, 32 G5
Corsica, *France*, 61 G6
Corum, *Turkey*, 63 K3
Corumba, *Brazil*, 32 G3
Cosenza, *Italy*, 62 F4
Cosmoledo Group, *Seychelles*, 73 J1
Costa Rica, *North America, country*, 27 G6
Cotonou, *Benin*, 69 F7
Cottbus, *Germany*, 60 H4
Cradock, *South Africa*, 72 E6
Craiova, *Romania*, 63 G2
Cravo Norte, *Colombia*, 30 D2
Crete, *Greece*, 63 H5
Criciuma, *Brazil*, 32 J5
Crimea, *Ukraine*, 63 K2
Cristobal Colon, *Colombia*, 30 D1
Croatia, *Europe, country*, 62 F2
Cruzeiro do Sul, *Brazil*, 30 D5
Cuamba, *Mozambique*, 73 G2
Cuangar, *Angola*, 72 C3
Cuango, *Africa*, 72 C1
Cuanza, *Angola*, 72 C2
Cuba, *North America, country*, 27 J3
Cucuta, *Colombia*, 30 D2
Cuenca, *Ecuador*, 30 C4
Cuiaba, *Brazil*, 32 G3
Culiacan, *Mexico*, 26 C3
Cumana, *Venezuela*, 30 F1
Cumberland Peninsula, *Canada*, 23 N2
Cunene, *Africa*, 72 C3
Curitiba, *Brazil*, 32 J5
Cusco, *Peru*, 30 D6
Cuttack, *India*, 49 F6
Cuxhaven, *Germany*, 60 G3
Cyclades, *Greece*, 63 H4
Cyprus, *Asia, country*, 63 J5
Cyrene, *Libya*, 66 F2
Czech Republic, *Europe, country*, 62 E1
Czestochowa, *Poland*, 59 F6

d

Dabeiba, *Colombia*, 30 C2
Dagupan, *Philippines*, 45 H4
Dahlak Archipelago, *Eritrea*, 67 K5
Dakar, *Senegal, national capital*, 69 B6
Dal, *Sweden*, 58 F3
Da Lat, *Vietnam*, 44 E5
Dali, *China*, 46 F5
Dalian, *China*, 47 K3
Dallas, *U.S.A.*, 25 G4
Daloa, *Ivory Coast*, 69 D7
Damascus, *Syria, national capital*, 50 C5
Damavand, *Iran*, 50 F4
Damongo, *Ghana*, 69 E7
Da Nang, *Vietnam*, 44 E4
Dandong, *China*, 47 K2
Danube, *Europe*, 59 F7
Danube, Mouths of the, *Europe*, 63 J2
Daqing, *China*, 47 L1
Darbhanga, *India*, 48 F5
Dar es Salaam, *Tanzania, national capital*, 71 G5
Darien, Gulf of, *Colombia*, 30 C2
Darjeeling, *India*, 48 F5
Darling, *Australia*, 38 H6
Darnah, *Libya*, 66 F2
Darwin, *Australia, internal capital*, 38 F2
Darwin, Mount, *Zimbabwe*, 72 F3
Dasht-e Kavir, *Iran*, 50 F5
Dasoguz, *Turkmenistan*, 50 G3
Datong, *China*, 47 H2
Daugavpils, *Latvia*, 59 H5
Davangere, *India*, 49 D8

Davao, *Philippines*, 45 J6
David, *Panama*, 27 H6
Davis Strait, *Canada*, 23 P2
Dawson, *Canada*, 22 F2
Dayr az Zawr, *Syria*, 50 D4
Daytona Beach, *U.S.A.*, 25 K5
De Aar, *South Africa*, 72 D6
Dease Lake, *Canada*, 22 G3
Death Valley, *U.S.A.*, 24 C3
Debrecen, *Hungary*, 59 G7
Debre Zeyit, *Ethiopia*, 71 G2
Deccan Plateau, *India*, 49 D7
Delaware, *U.S.A., internal admin. area*, 25 L3
Delgado, Cape, *Mozambique*, 73 H2
Delhi, *India*, 48 D5
Del Rio, *U.S.A.*, 24 F5
Democratic Republic of Congo, *Africa, country*, 70 D4
Denizli, *Turkey*, 63 J4
Denmark, *Europe, country*, 59 D5
Denpasar, *Indonesia*, 42 E5
D'Entrecasteaux Islands, *Papua New Guinea*, 43 M5
Denver, *U.S.A., internal capital*, 24 E3
Dera Ghazi Khan, *Pakistan*, 48 C4
Derbent, *Russia*, 50 E3
Dese, *Ethiopia*, 71 G1
Des Moines, *U.S.A., internal capital*, 25 H2
Desna, *Europe*, 56 C3
Detroit, *U.S.A.*, 25 K2
Devon Island, *Canada*, 23 L1
Devonport, *Australia*, 38 J8
Dhaka, *Bangladesh, national capital*, 49 G6
Dhamar, *Yemen*, 51 D9
Dhule, *India*, 49 C6
Dibrugarh, *India*, 48 G5
Dijon, *France*, 61 F5
Dikhil, *Djibouti*, 67 K6
Dili, *East Timor, national capital*, 43 G5
Dilolo, *Democratic Republic of Congo*, 70 D6
Dinaric Alps, *Europe*, 62 E2
Dire Dawa, *Ethiopia*, 71 H2
Divo, *Ivory Coast*, 69 D7
Diyarbakir, *Turkey*, 50 D4
Djado Plateau, *Africa*, 66 D4
Djambala, *Congo*, 70 B4
Djelfa, *Algeria*, 68 F2
Djema, *Central African Republic*, 70 E2
Djemila, *Algeria*, 68 G1
Djibouti, *Africa, country*, 67 K6
Djibouti, *Djibouti, national capital*, 67 K6
Djougou, *Benin*, 69 F7
Dnieper, *Europe*, 56 C4
Dniester, *Europe*, 59 H6
Dniprodzerzhynsk, *Ukraine*, 56 C4
Dnipropetrovsk, *Ukraine*, 56 D4
Doba, *Chad*, 70 C2
Dobrich, *Bulgaria*, 63 H3
Dodecanese, *Greece*, 63 H4
Dodoma, *Tanzania, national capital*, 71 G5
Doha, *Qatar, national capital*, 51 F6
Dolak, *Indonesia*, 43 J5
Dolores, *Argentina*, 33 G7
Dominica, *North America, country*, 26 M4
Dominican Republic, *North America, country*, 27 L3
Don, *Russia*, 56 E4
Dondo, *Angola*, 72 B1
Donets, *Europe*, 56 D4
Donetsk, *Ukraine*, 56 D4
Dongting Lake, *China*, 47 H5
Dori, *Burkina Faso*, 69 E6
Dosso, *Niger*, 69 F6
Douala, *Cameroon*, 70 A3
Douglas, *South Africa*, 72 D5
Dourados, *Brazil*, 32 H4
Douro, *Europe*, 61 C6
Dover, *United Kingdom*, 60 E4
Dover, *U.S.A., internal capital*, 25 L3

Dover, Strait of, *Europe*, 60 E4
Drakensberg, *South Africa*, 72 E6
Drake Passage, *South America*, 33 E11
Drammen, *Norway*, 58 D4
Dresden, *Germany*, 60 H4
Drobeta-Turnu Severin, *Romania*, 63 G2
Dryden, *Canada*, 23 K4
Dubai, *United Arab Emirates*, 51 G6
Dubawnt Lake, *Canada*, 22 J2
Dubbo, *Australia*, 39 J6
Dublin, *Ireland, national capital*, 60 C3
Dubrovnik, *Croatia*, 63 F3
Duisburg, *Germany*, 60 F4
Duitama, *Colombia*, 30 D2
Duluth, *U.S.A.*, 25 H1
Dumaguete, *Philippines*, 45 H6
Dundee, *United Kingdom*, 60 D2
Dunedin, *New Zealand*, 39 P9
Durango, *Mexico*, 26 D3
Durazno, *Uruguay*, 32 G6
Durban, *South Africa*, 72 F5
Durres, *Albania*, 63 F3
Dushanbe, *Tajikistan, national capital*, 48 B3
Dusseldorf, *Germany*, 60 F4
Dzhankoy, *Ukraine*, 63 K2
Dzungarian Basin, *China*, 48 F1

e

East Antarctica, *Antarctica*, 77 E3
East Cape, *New Zealand*, 39 Q7
East China Sea, *Asia*, 47 K5
Easter Island, *Pacific Ocean*, 37 N7
Eastern Cordillera, *Colombia*, 30 D3
Eastern Cordillera, *Peru*, 30 D6
Eastern Ghats, *India*, 49 D8
Eastern Sierra Madre, *Mexico*, 26 D2
East Falkland, *Falkland Islands*, 33 G10
East London, *South Africa*, 72 E6
East Siberian Sea, *Russia*, 53 J2
East Timor, *Asia, country*, 43 G5
Ebolowa, *Cameroon*, 70 B3
Ebro, *Spain*, 61 D6
Ecuador, *South America, country*, 30 B4
Edinburgh, *United Kingdom, internal capital*, 60 D2
Edirne, *Turkey*, 63 H3
Edmonton, *Canada, internal capital*, 22 H3
Edmundston, *Canada*, 23 N4
Edward, Lake, *Africa*, 70 E4
Edwards Plateau, *U.S.A.*, 24 F4
Efate, *Vanuatu*, 39 N3
Egypt, *Africa, country*, 67 G3
Eindhoven, *Netherlands*, 60 F4
Elat, *Israel*, 51 B6
Elazig, *Turkey*, 50 C4
Elba, *Italy*, 62 D3
Elbasan, *Albania*, 63 G3
Elbe, *Europe*, 60 G3
Elbrus, Mount, *Russia*, 50 D3
Elche, *Spain*, 61 D7
Eldorado, *Argentina*, 32 H5
Eldoret, *Kenya*, 71 G3
Elephant Island, *Atlantic Ocean*, 33 H12
Eleuthera, *The Bahamas*, 25 L5
El Fasher, *Sudan*, 67 G6
Elgon, Mount, *Uganda*, 71 F3
El Hierro, *Canary Islands*, 68 B3
Elista, *Russia*, 50 D2
El Jadida, *Morocco*, 68 D2
El Jem, *Tunisia*, 66 D1
Ellesmere Island, *Canada*, 75 R3
Ellsworth Land, *Antarctica*, 77 R3
El Mansura, *Egypt*, 67 H2
El Minya, *Egypt*, 67 H3
El Obeid, *Sudan*, 67 H6
El Oued, *Algeria*, 68 G2
El Paso, *U.S.A.*, 24 E4
El Salvador, *North America, country*, 26 G5
Embi, *Kazakhstan*, 50 G2
Emi Koussi, *Chad*, 66 E4
Empty Quarter, *Asia*, 51 E8
Encarnacion, *Paraguay*, 32 G5
Ende, *Indonesia*, 43 F5

Enderby Land, *Antarctica*, 77 E3
Engels, *Russia*, 57 F3
England, *United Kingdom, internal admin. area*, 60 D3
English Channel, *Europe*, 60 D4
Ennedi Plateau, *Africa*, 66 F5
Enschede, *Netherlands*, 60 F3
Entebbe, *Uganda*, 71 F3
Enugu, *Nigeria*, 69 G7
Ephesus, *Turkey*, 63 H4
Equatorial Guinea, *Africa, country*, 70 A3
Erenhot, *China*, 46 H2
Erfurt, *Germany*, 60 G4
Erie, *U.S.A.*, 25 K2
Erie, Lake, *U.S.A.*, 25 K2
Eritrea, *Africa, country*, 67 J5
Er Rachidia, *Morocco*, 68 E2
Ershovka, *Kazakhstan*, 57 K3
Erzurum, *Turkey*, 50 D4
Esbjerg, *Denmark*, 59 D5
Esfahan, *Iran*, 50 F5
Eskilstuna, *Sweden*, 58 F4
Eskisehir, *Turkey*, 63 J4
Esmeraldas, *Ecuador*, 30 C3
Esperance, *Australia*, 38 D6
Espinosa, *Brazil*, 32 K2
Espiritu Santo, *Vanuatu*, 39 N3
Espoo, *Finland*, 58 H3
Espungabera, *Mozambique*, 73 F4
Esquel, *Argentina*, 33 D8
Essaouira, *Morocco*, 68 D2
Es Semara, *Western Sahara*, 68 C3
Essen, *Germany*, 60 F4
Estevan, *Canada*, 22 J4
Estonia, *Europe, country*, 58 H4
Ethiopia, *Africa, country*, 71 G2
Ethiopian Highlands, *Ethiopia*, 71 G1
Etna, Mount, *Italy*, 62 E4
Etosha Pan, *Namibia*, 72 C3
Euboea, *Greece*, 63 G4
Eugene, *U.S.A.*, 24 B2
Eugenia, Point, *Mexico*, 26 A2
Euphrates, *Asia*, 51 E5
Europa Island, *Africa*, 73 H4
Europe, 19
Evansville, *U.S.A.*, 25 J3
Everest, Mount, *Asia*, 48 F5
Everglades, The, *U.S.A.*, 25 K5
Evora, *Portugal*, 61 C7
Evry, *France*, 60 E4
Exeter, *United Kingdom*, 60 D4
Eyl, *Somalia*, 71 J2
Eyre, Lake, *Australia*, 38 G5

f

Fada-Ngourma, *Burkina Faso*, 69 F6
Fairbanks, *U.S.A.*, 22 E2
Faisalabad, *Pakistan*, 48 C4
Fakfak, *Indonesia*, 43 H4
Falkland Islands, *Atlantic Ocean*, 33 F10
Farasan Islands, *Saudi Arabia*, 51 D8
Farewell, Cape, *New Zealand*, 39 P8
Fargo, *U.S.A.*, 25 G1
Fargona, *Uzbekistan*, 48 C2
Farmington, *U.S.A.*, 24 E3
Faro, *Portugal*, 61 C7
Farquhar Group, *Seychelles*, 73 K1
Faxafloi, *Iceland*, 58 N2
Faya-Largeau, *Chad*, 66 E5
Federated States of Micronesia, *Oceania, country*, 36 G5
Feira de Santana, *Brazil*, 32 L2
Feodosiya, *Ukraine*, 63 K2
Fernandina, *Ecuador*, 30 N10
Ferrara, *Italy*, 62 D2
Fes, *Morocco*, 68 E2
Fianarantsoa, *Madagascar*, 73 J4
Fiji, *Oceania, country*, 39 Q3
Finland, *Europe, country*, 58 H2
Finland, Gulf of, *Europe*, 58 H4
Flagstaff, *U.S.A.*, 24 D3
Flensburg, *Germany*, 60 G3
Flinders Island, *Australia*, 39 J7
Flin Flon, *Canada*, 22 J3
Florence, *Italy*, 62 D3

Florencia, Colombia, 30 C3
Flores, Azores, 68 J10
Flores, Indonesia, 43 F5
Flores Sea, Indonesia, 43 F5
Floresta, Brazil, 31 L5
Floriano, Brazil, 31 K5
Florianopolis, Brazil, 32 J5
Florida, U.S.A., internal admin. area, 25 K5
Florida Keys, U.S.A., 25 K6
Florida, Straits of, North America, 25 K6
Focsani, Romania, 63 H2
Foggia, Italy, 62 E3
Fogo, Cape Verde, 69 M12
Fomboni, Comoros, 73 H2
Formosa, Argentina, 32 G5
Fort Albany, Canada, 23 L3
Fortaleza, Brazil, 31 L4
Fort Chipewyan, Canada, 22 H3
Fort-de-France, Martinique, 26 M5
Fort Lauderdale, U.S.A., 25 K5
Fort McMurray, Canada, 22 H3
Fort Nelson, Canada, 22 G3
Fort Peck Lake, U.S.A., 24 E1
Fort Providence, Canada, 22 H2
Fort St. John, Canada, 22 G3
Fort Severn, Canada, 23 L3
Fort Vermilion, Canada, 22 H3
Fort Wayne, U.S.A., 25 J2
Fort Worth, U.S.A., 24 G4
Foumban, Cameroon, 70 B2
Foxe Basin, Canada, 23 M2
Foxe Peninsula, Canada, 23 M2
Fox Islands, U.S.A., 23 C3
Foz do Cunene, Angola, 72 B3
Foz do Iguacu, Brazil, 32 H5
France, Europe, country, 61 E5
Franceville, Gabon, 70 B4
Francistown, Botswana, 72 E4
Frankfort, U.S.A., internal capital, 25 K3
Frankfurt, Germany, 60 G4
Franz Josef Land, Russia, 52 C1
Fraser Island, Australia, 39 K5
Fredericton, Canada, internal capital, 23 N4
Fredrikstad, Norway, 58 D4
Freeport City, The Bahamas, 25 L5
Freetown, Sierra Leone, national capital, 69 C7
Freiburg, Germany, 60 F4
French Guiana, South America, dependency, 31 H3
French Polynesia, Oceania, dependency, 37 J6
Fresno, U.S.A., 24 C3
Frisian Islands, Europe, 60 F3
Froya, Norway, 58 D3
Fuerteventura, Canary Islands, 68 B3
Fuji, Mount, Japan, 47 N3
Fukui, Japan, 47 N3
Fukuoka, Japan, 47 M4
Fukushima, Japan, 47 P3
Funafuti, Tuvalu, national capital, 36 E5
Funchal, Madeira, 68 B2
Furnas Reservoir, Brazil, 32 J4
Fushun, China, 47 K2
Fuxin, China, 47 K2
Fyn, Denmark, 59 D5

g

Gabes, Tunisia, 66 D2
Gabes, Gulf of, Africa, 66 D2
Gabon, Africa, country, 70 B4
Gaborone, Botswana, national capital, 72 E4
Gafsa, Tunisia, 66 C2
Gagnoa, Ivory Coast, 69 D7
Gairdner, Lake, Australia, 38 F6
Galapagos Islands, Ecuador, 30 N9
Galati, Romania, 63 J2
Galdhopiggen, Norway, 58 D3
Galle, Sri Lanka, 49 E9
Gallinas, Cape, Colombia, 30 D1
Galveston, U.S.A., 25 H5
Galway, Ireland, 60 B3
Gambela, Ethiopia, 71 F2

Gambia, The, Africa, country, 69 B6
Ganca, Azerbaijan, 50 E3
Gander, Canada, 23 P4
Ganges, Asia, 48 E5
Ganges, Mouths of the, Asia, 49 F6
Ganzhou, China, 47 H5
Garda, Lake, Italy, 62 D2
Garissa, Kenya, 71 G4
Garonne, France, 61 E5
Garoua, Cameroon, 70 B2
Gaspe, Canada, 23 N4
Gatchina, Russia, 58 J4
Gavle, Sweden, 58 F3
Gaza, Israel, 51 B5
Gaziantep, Turkey, 50 C4
Gdansk, Poland, 59 F5
Gdansk, Gulf of, Poland, 59 F5
Gdynia, Poland, 59 F5
Gedaref, Sudan, 67 J6
Geelong, Australia, 38 H7
Gejiu, China, 46 F6
Gemena, Democratic Republic of Congo, 70 C3
General Roca, Argentina, 33 E7
General Santos, Philippines, 45 J6
General Villegas, Argentina, 32 F7
Geneva, Switzerland, 62 C2
Geneva, Lake, Europe, 62 C2
Genoa, Italy, 62 D2
Genoa, Gulf of, Italy, 62 D2
Gent, Belgium, 60 E4
Georgetown, Guyana, national capital, 31 G2
George Town, Malaysia, 42 B2
Georgia, Asia, country, 50 D3
Georgia, U.S.A., internal admin. area, 25 K4
Gera, Germany, 60 H4
Geraldton, Australia, 38 B5
Gerlachovsky stit, Slovakia, 59 G6
Germany, Europe, country, 60 G4
Gerona, Spain, 61 E6
Ghadamis, Libya, 66 C2
Ghana, Africa, country, 69 E7
Ghardaia, Algeria, 68 F2
Gharyan, Libya, 66 D2
Ghat, Libya, 66 D3
Gibraltar, Europe, 61 C7
Gibson Desert, Australia, 38 E4
Gijon, Spain, 61 C6
Gilbert Islands, Kiribati, 36 E5
Gilgit, Pakistan, 48 C3
Girardeau, Cape, U.S.A., 25 J3
Giza, Pyramids of, Egypt, 67 H3
Gladstone, Australia, 39 K4
Glama, Norway, 58 D3
Glasgow, United Kingdom, 60 C3
Glazov, Russia, 57 G2
Glorioso Islands, Africa, 73 J2
Gloucester, United Kingdom, 60 D4
Gobabis, Namibia, 72 C4
Gobi Desert, Asia, 46 F2
Gochas, Namibia, 72 C4
Godavari, India, 49 D7
Gode, Ethiopia, 71 H2
Goiania, Brazil, 32 J3
Gold Coast, Australia, 39 K5
Golmud, China, 48 G3
Goma, Democratic Republic of Congo, 70 E4
Gonaives, Haiti, 27 K4
Gonder, Ethiopia, 71 G1
Gongga Shan, China, 46 F5
Good Hope, Cape of, South Africa, 72 C6
Goose Lake, U.S.A., 24 B2
Gorakhpur, India, 49 E5
Gorgan, Iran, 50 F4
Gori, Georgia, 50 D3
Gorki Reservoir, Russia, 56 E2
Gorontalo, Indonesia, 43 F3
Gorzow Wielkopolski, Poland, 59 E5
Gothenburg, Sweden, 59 E4
Gotland, Sweden, 59 F4
Gottingen, Germany, 60 G4

Gouin Reservoir, Canada, 25 L1
Goundam, Mali, 69 E5
Governador Valadares, Brazil, 32 K3
Graaff-Reinet, South Africa, 72 D6
Grafton, Australia, 39 K5
Grahamstown, South Africa, 72 E6
Granada, Spain, 61 D7
Gran Canaria, Canary Islands, 68 B3
Gran Chaco, South America, 32 F4
Grand Bahama, The Bahamas, 25 L5
Grand Canal, China, 47 J4
Grand Canyon, U.S.A., 24 D3
Grand Comoro, Comoros, 73 H2
Grande Bay, Argentina, 33 E10
Grande Prairie, Canada, 22 H3
Grand Forks, U.S.A., 25 G1
Grand Island, U.S.A., 24 G2
Grand Junction, U.S.A., 24 E3
Grand Rapids, Canada, 23 K3
Grand Rapids, U.S.A., 25 J2
Grand Teton, U.S.A., 24 D2
Graskop, South Africa, 72 F5
Graz, Austria, 62 E2
Great Australian Bight, Australia, 38 F6
Great Barrier Reef, Australia, 38 J3
Great Basin, U.S.A., 24 C2
Great Bear Lake, Canada, 22 G2
Great Dividing Range, Australia, 39 J6
Great Eastern Erg, Algeria, 68 G3
Greater Antilles, North America, 27 J4
Greater Khingan Range, China, 47 J1
Greater Sunda Islands, Asia, 42 C4
Great Falls, U.S.A., 24 D1
Great Inagua, The Bahamas, 27 K3
Great Karoo, South Africa, 72 D6
Great Plains, U.S.A., 24 F2
Great Rift Valley, Africa, 71 F5
Great Salt Desert, Iran, 50 F5
Great Salt Lake, U.S.A., 24 D2
Great Salt Lake Desert, U.S.A., 24 D2
Great Sandy Desert, Australia, 38 D4
Great Slave Lake, Canada, 22 H2
Great Victoria Desert, Australia, 38 D5
Great Wall of China, China, 46 F3
Great Western Erg, Algeria, 68 E2
Greece, Europe, country, 63 G4
Green Bay, U.S.A., 25 J2
Greenland, North America, dependency, 75 P3
Greenland Sea, Atlantic Ocean, 75 M3
Greensboro, U.S.A., 25 L3
Greenville, U.S.A., 25 H4
Grenada, North America, country, 26 M5
Grenoble, France, 61 F5
Griffith, Australia, 38 J6
Groningen, Netherlands, 60 F3
Groot, South Africa, 72 D6
Groote Eylandt, Australia, 38 G2
Grossglockner, Austria, 62 E2
Groznyy, Russia, 50 E3
Grudziadz, Poland, 59 F5
Grunau, Namibia, 72 C5
Grytviken, South Georgia, 33 L10
Guadalajara, Mexico, 26 D3
Guadalquivir, Spain, 61 C7
Guadalupe Island, Mexico, 26 A2
Guadeloupe, North America, 26 M4
Guadiana, Europe, 61 C7
Gualeguaychu, Argentina, 32 G6
Guam, Oceania, 36 B3
Guangzhou, China, 47 H6
Guantanamo, Cuba, 27 J3
Guarapuava, Brazil, 32 H5
Guardafui, Cape, Somalia, 71 K1
Guatemala, North America, country, 26 F4
Guatemala City, Guatemala, national capital, 26 F5
Guaviare, Colombia, 30 E3
Guayaquil, Ecuador, 30 C4
Guayaquil, Gulf of, Ecuador, 30 B4
Gueckedou, Guinea, 69 C7
Guelma, Algeria, 62 C4
Guelph, Canada, 25 K2
Guiana Highlands, Venezuela, 30 E2
Guilin, China, 46 H5
Guinea, Africa, country, 69 C6

Guinea-Bissau, Africa, country, 69 B6
Guinea, Gulf of, Africa, 69 F8
Guiria, Venezuela, 30 F1
Guiyang, China, 46 G5
Gujranwala, Pakistan, 48 C4
Gujrat, Pakistan, 48 C4
Gulbarga, India, 49 D7
Gulf, The, Asia, 51 F6
Gulu, Uganda, 71 F3
Gunnbjorns Mountain, Greenland, 75 N2
Gunung Kerinci, Indonesia, 42 B4
Gunung Tahan, Malaysia, 42 B3
Gurupi, Brazil, 32 J2
Gusau, Nigeria, 69 G6
Guwahati, India, 48 G5
Guyana, South America, country, 31 G2
Gwalior, India, 48 D5
Gweru, Zimbabwe, 72 E3
Gympie, Australia, 39 K5
Gyor, Hungary, 59 F7

h

Haapsalu, Estonia, 58 G4
Haarlem, Netherlands, 60 F3
Hadhramaut, Yemen, 51 E9
Ha Giang, Vietnam, 44 E3
Hague, The, Netherlands, national capital, 60 F3
Haifa, Israel, 50 B5
Haikou, China, 46 H6
Hail, Saudi Arabia, 51 D6
Hailar, China, 47 J1
Hainan, China, 46 H7
Hai Phong, Vietnam, 44 E3
Haiti, North America, country, 27 K4
Hakodate, Japan, 47 P2
Halifax, Canada, internal capital, 23 N4
Halmahera, Indonesia, 43 G3
Halmstad, Sweden, 59 E4
Hamadan, Iran, 50 E5
Hamah, Syria, 50 C4
Hamamatsu, Japan, 47 N4
Hamburg, Germany, 60 G3
Hameenlinna, Finland, 58 H3
Hamhung, North Korea, 47 L3
Hami, China, 48 G2
Hamilton, Canada, 23 M4
Hamilton, New Zealand, 39 Q7
Hammerfest, Norway, 58 G1
Handan, China, 47 H3
Hangzhou, China, 47 K4
Hannover, Germany, 60 G3
Hanoi, Vietnam, national capital, 44 E3
Happy Valley-Goose Bay, Canada, 23 N3
Haradh, Saudi Arabia, 51 E7
Harare, Zimbabwe, national capital, 72 F3
Harbin, China, 47 L1
Harer, Ethiopia, 71 H2
Hargeysa, Somalia, 71 H2
Harney Basin, U.S.A., 24 C2
Harper, Liberia, 69 D8
Harrisburg, U.S.A., internal capital, 25 L2
Harrismith, South Africa, 72 E5
Hartford, U.S.A., internal capital, 25 M2
Hatteras, Cape, U.S.A., 25 L3
Hattiesburg, U.S.A., 25 J4
Hat Yai, Thailand, 44 D6
Hauki Lake, Finland, 58 J3
Havana, Cuba, national capital, 27 H3
Hawaii, Pacific Ocean, internal admin. area, 25 P7
Hawaiian Islands, Pacific Ocean, 25 P7
Hebrides, United Kingdom, 60 C2
Hefei, China, 47 J4
Hegang, China, 47 M1
Hejaz, Saudi Arabia, 51 C6
Helena, U.S.A., internal capital, 24 D1
Helmand, Asia, 48 B4
Helsingborg, Sweden, 59 E4
Helsinki, Finland, national capital, 58 H3
Hengyang, China, 46 H5
Henzada, Burma, 44 B4
Herat, Afghanistan, 48 A4
Hermosillo, Mexico, 26 B2
Hiiumaa, Estonia, 58 G4
Hilo, U.S.A., 25 P8

Himalayas, *Asia*, 48 E4
Hindu Kush, *Asia*, 48 B3
Hinton, *Canada*, 22 H3
Hiroshima, *Japan*, 47 M4
Hispaniola, *North America*, 27 K4
Hitra, *Norway*, 58 D3
Hobart, *Australia, internal capital*, 38 J8
Ho Chi Minh City, *Vietnam*, 44 E5
Hohhot, *China*, 46 H2
Hokkaido, *Japan*, 47 P2
Holguin, *Cuba*, 27 J3
Homs, *Syria*, 50 C5
Homyel, *Belarus*, 59 J5
Honduras, *North America, country*, 27 G4
Honduras, Gulf of, *North America*, 27 G4
Honefoss, *Norway*, 58 D3
Hong Kong, *China*, 47 H6
Honiara, *Solomon Islands, national capital*, 36 D5
Honolulu, *U.S.A., internal capital*, 25 P7
Honshu, *Japan*, 47 N3
Horlivka, *Ukraine*, 56 D4
Hormuz, Strait of, *Asia*, 51 G6
Horn, Cape, *Chile*, 33 D11
Horn Lake, *Sweden*, 58 F2
Hotan, *China*, 48 D3
Hotazel, *South Africa*, 72 D5
Houston, *U.S.A.*, 25 G5
Hradec Kralove, *Czech Republic*, 62 E1
Hrodna, *Belarus*, 59 G5
Huacrachuco, *Peru*, 30 C5
Huaihua, *China*, 46 H5
Huambo, *Angola*, 72 C2
Huancayo, *Peru*, 30 C6
Huang He, *China*, 47 H3
Huanuco, *Peru*, 30 C5
Huascaran, Mount, *Peru*, 30 C5
Hubli, *India*, 49 D7
Hudiksvall, *Sweden*, 58 F3
Hudson Bay, *Canada*, 23 L3
Hudson Strait, *Canada*, 23 M2
Hue, *Vietnam*, 44 E4
Huelva, *Spain*, 61 C7
Hull, *United Kingdom*, 60 D3
Hulun Lake, *China*, 47 J1
Hungary, *Europe, country*, 59 F7
Huntsville, *Canada*, 23 M4
Huntsville, *U.S.A.*, 25 J4
Hurghada, *Egypt*, 67 H3
Huron, Lake, *U.S.A.*, 25 K2
Hvannadalshnukur, *Iceland*, 58 P2
Hwange, *Zimbabwe*, 72 E3
Hyderabad, *India*, 49 D7
Hyderabad, *Pakistan*, 48 B5
Hyesan, *North Korea*, 47 L2

i

Iasi, *Romania*, 63 H2
Ibadan, *Nigeria*, 69 F7
Ibague, *Colombia*, 30 C3
Ibarra, *Ecuador*, 30 C3
Ibb, *Yemen*, 51 D9
Iberian Mountains, *Spain*, 61 D6
Ibiza, *Spain*, 61 E7
Ica, *Peru*, 30 C6
Iceland, *Europe, country*, 58 P2
Idaho, *U.S.A., internal admin. area*, 24 C2
Idaho Falls, *U.S.A.*, 24 D2
Ierapetra, *Greece*, 63 H5
Iguacu Falls, *South America*, 32 H5
Ihosy, *Madagascar*, 73 J4
Ikopa, *Madagascar*, 73 J3
Ilagan, *Philippines*, 45 H4
Ilebo, *Democratic Republic of Congo*, 70 D4
Ilheus, *Brazil*, 32 L2
Iliamna Lake, *U.S.A.*, 22 D2
Iligan, *Philippines*, 45 H6
Illapel, *Chile*, 32 D6
Illimani, Mount, *Bolivia*, 32 E3
Illinois, *U.S.A., internal admin. area*, 25 J2
Illizi, *Algeria*, 68 G3
Ilmen, Lake, *Russia*, 58 J4
Iloilo, *Philippines*, 45 H5
Ilonga, *Tanzania*, 71 G5
Ilorin, *Nigeria*, 69 F7

Imperatriz, *Brazil*, 31 J5
Imphal, *India*, 49 G6
Inari, Lake, *Finland*, 58 H1
Inchon, *South Korea*, 47 L3
Indals, *Sweden*, 58 E3
Inderbor, *Kazakhstan*, 57 G4
India, *Asia, country*, 49 D6
Indiana, *U.S.A., internal admin. area*, 25 J2
Indianapolis, *U.S.A., internal capital*, 25 J3
Indian Ocean, 19
Indonesia, *Asia, country*, 42 C5
Indore, *India*, 49 D6
Indus, *Asia*, 48 B5
Ingolstadt, *Germany*, 60 G4
Inhambane, *Mozambique*, 73 G4
Inner Mongolia, *China*, 47 H2
Innsbruck, *Austria*, 62 D2
Inukjuak, *Canada*, 23 M3
Inuvik, *Canada*, 22 F2
Invercargill, *New Zealand*, 39 N9
Inyangani, *Zimbabwe*, 73 F3
Ioannina, *Greece*, 63 G4
Ionian Sea, *Europe*, 63 F4
Iowa, *U.S.A., internal admin. area*, 25 H2
Ipiales, *Colombia*, 30 C3
Ipoh, *Malaysia*, 42 B3
Ipswich, *United Kingdom*, 60 E3
Iqaluit, *Canada, internal capital*, 23 N2
Iquique, *Chile*, 32 D4
Iquitos, *Peru*, 30 D4
Irakleio, *Greece*, 63 H5
Iran, *Asia, country*, 50 F5
Iranshahr, *Iran*, 51 H6
Iraq, *Asia, country*, 50 D5
Irbid, *Jordan*, 50 C5
Ireland, *Europe, country*, 60 B3
Iringa, *Tanzania*, 71 G5
Irish Sea, *Europe*, 60 C3
Irkutsk, *Russia*, 53 F3
Irrawaddy, *Burma*, 44 C4
Irrawaddy, Mouths of the, *Burma*, 44 B4
Irtysh, *Asia*, 52 D3
Isabela, *Ecuador*, 30 N10
Isafjordhur, *Iceland*, 58 N2
Isiro, *Democratic Republic of Congo*, 70 E3
Islamabad, *Pakistan, national capital*, 48 C4
Isle of Man, *Europe*, 60 C3
Isle of Wight, *United Kingdom*, 60 D4
Ismailia, *Egypt*, 67 H2
Isoka, *Zambia*, 73 F2
Isparta, *Turkey*, 63 J4
Israel, *Asia, country*, 51 B5
Issyk, Lake, *Kyrgyzstan*, 48 D2
Istanbul, *Turkey*, 63 J3
Itaituba, *Brazil*, 31 G4
Itajai, *Brazil*, 32 J5
Italy, *Europe, country*, 62 D2
Itapetininga, *Brazil*, 32 J4
Ivano-Frankivsk, *Ukraine*, 59 H6
Ivanovo, *Russia*, 56 E2
Ivdel, *Russia*, 57 J1
Ivory Coast, *Africa, country*, 69 D7
Ivujivik, *Canada*, 23 M2
Izhevsk, *Russia*, 57 G2
Izmir, *Turkey*, 63 H4

j

Jabalpur, *India*, 49 D6
Jackson, *Mississippi, U.S.A., internal capital*, 25 H4
Jackson, *Tennessee, U.S.A.*, 25 J3
Jacksonville, *U.S.A.*, 25 K4
Jaen, *Spain*, 61 D7
Jaffna, *Sri Lanka*, 49 E9
Jaipur, *India*, 48 D5
Jakarta, *Indonesia, national capital*, 42 C5
Jalalabad, *Afghanistan*, 48 C4
Jalal-Abad, *Kyrgyzstan*, 48 C2
Jamaica, *North America, country*, 27 J4
Jambi, *Indonesia*, 42 B4
James Bay, *Canada*, 23 L3
Jamestown, *U.S.A.*, 25 L2

Jammu, *India*, 48 C4
Jammu and Kashmir, *Asia*, 48 D4
Jamnagar, *India*, 49 C6
Jamshedpur, *India*, 49 F6
Japan, *Asia, country*, 47 N3
Japan, Sea of, *Asia*, 47 M2
Japura, *Brazil*, 30 E4
Jatai, *Brazil*, 32 H3
Java, *Indonesia*, 42 C5
Java Sea, *Indonesia*, 42 C5
Jayapura, *Indonesia*, 43 K4
Jedda, *Saudi Arabia*, 51 C7
Jefferson City, *U.S.A., internal capital*, 25 H3
Jekabpils, *Latvia*, 59 H4
Jelgava, *Latvia*, 59 G4
Jember, *Indonesia*, 42 D5
Jerba, *Tunisia*, 66 D2
Jerez de la Frontera, *Spain*, 61 C7
Jerusalem, *Israel, national capital*, 51 C5
Jhansi, *India*, 48 D5
Jiamusi, *China*, 47 M1
Jilin, *China*, 47 L2
Jima, *Ethiopia*, 71 G2
Jinhua, *China*, 47 J5
Jining, *China*, 47 J3
Jinja, *Uganda*, 71 F3
Jinzhou, *China*, 47 K2
Jixi, *China*, 47 M1
Jizzax, *Uzbekistan*, 48 B2
Joao Pessoa, *Brazil*, 31 M5
Jodhpur, *India*, 48 C5
Johannesburg, *South Africa*, 72 E5
Johnston Atoll, *Oceania*, 36 G3
Johor Bahru, *Malaysia*, 42 B3
Jolo, *Philippines*, 45 H6
Jonesboro, *U.S.A.*, 25 H3
Jonkoping, *Sweden*, 59 E4
Jordan, *Asia, country*, 51 C5
Jorhat, *India*, 48 G5
Jos, *Nigeria*, 70 A2
Juan de Nova, *Africa*, 73 H3
Juazeiro, *Brazil*, 31 K5
Juazeiro do Norte, *Brazil*, 31 L5
Juba, *Africa*, 71 H3
Juba, *Sudan*, 71 F3
Juchitan, *Mexico*, 26 E4
Juiz de Fora, *Brazil*, 32 K4
Juliaca, *Peru*, 30 D7
Juneau, *U.S.A., internal capital*, 22 F3
Jurmala, *Latvia*, 59 G4
Jurua, *Brazil*, 30 E5
Jutland, *Europe*, 59 D4
Jyvaskyla, *Finland*, 58 H3

k

K2, *Asia*, 48 D3
Kaamanen, *Finland*, 58 H1
Kabinda, *Democratic Republic of Congo*, 70 D5
Kabul, *Afghanistan, national capital*, 48 B4
Kabunda, *Democratic Republic of Congo*, 70 E6
Kabwe, *Zambia*, 72 E2
Kadoma, *Zimbabwe*, 72 E3
Kaduna, *Nigeria*, 69 G6
Kaedi, *Mauritania*, 69 C5
Kafakumba, *Democratic Republic of Congo*, 70 D5
Kafue, *Zambia*, 72 E3
Kagoshima, *Japan*, 47 M4
Kahramanmaras, *Turkey*, 50 C4
Kahului, *U.S.A.*, 25 P7
Kainji Reservoir, *Nigeria*, 69 F6
Kairouan, *Tunisia*, 66 D1
Kajaani, *Finland*, 58 H2
Kakhovske Reservoir, *Ukraine*, 56 C4
Kalahari Desert, *Africa*, 72 D4
Kalamata, *Greece*, 63 G4
Kalemie, *Democratic Republic of Congo*, 70 E5
Kalgoorlie, *Australia*, 38 D6
Kaliningrad, *Russia*, 59 G5
Kalisz, *Poland*, 59 F6
Kalkrand, *Namibia*, 72 C4

Kalmar, *Sweden*, 59 F4
Kaluga, *Russia*, 56 D3
Kamanjab, *Namibia*, 72 B3
Kama Reservoir, *Russia*, 57 H2
Kamativi, *Zimbabwe*, 72 E3
Kamchatka Peninsula, *Russia*, 53 H3
Kamenka, *Russia*, 56 E3
Kamina, *Democratic Republic of Congo*, 70 E5
Kamloops, *Canada*, 22 G3
Kampala, *Uganda, national capital*, 71 F3
Kampong Cham, *Cambodia*, 44 E5
Kampong Chhnang, *Cambodia*, 44 D5
Kampong Saom, *Cambodia*, 44 D5
Kamyanets-Podilskyy, *Ukraine*, 59 H6
Kamyshin, *Russia*, 56 F3
Kananga, *Democratic Republic of Congo*, 70 D5
Kanazawa, *Japan*, 47 N3
Kandahar, *Afghanistan*, 48 B4
Kandalaksha, *Russia*, 58 K2
Kandi, *Benin*, 69 F6
Kandy, *Sri Lanka*, 49 E9
Kang, *Botswana*, 72 D4
Kangaroo Island, *Australia*, 38 G7
Kanggye, *North Korea*, 47 L2
Kankan, *Guinea*, 69 D6
Kano, *Nigeria*, 66 C6
Kanpur, *India*, 48 E5
Kansas, *U.S.A., internal admin. area*, 24 G3
Kansas City, *U.S.A.*, 25 H3
Kanye, *Botswana*, 72 E4
Kaohsiung, *Taiwan*, 47 K6
Kaolack, *Senegal*, 69 B6
Kara-Balta, *Kyrgyzstan*, 48 C2
Karabuk, *Turkey*, 63 K3
Karachi, *Pakistan*, 49 B6
Karaj, *Iran*, 50 F4
Karakol, *Kyrgyzstan*, 48 D2
Karakorum Range, *Asia*, 48 D3
Karaman, *Turkey*, 63 K4
Karamay, *China*, 48 E1
Kara Kum Desert, *Turkmenistan*, 50 G3
Karasburg, *Russia*, 52 D2
Kariba, *Zimbabwe*, 72 E3
Kariba, Lake, *Africa*, 72 E3
Karibib, *Namibia*, 72 C4
Karimata Strait, *Indonesia*, 42 C4
Karlovac, *Croatia*, 62 E2
Karlovy Vary, *Czech Republic*, 62 E1
Karlshamn, *Sweden*, 59 F4
Karlsruhe, *Germany*, 60 G4
Karlstad, *Sweden*, 58 E4
Karmoy, *Norway*, 58 C4
Karonga, *Malawi*, 73 F1
Karora, *Eritrea*, 67 J5
Karpathos, *Greece*, 63 H5
Karratha, *Australia*, 38 C4
Kasai, *Africa*, 70 C4
Kasama, *Zambia*, 72 F2
Kashi, *China*, 48 D3
Kassala, *Sudan*, 67 J5
Kassel, *Germany*, 60 G4
Kasungu, *Malawi*, 73 F2
Kataba, *Zambia*, 72 E3
Kathmandu, *Nepal, national capital*, 48 F5
Katiola, *Ivory Coast*, 69 D7
Katowice, *Poland*, 59 F6
Katsina, *Nigeria*, 69 G6
Kattegat, *Europe*, 59 D4
Kauai, *U.S.A.*, 25 P7
Kaukau Veld, *Africa*, 72 C4
Kaunas, *Lithuania*, 59 G5
Kavala, *Greece*, 63 H3
Kawambwa, *Zambia*, 72 E1
Kayes, *Mali*, 69 C6
Kayseri, *Turkey*, 50 C4
Kazakhstan, *Asia, country*, 52 C3
Kazan, *Russia*, 57 F2
Kaztalovka, *Kazakhstan*, 57 F4
Kebnekaise, *Sweden*, 58 F2
Kecskemet, *Hungary*, 59 F7
Kedougou, *Senegal*, 69 C6
Keetmanshoop, *Namibia*, 72 C5

Liverpool, *United Kingdom*, 60 D3
Livingstone, *Zambia*, 72 E3
Livorno, *Italy*, 62 D3
Liwale, *Tanzania*, 71 G5
Ljubljana, *Slovenia, national capital*, 62 E2
Llanos, *South America*, 30 D2
Lloydminster, *Canada*, 22 J3
Lobamba, *Lesotho, national capital*, 72 F5
Lodz, *Poland*, 59 F6
Lofoten, *Norway*, 58 E1
Logan, Mount, *Canada*, 22 F2
Logrono, *Spain*, 61 D6
Loire, *France*, 60 E5
Loja, *Ecuador*, 30 C4
Lokan Reservoir, *Finland*, 58 H2
Lolland, *Denmark*, 59 D5
Lombok, *Indonesia*, 42 E5
Lome, *Togo, national capital*, 69 F7
London, *Canada*, 23 L4
London, *United Kingdom, national capital*, 60 D4
Londonderry, *United Kingdom*, 60 C3
Londrina, *Brazil*, 32 H4
Long Island, *The Bahamas*, 25 L6
Long Xuyen, *Vietnam*, 44 E5
Lopez, Cape, *Gabon*, 70 A4
Lop Lake, *China*, 48 G2
Lord Howe Island, *Australia*, 39 L6
Los Angeles, *Chile*, 33 D7
Los Angeles, *U.S.A.*, 24 C4
Los Mochis, *Mexico*, 26 C2
Louangphrabang, *Laos*, 44 D4
Loubomo, *Congo*, 70 B4
Louga, *Senegal*, 69 B5
Louisiana, *U.S.A., internal admin. area*, 25 H4
Lower California, *Mexico*, 26 B2
Loyalty Islands, *New Caledonia*, 39 N4
Luacano, *Angola*, 72 D2
Luanda, *Angola, national capital*, 72 B1
Luangwa, *Africa*, 72 F2
Luanshya, *Zambia*, 72 E2
Lubango, *Angola*, 72 B2
Lubbock, *U.S.A.*, 24 F4
Lublin, *Poland*, 59 G6
Lubny, *Ukraine*, 56 C3
Lubumbashi, *Democratic Republic of Congo*, 70 E6
Lucena, *Philippines*, 45 H5
Lucerne, *Switzerland*, 62 D2
Lucira, *Angola*, 72 B2
Lucknow, *India*, 48 E5
Luderitz, *Namibia*, 72 C5
Ludhiana, *India*, 48 D4
Ludza, *Latvia*, 59 H4
Luena, *Angola*, 72 C2
Luganville, *Vanuatu*, 39 N3
Lugo, *Spain*, 61 C6
Luhansk, *Ukraine*, 56 D4
Luiana, *Angola*, 72 D3
Lukulu, *Zambia*, 72 D2
Lumbala Kaquengue, *Angola*, 72 D2
Lumbala Nguimbo, *Angola*, 72 D2
Lundazi, *Zambia*, 73 F2
Lupilichi, *Mozambique*, 73 G2
Lusaka, *Zambia, national capital*, 72 E3
Lutsk, *Ukraine*, 59 H6
Luxembourg, *Europe, country*, 60 F4
Luxembourg, *Luxembourg, national capital*, 60 F4
Luxor, *Egypt*, 67 H3
Luzhou, *China*, 46 G5
Luzon, *Philippines*, 45 H4
Luzon Strait, *Philippines*, 45 H4
Lviv, *Ukraine*, 59 H6
Lyon, *France*, 61 F5
Lysychansk, *Ukraine*, 56 D4

m

Maan, *Jordan*, 51 C5
Maastricht, *Netherlands*, 60 F4
Macae, *Brazil*, 32 K4
Macapa, *Brazil*, 31 H3
Macau, *China*, 47 H6

Macedonia, *Europe, country*, 63 G3
Maceio, *Brazil*, 31 L5
Machakos, *Kenya*, 71 G4
Machala, *Ecuador*, 30 C4
Machu Picchu, *Peru*, 30 D6
Mackay, *Australia*, 39 J4
Mackenzie, *Canada*, 22 G2
Mackenzie Bay, *Canada*, 22 F2
Mackenzie Mountains, *Canada*, 22 F2
Macon, *U.S.A.*, 25 K4
Madagascar, *Africa, country*, 73 J4
Madang, *Papua New Guinea*, 43 L5
Madeira, *Atlantic Ocean*, 68 B2
Madeira, *Brazil*, 30 F5
Madingou, *Congo*, 70 B4
Madison, *U.S.A., internal capital*, 25 J2
Madras, *India*, 49 E8
Madrid, *Spain, national capital*, 61 D6
Madurai, *India*, 49 D9
Maevatanana, *Madagascar*, 73 J3
Mafeteng, *Lesotho*, 72 E5
Mafia Island, *Tanzania*, 71 H5
Magadan, *Russia*, 53 H3
Magangue, *Colombia*, 30 D2
Magdalena, *Bolivia*, 32 F2
Magdeburg, *Germany*, 60 G3
Magellan, Strait of, *South America*, 33 E10
Magnitogorsk, *Russia*, 57 H3
Mahajanga, *Madagascar*, 73 J3
Mahalapye, *Botswana*, 72 E4
Mahilyow, *Belarus*, 59 J5
Mahon, *Spain*, 61 F7
Maiduguri, *Nigeria*, 66 D6
Mai-Ndombe, Lake, *Democratic Republic of Congo*, 70 C4
Maine, *U.S.A., internal admin. area*, 25 N1
Maine, Gulf of, *U.S.A.*, 25 N2
Maio, *Cape Verde*, 69 M11
Majorca, *Spain*, 61 E7
Majuro, *Marshall Islands, national capital*, 36 E4
Makarikari, *Botswana*, 72 D4
Makassar Strait, *Indonesia*, 43 E4
Makeni, *Sierra Leone*, 69 C7
Makgadikgadi Pans, *Botswana*, 72 D4
Makhachkala, *Russia*, 50 E3
Makkovik, *Canada*, 23 P3
Makokou, *Gabon*, 70 B3
Makumbako, *Tanzania*, 71 F5
Makurdi, *Nigeria*, 70 A2
Mala, *Peru*, 30 C6
Malabo, *Equatorial Guinea, national capital*, 70 A3
Maladzyechna, *Belarus*, 59 H5
Malaga, *Spain*, 61 C7
Malaimbandy, *Madagascar*, 73 J4
Malakal, *Sudan*, 71 F2
Malakula, *Vanuatu*, 39 N3
Malang, *Indonesia*, 42 D5
Malanje, *Angola*, 72 C1
Malar, Lake, *Sweden*, 58 F4
Malatya, *Turkey*, 50 C4
Malawi, *Africa, country*, 73 F2
Malawi, Lake, *Africa*, 71 F6
Malaysia, *Asia, country*, 42 B2
Maldives, *Asia, country*, 49 C9
Male, *Maldives, national capital*, 49 C10
Malegaon, *India*, 49 C6
Mali, *Africa, country*, 68 E5
Malindi, *Kenya*, 71 H4
Malmo, *Sweden*, 59 E5
Malpelo Island, *Colombia*, 30 B3
Malta, *Europe, country*, 62 E4
Mamoudzou, *Mayotte*, 73 J2
Mamuno, *Botswana*, 72 D4
Man, *Ivory Coast*, 69 D7
Manado, *Indonesia*, 43 F3
Managua, *Nicaragua, national capital*, 27 G5
Manakara, *Madagascar*, 73 J4
Manama, *Bahrain, national capital*, 51 F6
Manaus, *Brazil*, 31 G4
Manchester, *United Kingdom*, 60 D3
Manchuria, *China*, 47 K2
Mandalay, *Burma*, 44 C3

Mandera, *Kenya*, 71 H3
Mandritsara, *Madagascar*, 73 J3
Mandurah, *Australia*, 38 C6
Mangalore, *India*, 49 C8
Mania, *Madagascar*, 73 J3
Manicouagan Reservoir, *Canada*, 23 N3
Manila, *Philippines, national capital*, 45 H5
Manisa, *Turkey*, 63 H4
Man, Isle of, *Europe*, 60 C3
Manitoba, *Canada, internal admin. area*, 23 K3
Manitoba, Lake, *Canada*, 23 K3
Manizales, *Colombia*, 30 C2
Manja, *Madagascar*, 73 H4
Mannar, *Sri Lanka*, 49 E9
Mannar, Gulf of, *Asia*, 49 D9
Mannheim, *Germany*, 60 G4
Mansa, *Zambia*, 72 E2
Manta, *Ecuador*, 30 B4
Manzhouli, *China*, 53 F3
Mao, *Chad*, 66 E6
Maoke Range, *Indonesia*, 43 J4
Maputo, *Mozambique, national capital*, 73 F5
Maraba, *Brazil*, 31 J5
Maracaibo, *Venezuela*, 30 D1
Maracaibo, Lake, *Venezuela*, 30 D2
Maracay, *Venezuela*, 30 E1
Maradi, *Niger*, 66 C6
Maranon, *Peru*, 30 D4
Marathon, *Canada*, 23 L4
Mar del Plata, *Argentina*, 33 G7
Margarita Island, *Venezuela*, 30 F1
Margherita Peak, *Africa*, 70 E3
Marib, *Yemen*, 51 E8
Maribor, *Slovenia*, 62 E2
Marie Byrd Land, *Antarctica*, 77 Q3
Mariental, *Namibia*, 72 C4
Marijampole, *Lithuania*, 59 G5
Marilia, *Brazil*, 32 J4
Marimba, *Angola*, 72 C1
Mariupol, *Ukraine*, 56 D4
Marka, *Somalia*, 71 H3
Marmara, Sea of, *Turkey*, 63 J3
Maroantsetra, *Madagascar*, 73 J3
Maroua, *Cameroon*, 70 B1
Marquesas Islands, *French Polynesia*, 37 K5
Marrakech, *Morocco*, 68 D2
Marra, Mount, *Sudan*, 66 F6
Marsa Matruh, *Egypt*, 67 G2
Marseille, *France*, 61 F6
Marshall Islands, *Oceania, country*, 36 D3
Martapura, *Indonesia*, 42 D4
Martinique, *North America*, 26 M5
Mary, *Turkmenistan*, 50 H4
Maryland, *U.S.A., internal admin. area*, 25 L3
Masaka, *Uganda*, 71 F4
Masasi, *Tanzania*, 71 G6
Masbate, *Philippines*, 45 H5
Maseru, *Lesotho, national capital*, 72 E5
Mashhad, *Iran*, 50 G4
Masirah Island, *Oman*, 51 G7
Massachusetts, *U.S.A., internal admin. area*, 25 M2
Massangena, *Mozambique*, 73 F4
Massawa, *Eritrea*, 67 J5
Massif Central, *France*, 61 E5
Massinga, *Mozambique*, 73 G4
Masvingo, *Zimbabwe*, 72 F4
Matagalpa, *Nicaragua*, 27 G5
Matala, *Angola*, 72 B2
Matamoros, *Mexico*, 26 E2
Matanzas, *Cuba*, 27 H3
Mataram, *Indonesia*, 42 E5
Mataro, *Spain*, 61 E6
Matehuala, *Mexico*, 26 D3
Mato Grosso, Plateau of, *Brazil*, 31 G6
Matsuyama, *Japan*, 47 M4
Maturin, *Venezuela*, 30 F2
Maui, *U.S.A.*, 25 P7
Maun, *Botswana*, 72 D3
Mauritania, *Africa, country*, 68 C5
Mauritius, *Indian Ocean, country*, 73 L3

Mavinga, *Angola*, 72 D3
Mayotte, *Africa*, 73 J2
Mazar-e Sharif, *Afghanistan*, 48 B3
Mazatlan, *Mexico*, 26 C3
Mazyr, *Belarus*, 59 J5
Mbabane, *Swaziland, national capital*, 72 F5
Mbala, *Zambia*, 72 F1
Mbale, *Uganda*, 71 F3
Mbandaka, *Democratic Republic of Congo*, 70 C3
Mbarara, *Uganda*, 71 F4
Mbeya, *Tanzania*, 71 F5
Mbuji-Mayi, *Democratic Republic of Congo*, 70 D5
McClintock Channel, *Canada*, 22 J1
McClure Strait, *Canada*, 22 G1
McKinley, Mount, *U.S.A.*, 22 D2
Mead, Lake, *U.S.A.*, 24 C3
Mecca, *Saudi Arabia*, 51 C7
Mecula, *Mozambique*, 73 G2
Medan, *Indonesia*, 42 A3
Medellin, *Colombia*, 30 C2
Medford, *U.S.A.*, 24 B2
Medina, *Saudi Arabia*, 51 C7
Mediterranean Sea, *Africa/Europe*, 19
Medvezhyegorsk, *Russia*, 58 K3
Meerut, *India*, 48 D5
Meiktila, *Burma*, 44 C3
Meizhou, *China*, 47 J6
Mekele, *Ethiopia*, 71 G1
Meknes, *Morocco*, 68 D2
Mekong, *Asia*, 44 E5
Melaka, *Malaysia*, 42 B3
Melamo, Cape, *Mozambique*, 73 H2
Melanesia, *Oceania*, 36 D5
Melbourne, *Australia, internal capital*, 38 H7
Melilla, *Africa*, 61 D7
Melitopol, *Ukraine*, 56 D4
Melo, *Uruguay*, 32 H6
Melville Island, *Australia*, 38 F2
Melville Island, *Canada*, 22 H1
Melville Peninsula, *Canada*, 23 L2
Memphis, *U.S.A.*, 25 J3
Mendoza, *Argentina*, 32 E6
Menongue, *Angola*, 72 C2
Mentawai Islands, *Indonesia*, 42 A4
Menzel Bourguiba, *Tunisia*, 66 C1
Mergui, *Burma*, 44 C5
Mergui Archipelago, *Burma*, 44 C5
Merida, *Mexico*, 26 G3
Meridian, *U.S.A.*, 25 J4
Merlo, *Argentina*, 32 E6
Mersin, *Turkey*, 50 B4
Meru, *Kenya*, 71 G3
Messina, *Italy*, 62 E4
Messina, *South Africa*, 72 F4
Metz, *France*, 60 F4
Mexicali, *Mexico*, 26 A1
Mexico, *North America, country*, 26 D3
Mexico City, *Mexico, national capital*, 26 E4
Mexico, Gulf of, *North America*, 26 F3
Mexico, Plateau of, *Mexico*, 26 D2
Miami, *U.S.A.*, 25 K5
Michigan, *U.S.A., internal admin. area*, 25 J2
Michigan, Lake, *U.S.A.*, 25 J2
Michurinsk, *Russia*, 56 E3
Micronesia, *Oceania*, 36 C4
Micronesia, Federated States of, *Oceania, country*, 36 C4
Middlesbrough, *United Kingdom*, 60 D3
Midway Islands, *Pacific Ocean*, 36 F2
Mikkeli, *Finland*, 58 H3
Milan, *Italy*, 62 D2
Milange, *Mozambique*, 73 G3
Mildura, *Australia*, 38 H6
Milwaukee, *U.S.A.*, 25 J2
Minas, *Uruguay*, 32 G6
Mindanao, *Philippines*, 45 H6
Mindelo, *Cape Verde*, 69 M11
Mindoro, *Philippines*, 45 H5
Mingacevir, *Azerbaijan*, 50 E3
Minna, *Nigeria*, 69 G7

Minneapolis, *U.S.A.*, **25 H2**
Minnesota, *U.S.A., internal admin. area*, **25 G1**
Minorca, *Spain*, **61 E6**
Minot, *U.S.A.*, **24 F1**
Minsk, *Belarus, national capital*, **59 H5**
Miri, *Malaysia*, **42 D3**
Mirim Lake, *Brazil*, **32 H6**
Miskolc, *Hungary*, **59 G6**
Misool, *Indonesia*, **43 H4**
Misratah, *Libya*, **66 E2**
Mississippi, *U.S.A.*, **25 H4**
Mississippi, *U.S.A., internal admin. area*, **25 H4**
Mississippi Delta, *U.S.A.*, **25 J5**
Missoula, *U.S.A.*, **24 D1**
Missouri, *U.S.A.*, **24 G2**
Missouri, *U.S.A., internal admin. area*, **25 H3**
Mistassini, Lake, *Canada*, **23 M3**
Mitwaba, *Democratic Republic of Congo*, **70 E5**
Mkushi, *Zambia*, **72 E2**
Mmabatho, *South Africa*, **72 E5**
Moanda, *Gabon*, **70 B4**
Mobile, *U.S.A.*, **25 J4**
Mochudi, *Botswana*, **72 E4**
Mocuba, *Mozambique*, **73 G3**
Modena, *Italy*, **62 D2**
Mogadishu, *Somalia, national capital*, **71 J3**
Mogao Caves, *China*, **46 E2**
Mohilla Island, *Comoros*, **73 H2**
Mo i Rana, *Norway*, **58 E2**
Mojave Desert, *U.S.A.*, **24 C4**
Moldova, *Europe, country*, **63 J2**
Moldoveanu, Mount, *Romania*, **56 C4**
Molepolole, *Botswana*, **72 E4**
Mollendo, *Peru*, **30 D7**
Molokai, *U.S.A.*, **25 P7**
Molopo, *Africa*, **72 D5**
Molucca Sea, *Indonesia*, **43 F4**
Mombasa, *Kenya*, **71 G4**
Monaco, *Europe, country*, **61 F6**
Monastir, *Tunisia*, **66 D1**
Monchegorsk, *Russia*, **58 K2**
Monclova, *Mexico*, **26 D2**
Moncton, *Canada*, **23 N4**
Mongo, *Chad*, **66 E6**
Mongolia, *Asia, country*, **46 F1**
Mongu, *Zambia*, **72 D3**
Monrovia, *Liberia, national capital*, **69 C7**
Montalvo, *Ecuador*, **30 C4**
Montana, *U.S.A., internal admin. area*, **24 E1**
Montauban, *France*, **61 E5**
Montego Bay, *Jamaica*, **27 J4**
Monterrey, *Mexico*, **26 D2**
Montes Claros, *Brazil*, **32 K3**
Montevideo, *Uruguay, national capital*, **32 G6**
Montgomery, *U.S.A., internal capital*, **25 J4**
Montpelier, *U.S.A., internal capital*, **25 M2**
Montpellier, *France*, **61 E6**
Montreal, *Canada*, **23 M4**
Montserrat, *North America*, **26 M4**
Monywa, *Burma*, **44 C3**
Moose Jaw, *Canada*, **22 J3**
Mopti, *Mali*, **69 E6**
Moree, *Australia*, **39 J5**
Morelia, *Mexico*, **26 D4**
Morocco, *Africa, country*, **68 D2**
Morogoro, *Tanzania*, **71 G5**
Morombe, *Madagascar*, **73 H4**
Moroni, *Comoros, national capital*, **73 H2**
Morotai, *Indonesia*, **43 G3**
Morpara, *Brazil*, **32 K2**
Moscow, *Russia, national capital*, **56 D2**
Moshi, *Tanzania*, **71 G4**
Mosquitos, Gulf of, *North America*, **27 H5**
Mossendjo, *Congo*, **70 B4**
Mossoro, *Brazil*, **31 L5**
Most, *Czech Republic*, **62 E1**

Mostaganem, *Algeria*, **68 F1**
Mostar, *Bosnia and Herzegovina*, **62 F3**
Mosul, *Iraq*, **50 D4**
Moulmein, *Burma*, **44 C4**
Moundou, *Chad*, **70 C2**
Mount Gambier, *Australia*, **38 H7**
Mount Hagen, *Papua New Guinea*, **43 K5**
Mount Isa, *Australia*, **38 G4**
Mount Li, *China*, **46 G4**
Moyale, *Ethiopia*, **71 G3**
Moyobamba, *Peru*, **30 C5**
Mozambique, *Africa, country*, **73 F3**
Mozambique, *Mozambique*, **73 H3**
Mozambique Channel, *Africa*, **73 G4**
Mpika, *Zambia*, **72 F2**
Mtwara, *Tanzania*, **71 H6**
Mudanjiang, *China*, **47 L2**
Mueda, *Mozambique*, **73 G2**
Mufulira, *Zambia*, **72 E2**
Multan, *Pakistan*, **48 C4**
Mumbai, *India*, **49 C7**
Mumbue, *Angola*, **72 C2**
Munhango, *Angola*, **72 C2**
Munich, *Germany*, **60 G4**
Munster, *Germany*, **60 F4**
Murcia, *Spain*, **61 D7**
Murmansk, *Russia*, **58 K1**
Murom, *Russia*, **56 E2**
Murray, *Australia*, **38 G6**
Murzuq, *Libya*, **66 D3**
Muscat, *Oman, national capital*, **51 G7**
Mutare, *Zimbabwe*, **73 F3**
Mutoko, *Zimbabwe*, **72 F3**
Mutsamudu, *Comoros*, **73 H2**
Mutshatsha, *Democratic Republic of Congo*, **70 D6**
Mwali, *Comoros*, **73 H2**
Mwanza, *Tanzania*, **71 F4**
Mwene-Ditu, *Democratic Republic of Congo*, **70 D5**
Mweru, Lake, *Africa*, **72 E1**
Mwinilunga, *Zambia*, **72 D2**
Myanmar, *Asia, country*, **44 C3**
Myitkyina, *Burma*, **44 C2**
Mykolayiv, *Ukraine*, **56 C4**
Mysore, *India*, **49 D8**
Mzuzu, *Malawi*, **73 F2**

n

Naberezhnyye Chelny, *Russia*, **57 G2**
Nabeul, *Tunisia*, **62 D4**
Nacala, *Mozambique*, **73 H2**
Nador, *Morocco*, **61 D8**
Naga, *Philippines*, **45 H5**
Nagasaki, *Japan*, **47 L4**
Nagoya, *Japan*, **47 N3**
Nagpur, *India*, **49 D6**
Nain, *Canada*, **23 N3**
Nairobi, *Kenya, national capital*, **71 G4**
Najran, *Saudi Arabia*, **51 D8**
Nakhodka, *Russia*, **47 M2**
Nakhon Ratchasima, *Thailand*, **44 D5**
Nakhon Sawan, *Thailand*, **44 D4**
Nakhon Si Thammarat, *Thailand*, **44 D6**
Nakuru, *Kenya*, **71 G4**
Nalchik, *Russia*, **50 D3**
Namangan, *Uzbekistan*, **48 C2**
Namib Desert, *Africa*, **72 B3**
Namibe, *Angola*, **72 B3**
Namibia, *Africa, country*, **72 C4**
Nam Lake, *China*, **48 G4**
Nampo, *North Korea*, **47 L3**
Nampula, *Mozambique*, **73 G3**
Namsos, *Norway*, **58 D2**
Namur, *Belgium*, **60 F4**
Nanaimo, *Canada*, **22 G4**
Nanchang, *China*, **47 J5**
Nancy, *France*, **60 F4**
Nanded, *India*, **49 D7**
Nanjing, *China*, **47 J4**
Nanning, *China*, **46 G6**
Nanping, *China*, **47 J5**
Nantes, *France*, **61 D5**
Napier, *New Zealand*, **39 Q7**
Naples, *Italy*, **62 E3**

Narmada, *India*, **49 C6**
Narva, *Estonia*, **58 J4**
Narvik, *Norway*, **58 F1**
Nashik, *India*, **49 C6**
Nashville, *U.S.A., internal capital*, **25 J3**
Nasi Lake, *Finland*, **58 G3**
Nassau, *The Bahamas, national capital*, **25 L5**
Nasser, Lake, *Egypt*, **67 H4**
Natal, *Brazil*, **31 L5**
Natitingou, *Benin*, **69 F6**
Natuna Islands, *Indonesia*, **42 C3**
Nauru, *Oceania, country*, **36 D5**
Navapolatsk, *Belarus*, **59 J5**
Navoiy, *Uzbekistan*, **48 B2**
Nawabshah, *Pakistan*, **48 B5**
Naxcivan, *Azerbaijan*, **50 E4**
Nazca, *Peru*, **30 D6**
Nazret, *Ethiopia*, **71 G2**
Ndalatando, *Angola*, **72 B1**
Ndele, *Central African Republic*, **70 D2**
Ndjamena, *Chad, national capital*, **66 E6**
Ndola, *Zambia*, **72 E2**
Near Islands, *U.S.A.*, **23 A3**
Nebraska, *U.S.A., internal admin. area*, **24 F2**
Necochea, *Argentina*, **33 G7**
Negombo, *Sri Lanka*, **49 D9**
Negro, *Brazil*, **30 F4**
Negro, Cape, *Peru*, **30 B5**
Negros, *Philippines*, **45 H6**
Neiva, *Colombia*, **30 C3**
Nekemte, *Ethiopia*, **71 G2**
Nellore, *India*, **49 E8**
Nelson, *New Zealand*, **39 P8**
Nelspruit, *South Africa*, **72 F5**
Nema, *Mauritania*, **69 D5**
Neman, *Europe*, **59 G5**
Nepal, *Asia, country*, **48 E5**
Netherlands, *Europe, country*, **60 F3**
Netherlands Antilles, *North America, dependency*, **27 L5**
Nettilling Lake, *Canada*, **23 M2**
Neuquen, *Argentina*, **33 E7**
Nevada, *U.S.A., internal admin. area*, **24 C3**
Nevers, *France*, **61 E5**
New Amsterdam, *Guyana*, **31 G2**
Newark, *U.S.A.*, **25 M2**
New Britain, *Papua New Guinea*, **43 M5**
New Brunswick, *Canada, internal admin. area*, **23 N4**
New Caledonia, *Oceania*, **39 M4**
Newcastle, *Australia*, **39 K6**
Newcastle upon Tyne, *United Kingdom*, **60 D3**
New Delhi, *India, national capital*, **48 D5**
Newfoundland, *Canada*, **23 P4**
Newfoundland, *Canada, internal admin. area*, **23 N3**
New Guinea, *Asia/Oceania*, **43 J4**
New Hampshire, *U.S.A., internal admin. area*, **25 M2**
New Ireland, *Papua New Guinea*, **43 M4**
New Jersey, *U.S.A., internal admin. area*, **25 M3**
New Mexico, *U.S.A., internal admin. area*, **24 E4**
New Orleans, *U.S.A.*, **25 J5**
New Plymouth, *New Zealand*, **39 P7**
Newport, *United Kingdom*, **60 D4**
New Siberia Islands, *Russia*, **53 H2**
New South Wales, *Australia, internal admin. area*, **38 H6**
New York, *U.S.A.*, **25 M2**
New York, *U.S.A., internal admin. area*, **25 M2**
New Zealand, *Australasia, country*, **39 Q8**
Ngami, Lake, *Botswana*, **72 D4**
Ngaoundere, *Cameroon*, **70 B2**
Ngoma, *Zambia*, **72 E3**
Nha Trang, *Vietnam*, **44 E5**
Niagara Falls, *North America*, **23 M4**
Niamey, *Niger, national capital*, **69 F6**
Nias, *Indonesia*, **42 A3**
Nicaragua, *North America, country*, **27 G5**

Nicaragua, Lake, *Nicaragua*, **27 H5**
Nice, *France*, **61 F6**
Nicobar Islands, *India*, **49 G9**
Nicosia, *Cyprus, national capital*, **63 K5**
Nieuw Nickerie, *Surinam*, **31 G2**
Niger, *Africa*, **69 G7**
Niger, *Africa, country*, **66 D5**
Niger Delta, *Nigeria*, **69 G8**
Nigeria, *Africa, country*, **69 F7**
Niigata, *Japan*, **47 N3**
Nikopol, *Ukraine*, **56 C4**
Niksic, *Serbia and Montenegro*, **63 F3**
Nile, *Africa*, **67 H3**
Nile Delta, *Egypt*, **67 H2**
Nimes, *France*, **61 F6**
Ningbo, *China*, **47 K5**
Niono, *Mali*, **69 D6**
Nioro du Sahel, *Mali*, **69 D5**
Nipigon, Lake, *Canada*, **23 L4**
Nis, *Serbia and Montenegro*, **63 G3**
Nitra, *Slovakia*, **59 F6**
Niue, *Oceania*, **36 G6**
Nizhniy Novgorod, *Russia*, **56 E2**
Nizhniy Tagil, *Russia*, **57 H2**
Njazidja, *Comoros*, **73 H2**
Njinjo, *Tanzania*, **71 G5**
Nkongsamba, *Cameroon*, **70 A3**
Nogales, *Mexico*, **26 B1**
Nokaneng, *Botswana*, **72 D3**
Norfolk Island, *Australia*, **39 N5**
Norilsk, *Russia*, **52 E2**
Norrkoping, *Sweden*, **58 F4**
North America, **18**
North Bay, *Canada*, **23 M4**
North Cape, *New Zealand*, **39 P6**
North Cape, *Norway*, **58 J1**
North Carolina, *U.S.A., internal admin. area*, **25 K3**
North Dakota, *U.S.A., internal admin. area*, **24 F1**
Northern Ireland, *United Kingdom, internal admin. area*, **60 C3**
Northern Mariana Islands, *Oceania*, **36 B3**
Northern Territory, *Australia, internal admin. area*, **38 F3**
North European Plain, *Russia*, **56 C2**
North Frisian Islands, *Europe*, **60 F3**
North Island, *New Zealand*, **39 Q7**
North Korea, *Asia, country*, **47 L2**
North Sea, *Europe*, **60 E2**
North West Cape, *Australia*, **38 B4**
Northwest Territories, *Canada, internal admin. area*, **22 G2**
Norway, *Europe, country*, **58 D3**
Norwegian Sea, *Europe*, **58 C2**
Norwich, *United Kingdom*, **60 E3**
Nosy Be, *Madagascar*, **73 J2**
Nosy Boraha, *Madagascar*, **73 J3**
Nottingham, *United Kingdom*, **60 D3**
Nouadhibou, *Mauritania*, **68 B4**
Nouakchott, *Mauritania, national capital*, **68 B5**
Noumea, *New Caledonia*, **39 N4**
Nova Iguacu, *Brazil*, **32 K4**
Nova Mambone, *Mozambique*, **73 G4**
Novara, *Italy*, **62 D2**
Nova Scotia, *Canada, internal admin. area*, **23 N4**
Novaya Zemlya, *Russia*, **52 C2**
Novgorod, *Russia*, **58 J4**
Novi Sad, *Serbia and Montenegro*, **63 F2**
Novocherkassk, *Russia*, **56 E4**
Novo Mesto, *Slovenia*, **62 E2**
Novorossiysk, *Russia*, **50 C3**
Novosibirsk, *Russia*, **52 E3**
Novyy Urengoy, *Russia*, **52 D2**
Nubian Desert, *Africa*, **67 H4**
Nueva Loja, *Ecuador*, **30 C3**
Nukualofa, *Tonga, national capital*, **36 F7**
Nukus, *Uzbekistan*, **50 G3**
Nullarbor Plain, *Australia*, **38 E6**
Nunavut, *Canada, internal admin. area*, **23 K2**
Nungo, *Mozambique*, **73 G2**
Nunivak Island, *U.S.A.*, **22 C3**
Nuqui, *Colombia*, **30 C2**

Nuremberg, *Germany*, 60 G4
Nyala, *Sudan*, 66 F6
Nyasa, Lake, *Africa*, 71 F6
Nyeri, *Kenya*, 71 G4
Nykobing, *Denmark*, 59 D5
Nzerekore, *Guinea*, 69 D7
Nzwani, *Comoros*, 73 H2

O

Oahu, *U.S.A.*, 25 P7
Oaxaca, *Mexico*, 26 E4
Ob, *Russia*, 52 D2
Obi, *Indonesia*, 43 G4
Obninsk, *Russia*, 56 D2
Obo, *Central African Republic*, 70 E2
Odda, *Norway*, 58 C3
Odemis, *Turkey*, 63 J4
Odense, *Denmark*, 59 D5
Oder, *Europe*, 59 E5
Odesa, *Ukraine*, 56 C4
Odienne, *Ivory Coast*, 69 D7
Ogbomoso, *Nigeria*, 69 F7
Ogden, *U.S.A.*, 24 D2
Ohio, *U.S.A.*, 25 J3
Ohio, *U.S.A., internal admin. area*, 25 K2
Ojinaga, *Mexico*, 26 D2
Ojos del Salado, Mount, *South America*, 32 E5
Oka, *Russia*, 56 E2
Okahandja, *Namibia*, 72 C4
Okaukuejo, *Namibia*, 72 C3
Okavango, *Africa*, 72 D3
Okavango Swamp, *Botswana*, 72 D3
Okayama, *Japan*, 47 M4
Okeechobee, Lake, *U.S.A.*, 25 K5
Okhotsk, Sea of, *Asia*, 53 H3
Okinawa, *Japan*, 47 L5
Oklahoma, *U.S.A., internal admin. area*, 24 G4
Oklahoma City, *U.S.A., internal capital*, 24 G3
Oktyabrskiy, *Russia*, 57 G3
Oland, *Sweden*, 59 F4
Olavarria, *Argentina*, 33 F7
Olbia, *Italy*, 62 D3
Oleksandriya, *Ukraine*, 56 C4
Ollague, *Chile*, 32 E4
Olomouc, *Czech Republic*, 62 F1
Olongapo, *Philippines*, 45 H5
Olsztyn, *Poland*, 59 G5
Olympia, *U.S.A., internal capital*, 24 B1
Olympus, Mount, *Greece*, 63 G3
Omaha, *U.S.A.*, 25 G2
Oman, *Asia, country*, 51 G7
Oman, Gulf of, *Asia*, 51 G7
Omdurman, *Sudan*, 67 H5
Omsk, *Russia*, 52 D3
Ondangwa, *Namibia*, 72 C3
Onega, Lake, *Russia*, 58 K3
Onitsha, *Nigeria*, 69 G7
Ontario, *Canada, internal admin. area*, 23 L3
Ontario, Lake, *U.S.A.*, 25 L2
Opochka, *Russia*, 59 J4
Opole, *Poland*, 59 F6
Oporto, *Portugal*, 61 B6
Oppdal, *Norway*, 58 D3
Opuwo, *Namibia*, 72 B3
Oradea, *Romania*, 63 G2
Oral, *Kazakhstan*, 57 G3
Oran, *Algeria*, 68 E1
Orange, *Africa*, 72 C5
Orange, Cape, *Brazil*, 31 H3
Orapa, *Botswana*, 72 E4
Orebro, *Sweden*, 58 E4
Oregon, *U.S.A., internal admin. area*, 24 B2
Orel, *Russia*, 56 D3
Orenburg, *Russia*, 57 H3
Orense, *Spain*, 61 C6
Orinoco, *Venezuela*, 30 F2
Orinoco Delta, *Venezuela*, 30 F2
Oristano, *Italy*, 62 D4
Orizaba, *Mexico*, 26 E4
Orkney, *South Africa*, 72 E5

Orkney Islands, *United Kingdom*, 60 D2
Orlando, *U.S.A.*, 25 K5
Orleans, *France*, 60 E5
Orsha, *Belarus*, 59 J5
Orsk, *Russia*, 57 H3
Oruro, *Bolivia*, 32 E3
Osaka, *Japan*, 47 N4
Osh, *Kyrgyzstan*, 48 C2
Osijek, *Croatia*, 63 F2
Oskarshamn, *Sweden*, 59 F4
Oslo, *Norway, national capital*, 58 D4
Osnabruck, *Germany*, 60 G3
Osorno, *Chile*, 33 D8
Ostersund, *Sweden*, 58 E3
Ostrava, *Czech Republic*, 63 F1
Otavi, *Namibia*, 72 C3
Otjiwarongo, *Namibia*, 72 C4
Ottawa, *Canada, national capital*, 23 M4
Ouadda, *Central African Republic*, 70 D2
Ouagadougou, *Burkina Faso, national capital*, 69 E6
Ouahigouya, *Burkina Faso*, 69 E6
Ouargla, *Algeria*, 68 G2
Ouarzazate, *Morocco*, 68 D2
Oudtshoorn, *South Africa*, 72 D6
Ouesso, *Congo*, 70 C3
Oujda, *Morocco*, 68 E2
Oulu, *Finland*, 58 H2
Oulu Lake, *Finland*, 58 H2
Ovalle, *Chile*, 32 D6
Oviedo, *Spain*, 61 C6
Owando, *Congo*, 70 C4
Owen Sound, *Canada*, 23 L4
Owo, *Nigeria*, 69 G7
Oxford, *United Kingdom*, 60 D4
Oyem, *Gabon*, 70 B3
Ozark Plateau, *U.S.A.*, 25 H3

P

Paarl, *South Africa*, 72 C6
Pacasmayo, *Peru*, 30 C5
Pacific Ocean, 18
Padang, *Indonesia*, 42 B4
Pafuri, *Mozambique*, 72 F4
Pagadian, *Philippines*, 45 H6
Paijanne Lake, *Finland*, 58 H3
Pakxe, *Laos*, 44 E4
Pakistan, *Asia, country*, 48 B5
Palangkaraya, *Indonesia*, 42 D4
Palau, *Oceania, country*, 36 A4
Palawan, *Philippines*, 45 G6
Palembang, *Indonesia*, 42 B4
Palencia, *Spain*, 61 C6
Palermo, *Italy*, 62 E4
Palikir, *Federated States of Micronesia, national capital*, 36 C4
Palk Strait, *Asia*, 49 D9
Palma, *Mozambique*, 73 H2
Palma, *Spain*, 61 E7
Palmas, Cape, *Africa*, 69 D8
Palmyra Atoll, *Oceania*, 36 G4
Palopo, *Indonesia*, 43 F4
Palu, *Indonesia*, 43 E4
Pampas, *Argentina*, 33 F7
Pamplona, *Colombia*, 30 D2
Pamplona, *Spain*, 61 D6
Panama, *North America, country*, 27 H6
Panama Canal, *Panama*, 27 J6
Panama City, *Panama, national capital*, 27 J6
Panama, Gulf of, *North America*, 27 J6
Panay, *Philippines*, 45 H5
Panevezys, *Lithuania*, 59 H4
Pangkalpinang, *Indonesia*, 42 C4
Panjgur, *Pakistan*, 48 A5
Pantelleria, *Italy*, 62 E4
Panzhihua, *China*, 46 F5
Papeete, *French Polynesia*, 37 J6
Paphos, *Cyprus*, 63 K5
Papua, Gulf of, *Papua New Guinea*, 43 K5
Papua New Guinea, *Oceania, country*, 43 L5
Paracel Islands, *Asia*, 45 F4
Paraguaipoa, *Venezuela*, 30 D1
Paraguay, *South America*, 32 G4

Paraguay, *South America, country*, 32 F4
Parakou, *Benin*, 69 F7
Paramaribo, *Surinam, national capital*, 31 G2
Parana, *South America*, 32 G6
Paranagua, *Brazil*, 32 J5
Parepare, *Indonesia*, 43 E4
Paris, *France, national capital*, 60 E4
Parma, *Italy*, 62 D2
Parnaiba, *Brazil*, 31 K4
Parnu, *Estonia*, 58 H4
Parry Islands, *Canada*, 22 J1
Pasadena, *U.S.A.*, 24 C4
Passo Fundo, *Brazil*, 32 H5
Pasto, *Colombia*, 30 C3
Patagonia, *Argentina*, 33 E9
Pathein, *Burma*, 44 B4
Patna, *India*, 48 F5
Patos de Minas, *Brazil*, 32 J3
Patos Lagoon, *Brazil*, 32 H6
Patra, *Greece*, 63 G4
Pattaya, *Thailand*, 44 D5
Pau, *France*, 61 D6
Pavlodar, *Kazakhstan*, 52 D3
Paysandu, *Uruguay*, 32 G6
Peace River, *Canada*, 22 H3
Pecos, *U.S.A.*, 24 F4
Pecs, *Hungary*, 59 F7
Pedro Juan Caballero, *Paraguay*, 32 G4
Pegu, *Burma*, 44 C4
Peipus, Lake, *Europe*, 58 H4
Peiraias, *Greece*, 63 G4
Pekanbaru, *Indonesia*, 42 B3
Pelagian Islands, *Italy*, 62 E5
Peleng, *Indonesia*, 43 F4
Pelotas, *Brazil*, 32 H6
Pematangsiantar, *Indonesia*, 42 A3
Pemba, *Mozambique*, 73 H2
Pemba Island, *Tanzania*, 71 G5
Penang, *Malaysia*, 42 B2
Penas, Gulf of, *Chile*, 33 C9
Pennsylvania, *U.S.A., internal admin. area*, 25 L2
Pensacola, *U.S.A.*, 25 J4
Penza, *Russia*, 56 F3
Penzance, *United Kingdom*, 60 C4
Peoria, *U.S.A.*, 25 J2
Pereira, *Colombia*, 30 C3
Perm, *Russia*, 57 H2
Perpignan, *France*, 61 E6
Persepolis, *Iran*, 51 F6
Persian Gulf, *Asia*, 51 F6
Perth, *Australia, internal capital*, 38 C6
Peru, *South America, country*, 30 C5
Perugia, *Italy*, 62 E3
Pescara, *Italy*, 62 E3
Peshawar, *Pakistan*, 48 C4
Petauke, *Zambia*, 72 F2
Petra, *Jordan*, 51 C5
Petrolina, *Brazil*, 31 K5
Petropavlovsk-Kamchatskiy, *Russia*, 53 H3
Petrozavodsk, *Russia*, 58 K3
Philadelphia, *U.S.A.*, 25 L3
Philippines, *Asia, country*, 45 J5
Philippine Sea, *Asia*, 45 H5
Phitsanulok, *Thailand*, 44 D4
Phnom Penh, *Cambodia, national capital*, 44 D5
Phoenix, *U.S.A., internal capital*, 24 D4
Phongsali, *Laos*, 44 D3
Piatra Neamt, *Romania*, 63 H2
Pica, *Chile*, 32 E4
Pico, *Azores*, 68 K10
Pielis Lake, *Finland*, 58 J3
Pierre, *U.S.A., internal capital*, 24 F2
Pietermaritzburg, *South Africa*, 72 F5
Pietersburg, *South Africa*, 72 E4
Pihlaja Lake, *Finland*, 58 J3
Pik Pobedy, *Asia*, 48 E2
Pilcomayo, *South America*, 32 F4
Pilsen, *Czech Republic*, 62 E1
Pinar del Rio, *Cuba*, 27 H3
Pindus Mountains, *Greece*, 63 G4
Pingdingshan, *China*, 47 H4
Pinsk, *Belarus*, 59 H5
Pisa, *Italy*, 62 D3

Pitcairn Islands, *Oceania*, 37 L7
Pitesti, *Romania*, 63 H2
Pittsburgh, *U.S.A.*, 25 L2
Piura, *Peru*, 30 B5
Platte, *U.S.A.*, 24 F2
Pleven, *Bulgaria*, 63 H3
Plock, *Poland*, 59 F5
Ploiesti, *Romania*, 63 H2
Plovdiv, *Bulgaria*, 63 H3
Plumtree, *Zimbabwe*, 72 E4
Plymouth, *United Kingdom*, 60 C4
Po, *Italy*, 62 D2
Pocos de Caldas, *Brazil*, 32 J4
Podgorica, *Serbia and Montenegro*, 56 C4
Podolsk, *Russia*, 56 D2
Pointe-Noire, *Congo*, 70 B4
Poitiers, *France*, 61 E5
Pokhara, *Nepal*, 48 E5
Poland, *Europe, country*, 59 F6
Polatsk, *Belarus*, 59 J5
Poltava, *Ukraine*, 56 C4
Polynesia, *Oceania*, 36 G5
Pompeii, *Italy*, 62 E3
Ponta Delgada, *Azores*, 68 K10
Ponta Pora, *Brazil*, 32 G4
Pontianak, *Indonesia*, 42 C3
Poole, *United Kingdom*, 60 D4
Poopo, Lake, *Bolivia*, 32 E3
Popayan, *Colombia*, 30 C3
Porbandar, *India*, 49 B6
Pori, *Finland*, 58 G3
Porlamar, *Venezuela*, 26 M5
Port-au-Prince, *Haiti, national capital*, 27 K4
Port Blair, *India*, 49 G8
Port Elizabeth, *South Africa*, 72 E6
Port-Gentil, *Gabon*, 70 A4
Port Harcourt, *Nigeria*, 69 G8
Port Hardy, *Canada*, 22 G3
Port Hedland, *Australia*, 38 C4
Portland, *Australia*, 38 H7
Portland, *Maine, U.S.A.*, 25 M2
Portland, *Oregon, U.S.A.*, 24 B1
Port Louis, *Mauritius, national capital*, 73 L4
Port Macquarie, *Australia*, 39 K6
Port McNeill, *Canada*, 22 G3
Port Moresby, *Papua New Guinea, national capital*, 43 L5
Porto Alegre, *Brazil*, 32 H5
Port-of-Spain, *Trinidad and Tobago, national capital*, 26 M5
Porto-Novo, *Benin, national capital*, 69 F7
Porto-Vecchio, *France*, 61 G6
Porto Velho, *Brazil*, 30 F5
Port Said, *Egypt*, 67 H2
Portsmouth, *United Kingdom*, 60 D4
Port Sudan, *Sudan*, 67 J5
Portugal, *Europe, country*, 61 B7
Port-Vila, *Vanuatu, national capital*, 39 N3
Porvenir, *Chile*, 33 D10
Posadas, *Argentina*, 32 G5
Poti, *Georgia*, 50 D3
Potiskum, *Nigeria*, 66 D6
Potosi, *Bolivia*, 32 E3
Potsdam, *Germany*, 60 H3
Poyang Lake, *China*, 47 J5
Poznan, *Poland*, 59 F5
Prachuap Khiri Khan, *Thailand*, 44 C5
Prague, *Czech Republic, national capital*, 62 E1
Praia, *Cape Verde, national capital*, 69 M12
Presidente Prudente, *Brazil*, 32 H4
Presov, *Slovakia*, 59 G6
Pretoria, *South Africa, national capital*, 72 E5
Preveza, *Greece*, 63 G4
Prieska, *South Africa*, 72 D5
Prilep, *Macedonia*, 63 G3
Prince Albert, *Canada*, 22 J3
Prince Edward Island, *Canada, internal admin. area*, 23 N4
Prince George, *Canada*, 22 G3

Prince of Wales Island, *Canada,* 23 K1
Prince Rupert, *Canada,* 22 F3
Principe, *Sao Tome and Principe,* 69 G8
Pripet, *Europe,* 59 J6
Pripet Marshes, *Europe,* 59 H5
Pristina, *Serbia and Montenegro,* 63 G3
Providence, *Seychelles,* 73 K1
Providence, *U.S.A., internal capital,* 25 M2
Providence, Cape, *New Zealand,* 39 N9
Provo, *U.S.A.,* 24 D2
Prudhoe Bay, *U.S.A.,* 22 E1
Pskov, *Russia,* 59 J4
Pskov, Lake, *Europe,* 58 J4
Pucallpa, *Peru,* 30 D5
Puebla, *Mexico,* 26 E4
Pueblo, *U.S.A.,* 24 F3
Puerto Ayora, *Ecuador,* 30 N10
Puerto Cabezas, *Nicaragua,* 27 H5
Puerto Deseado, *Argentina,* 33 E9
Puerto Inirida, *Colombia,* 30 E3
Puerto Leguizamo, *Colombia,* 30 D4
Puerto Maldonado, *Peru,* 30 E6
Puerto Montt, *Chile,* 33 D8
Puerto Natales, *Chile,* 33 D10
Puerto Paez, *Venezuela,* 30 E2
Puerto Princesa, *Philippines,* 45 G6
Puerto Rico, *North America,* 26 L4
Puerto Suarez, *Bolivia,* 32 G3
Puerto Vallarta, *Mexico,* 26 C3
Pula, *Croatia,* 62 E2
Pulog, Mount, *Philippines,* 45 H4
Puncak Jaya, *Indonesia,* 43 J4
Pune, *India,* 49 C7
Puno, *Peru,* 30 D7
Punta Arenas, *Chile,* 33 D10
Puntarenas, *Costa Rica,* 27 H5
Purus, *Brazil,* 30 E5
Pusan, *South Korea,* 47 L3
Pushkin, *Russia,* 58 J4
Puula Lake, *Finland,* 58 H3
Pweto, *Democratic Republic of Congo,* 70 E5
Pya, Lake, *Russia,* 58 J2
Pye, *Burma,* 44 C4
Pyinmana, *Burma,* 44 C4
Pyongyang, *North Korea, national capital,* 47 L3
Pyramids of Giza, *Egypt,* 67 H3
Pyrenees, *Europe,* 61 D6
Pyrgos, *Greece,* 63 G4

q

Qaidam Basin, *China,* 48 G3
Qaraghandy, *Kazakhstan,* 52 D3
Qatar, *Asia, country,* 51 F6
Qattara Depression, *Egypt,* 67 G3
Qazvin, *Iran,* 50 E4
Qena, *Egypt,* 67 H3
Qingdao, *China,* 47 K3
Qinghai Lake, *China,* 46 F3
Qinhuangdao, *China,* 47 J3
Qiqihar, *China,* 47 K1
Qom, *Iran,* 50 F5
Qostanay, *Kazakhstan,* 57 J3
Quanzhou, *China,* 47 J6
Quebec, *Canada, internal admin. area,* 23 M3
Quebec, *Canada, internal capital,* 23 M4
Queen Charlotte Islands, *Canada,* 22 F3
Queen Elizabeth Islands, *Canada,* 22 H1
Queen Maud Land, *Antarctica,* 77 C3
Queensland, *Australia, internal admin. area,* 38 H4
Quelimane, *Mozambique,* 73 G3
Quellon, *Chile,* 33 D8
Quetta, *Pakistan,* 48 B4
Quevedo, *Ecuador,* 30 C4
Quezaltenango, *Guatemala,* 26 F4
Quezon City, *Philippines,* 45 H5
Quibdo, *Colombia,* 30 C2
Quillabamba, *Peru,* 30 D6
Quimper, *France,* 60 C5
Quincy, *U.S.A.,* 25 H3
Qui Nhon, *Vietnam,* 44 E5
Quirima, *Angola,* 72 C2

Quito, *Ecuador, national capital,* 30 C4
Qurghonteppa, *Tajikistan,* 48 B3
Qyzylorda, *Kazakhstan,* 50 J3

r

Raahe, *Finland,* 58 H2
Rabat, *Morocco, national capital,* 68 D2
Rabaul, *Papua New Guinea,* 43 M4
Rabnita, *Moldova,* 63 J2
Radisson, *Canada,* 23 M3
Radom, *Poland,* 59 G6
Ragusa, *Italy,* 62 E4
Rahimyar Khan, *Pakistan,* 48 C5
Raipur, *India,* 49 E6
Rajahmundry, *India,* 49 E7
Rajkot, *India,* 49 C6
Rajshahi, *Bangladesh,* 49 F6
Rakops, *Botswana,* 72 D4
Raleigh, *U.S.A., internal capital,* 25 L3
Ralik Islands, *Marshall Islands,* 36 D3
Ramnicu Valcea, *Romania,* 63 H2
Rancagua, *Chile,* 32 D6
Ranchi, *India,* 49 F6
Randers, *Denmark,* 59 D4
Rangoon, *Burma, national capital,* 44 C4
Rangpur, *Bangladesh,* 48 F5
Rapid City, *U.S.A.,* 24 F2
Ras Dashen, *Ethiopia,* 71 G1
Rasht, *Iran,* 50 E4
Ratak Islands, *Marshall Islands,* 36 E3
Rat Islands, *U.S.A.,* 23 A3
Rauma, *Finland,* 58 G3
Ravenna, *Italy,* 62 E2
Rawson, *Argentina,* 33 E8
Rechytsa, *Belarus,* 59 J5
Recife, *Brazil,* 31 M5
Reconquista, *Argentina,* 32 G5
Red, *Asia,* 46 F6
Red, *U.S.A.,* 25 G4
Red Deer, *Canada,* 22 H3
Redding, *U.S.A.,* 24 B2
Red Sea, *Africa/Asia,* 67 J4
Regensburg, *Germany,* 60 H4
Regina, *Canada, internal capital,* 22 J3
Regina, *French Guiana,* 31 H3
Rehoboth, *Namibia,* 72 C4
Reims, *France,* 60 F4
Reindeer Lake, *Canada,* 22 J3
Rennell Island, *Solomon Islands,* 39 M2
Rennes, *France,* 60 D4
Reno, *U.S.A.,* 24 C3
Reunion, *Indian Ocean,* 73 L4
Revelstoke, *Canada,* 22 H3
Revillagigedo Islands, *Mexico,* 26 B4
Reykjavik, *Iceland, national capital,* 58 N2
Rhine, *Europe,* 60 F4
Rhode Island, *U.S.A., internal admin. area,* 25 M2
Rhodes, *Greece,* 63 J4
Rhone, *Europe,* 61 F5
Riau Islands, *Indonesia,* 42 B3
Ribeirao Preto, *Brazil,* 32 J4
Riberalta, *Bolivia,* 32 F2
Richards Bay, *South Africa,* 72 F5
Richmond, *U.S.A., internal capital,* 25 L3
Riga, *Latvia, national capital,* 59 H4
Riga, Gulf of, *Europe,* 59 G4
Rijeka, *Croatia,* 62 E2
Rimini, *Italy,* 62 E2
Rio Branco, *Brazil,* 30 E5
Rio Cuarto, *Argentina,* 32 F6
Rio de Janeiro, *Brazil,* 32 K4
Rio Gallegos, *Argentina,* 33 E10
Rio Grande, *Argentina,* 33 E10
Rio Grande, *Brazil,* 32 H6
Rio Grande, *U.S.A.,* 24 F5
Riohacha, *Colombia,* 30 D1
Rivas, *Nicaragua,* 27 G5
Rivera, *Uruguay,* 32 G6
Riverside, *U.S.A.,* 24 C4
Rivne, *Ukraine,* 59 H6
Riyadh, *Saudi Arabia, national capital,* 51 E7
Roanoke, *U.S.A.,* 25 L3
Robson, Mount, *Canada,* 22 H3

Rochester, *U.S.A.,* 25 L2
Rockford, *U.S.A.,* 25 J2
Rockhampton, *Australia,* 39 K4
Rocky Mountains, *U.S.A.,* 24 D1
Romania, *Europe, country,* 63 G2
Rome, *Italy, national capital,* 62 E3
Rondonopolis, *Brazil,* 32 H3
Ronne, *Denmark,* 59 E5
Ronne Ice Shelf, *Antarctica,* 77 S3
Roraima, Mount, *South America,* 30 F2
Rosario, *Argentina,* 32 F6
Roseau, *Dominica, national capital,* 26 M4
Roslavl, *Russia,* 59 K5
Ross Ice Shelf, *Antarctica,* 77 M4
Rosso, *Mauritania,* 69 B5
Ross Sea, *Antarctica,* 77 M3
Rostock, *Germany,* 60 H3
Rostov, *Russia,* 56 D4
Roti, *Indonesia,* 43 F6
Rotorua, *Australia,* 39 Q7
Rotterdam, *Netherlands,* 60 F4
Rouen, *France,* 60 E4
Rovaniemi, *Finland,* 58 H2
Roxas, *Philippines,* 45 H5
Rub al Khali, *Asia,* 51 E8
Rudnyy, *Kazakhstan,* 57 J3
Rufino, *Argentina,* 32 F6
Rufunsa, *Zambia,* 72 E3
Rukwa, Lake, *Tanzania,* 71 F5
Rundu, *Namibia,* 72 C3
Rurrenabaque, *Bolivia,* 32 E2
Ruse, *Bulgaria,* 63 H3
Russia, *Asia/Europe, country,* 52 E3
Ruvuma, *Africa,* 71 G6
Rwanda, *Africa, country,* 70 E4
Ryazan, *Russia,* 56 D3
Rybinsk, *Russia,* 56 D2
Rybinsk Reservoir, *Russia,* 56 D2
Rybnik, *Poland,* 59 F6
Ryukyu Islands, *Japan,* 47 L5
Rzeszow, *Poland,* 59 G6
Rzhev, *Russia,* 56 C2

s

Saarbrucken, *Germany,* 60 F4
Saarijarvi, *Finland,* 58 H3
Sabha, *Libya,* 66 F6
Sabzevar, *Iran,* 50 G4
Sacramento, *U.S.A., internal capital,* 24 B3
Sadah, *Yemen,* 51 E8
Safi, *Morocco,* 68 D2
Sahara, *Africa,* 66 C5
Saharanpur, *India,* 48 D5
Sahel, *Africa,* 66 C6
Sahiwal, *Pakistan,* 48 C4
Saida, *Algeria,* 68 F2
Saigon, *Vietnam,* 44 E5
Saimaa Lake, *Finland,* 58 H3
St. Andrew, Cape, *Madagascar,* 73 H3
St. Denis, *Reunion,* 73 L4
St. Etienne, *France,* 61 F5
St. Francis, Cape, *South Africa,* 72 D6
St. George, *U.S.A.,* 24 D3
St. George's, *Grenada, national capital,* 26 M5
St. Helier, *Channel Islands,* 60 D4
Saint John, *Canada,* 23 N4
St. John's, *Antigua and Barbuda, national capital,* 26 M4
St. John's, *Canada, internal capital,* 23 P4
St. Kitts and Nevis, *North America, country,* 26 M4
St. Lawrence, *Canada,* 23 M4
St. Lawrence, Gulf of, *Canada,* 23 N4
St. Lawrence Island, *U.S.A.,* 22 B2
St. Louis, *Senegal,* 69 B5
St. Louis, *U.S.A.,* 25 H3
St. Lucia, *North America, country,* 26 M5
St. Lucia, Cape, *South Africa,* 73 F5
St. Malo, *France,* 60 D4
St. Martha, Cape, *Angola,* 72 B2
St. Martin, *North America,* 26 M4
St. Mary, Cape, *Madagascar,* 73 J5
St. Paul, *U.S.A., internal capital,* 25 H1

St. Petersburg, *Russia,* 58 J4
St. Petersburg, *U.S.A.,* 25 K5
St. Pierre, *Seychelles,* 73 J1
St. Pierre and Miquelon, *North America,* 23 P4
St. Polten, *Austria,* 62 E1
St. Vincent and the Grenadines, *North America, country,* 26 M5
St. Vincent, Cape, *Portugal,* 61 B7
Sakhalin, *Russia,* 53 H3
Saki, *Azerbaijan,* 50 E3
Saki, *Nigeria,* 69 F7
Sakishima Islands, *Japan,* 47 K6
Sal, *Cape Verde,* 69 M11
Salado, *Argentina,* 32 F5
Salalah, *Oman,* 51 F8
Salamanca, *Spain,* 61 C6
Salem, *India,* 49 D8
Salem, *U.S.A., internal capital,* 24 B1
Salerno, *Italy,* 62 E3
Salihorsk, *Belarus,* 59 H5
Salinas, *U.S.A.,* 24 B3
Salta, *Argentina,* 32 E4
Saltillo, *Mexico,* 26 D2
Salt Lake City, *U.S.A., internal capital,* 24 D2
Salto, *Uruguay,* 32 G6
Salton Sea, *U.S.A.,* 24 C4
Salvador, *Brazil,* 31 L6
Salween, *Asia,* 44 C4
Salzburg, *Austria,* 62 E2
Samar, *Philippines,* 45 J5
Samara, *Russia,* 57 G3
Samarinda, *Indonesia,* 42 E4
Samarqand, *Uzbekistan,* 48 B3
Sambalpur, *India,* 49 E6
Samoa, *Oceania, country,* 36 F6
Sampwe, *Democratic Republic of Congo,* 70 E5
Sam Rayburn Reservoir, *U.S.A.,* 25 H4
Samsun, *Turkey,* 50 C3
San, *Mali,* 69 E6
Sana, *Yemen, national capital,* 51 D8
Sanandaj, *Iran,* 50 E4
San Andres Island, *Colombia,* 27 H5
San Antonio, *U.S.A.,* 24 G5
San Antonio, Cape, *Argentina,* 33 G7
San Antonio Oeste, *Argentina,* 33 F8
San Cristobal, *Ecuador,* 30 P10
San Cristobal, *Venezuela,* 30 D2
Sandakan, *Malaysia,* 43 E2
San Diego, *U.S.A.,* 24 C4
Sandoway, *Burma,* 44 B4
San Fernando, *Chile,* 32 D6
San Fernando de Apure, *Venezuela,* 30 E2
San Francisco, *Argentina,* 32 F6
San Francisco, *U.S.A.,* 24 B3
San Francisco, Cape, *Ecuador,* 30 B3
Sangihe Islands, *Indonesia,* 43 G3
San Jorge, Gulf of, *Argentina,* 33 E9
San Jose, *Costa Rica, national capital,* 27 H6
San Jose, *U.S.A.,* 24 B3
San Jose de Chiquitos, *Bolivia,* 32 F3
San Jose del Guaviare, *Colombia,* 30 D3
San Juan, *Argentina,* 32 E6
San Juan, *Puerto Rico,* 26 L4
San Julian, *Argentina,* 33 E9
Sanliurfa, *Turkey,* 50 C4
San Lucas, Cape, *Mexico,* 26 B3
San Luis, *Argentina,* 32 E6
San Luis Obispo, *U.S.A.,* 24 B3
San Luis Potosi, *Mexico,* 26 D3
San Marino, *Europe, country,* 62 E3
San Matias, Gulf of, *Argentina,* 33 F8
San Miguel de Tucuman, *Argentina,* 32 E5
San Nicolas de los Arroyos, *Argentina,* 32 F6
San Pedro, *Ivory Coast,* 69 D8
San Pedro de Atacama, *Chile,* 32 E4
San Rafael, *Argentina,* 32 E6
San Remo, *Italy,* 62 C3
San Salvador, *Ecuador,* 30 N10
San Salvador, *El Salvador, national capital,* 26 G5

San Salvador de Jujuy, *Argentina*, 32 E4
San Sebastian, *Spain*, 61 D6
Santa Clara, *Cuba*, 27 H3
Santa Cruz, *Bolivia*, 32 F3
Santa Cruz, *Ecuador*, 30 N10
Santa Cruz Islands, *Solomon Islands*, 39 N2
Santa Elena, *Venezuela*, 30 F3
Santa Fe, *Argentina*, 32 F6
Santa Fe, *U.S.A., internal capital*, 24 E3
Santa Maria, *Brazil*, 32 H5
Santa Marta, *Colombia*, 30 D1
Santander, *Spain*, 61 D6
Santarem, *Brazil*, 31 H4
Santa Rosa, *Argentina*, 33 F7
Santiago, *Chile, national capital*, 32 D6
Santiago, *Dominican Republic*, 27 K4
Santiago, *Panama*, 27 H6
Santiago de Compostela, *Spain*, 61 B6
Santiago de Cuba, *Cuba*, 27 J3
Santiago del Estero, *Argentina*, 32 F5
Santo Antao, *Cape Verde*, 69 L11
Santo Domingo, *Dominican Republic, national capital*, 27 L4
Santo Domingo de los Colorados, *Ecuador*, 30 N10
San Valentin, Mount, *Chile*, 33 D9
Sanya, *China*, 46 G7
Sao Francisco, *Brazil*, 31 L5
Sao Jose do Rio Preto, *Brazil*, 32 J4
Sao Luis, *Brazil*, 31 K4
Sao Miguel, *Azores*, 68 K10
Sao Nicolau, *Cape Verde*, 69 M11
Sao Paulo, *Brazil*, 32 J4
Sao Roque, Cape, *Brazil*, 31 L4
Sao Tiago, *Cape Verde*, 69 M11
Sao Tome, *Sao Tome and Principe, national capital*, 69 G8
Sao Tome and Principe, *Africa, country*, 69 G8
Sapporo, *Japan*, 47 P2
Saqqara, *Egypt*, 67 H3
Sarajevo, *Bosnia and Herzegovina, national capital*, 63 F3
Saransk, *Russia*, 56 F3
Sarapul, *Russia*, 57 G2
Saratov, *Russia*, 57 F3
Saratov Reservoir, *Russia*, 57 F3
Sardinia, *Italy*, 62 D3
Sargodha, *Pakistan*, 48 C4
Sarh, *Chad*, 70 C2
Sarremaa, *Estonia*, 58 G4
Saskatchewan, *Canada, internal admin. area*, 22 J3
Saskatoon, *Canada*, 22 J3
Sassari, *Italy*, 62 D3
Satu Mare, *Romania*, 63 G2
Saudi Arabia, *Asia, country*, 51 E7
Sault Ste. Marie, *Canada*, 23 L4
Saurimo, *Angola*, 72 D1
Savannah, *U.S.A.*, 25 K4
Savannakhet, *Laos*, 44 D4
Sawu, *Indonesia*, 43 F6
Sawu Sea, *Indonesia*, 43 F5
Schwerin, *Germany*, 60 G3
Scotland, *United Kingdom, internal admin. area*, 60 C2
Seattle, *U.S.A.*, 24 B1
Seeheim, *Namibia*, 72 C5
Sefadu, *Sierra Leone*, 69 C7
Seg, Lake, *Russia*, 58 K3
Segou, *Mali*, 69 D6
Seine, *France*, 60 E4
Sekondi-Takoradi, *Ghana*, 69 E8
Selebi-Phikwe, *Botswana*, 72 E4
Selibabi, *Mauritania*, 69 C5
Selvas, *Brazil*, 30 E5
Semarang, *Indonesia*, 42 D5
Semenov, *Russia*, 56 E2
Semiozernoe, *Kazakhstan*, 57 J3
Sendai, *Japan*, 47 P3
Senegal, *Africa*, 69 C5
Senegal, *Africa, country*, 69 B6
Seoul, *South Korea, national capital*, 47 L3
Serang, *Indonesia*, 42 C5

Serbia and Montenegro, *Europe, country*, 63 G2
Seremban, *Malaysia*, 42 B3
Sergiyev Posad, *Russia*, 56 D2
Serov, *Russia*, 57 J2
Serowe, *Botswana*, 72 E4
Serpukhov, *Russia*, 56 D3
Serres, *Greece*, 63 G3
Sesheke, *Zambia*, 72 D3
Setif, *Algeria*, 68 G1
Setubal, *Portugal*, 61 B7
Sevastopol, *Ukraine*, 63 K2
Severn, *United Kingdom*, 60 D3
Severnaya Zemlya, *Russia*, 53 F2
Severomorsk, *Russia*, 58 K1
Sevettijarvi, *Finland*, 58 J1
Seville, *Spain*, 61 C7
Seward, *U.S.A.*, 22 E2
Seward Peninsula, *U.S.A.*, 22 C2
Seychelles, *Indian Ocean, country*, 73 J1
Seydhisfjordhur, *Iceland*, 58 Q2
Sfax, *Tunisia*, 66 D2
Shalqar, *Kazakhstan*, 50 G2
Shanghai, *China*, 47 K4
Shannon, *Ireland*, 60 C3
Shantou, *China*, 47 J6
Shaoguan, *China*, 47 H6
Sharjah, *United Arab Emirates*, 51 G6
Sharm el Sheikh, *Egypt*, 67 H3
Shasta, Mount, *U.S.A.*, 24 B2
Sheffield, *United Kingdom*, 60 D3
Shenyang, *China*, 47 K2
Shepetivka, *Ukraine*, 59 H6
Shetland Islands, *United Kingdom*, 60 D1
Shieli, *Kazakhstan*, 50 J3
Shihezi, *China*, 48 F2
Shijiazhuang, *China*, 47 H3
Shikoku, *Japan*, 47 M4
Shillong, *India*, 48 G5
Shiraz, *Iran*, 51 F6
Shishaldin Volcano, *U.S.A.*, 23 C3
Shiyan, *China*, 46 H4
Shizuoka, *Japan*, 47 N3
Shkoder, *Albania*, 63 F3
Shreveport, *U.S.A.*, 25 H4
Shumen, *Bulgaria*, 63 H3
Shymkent, *Kazakhstan*, 48 B2
Sialkot, *Pakistan*, 48 C4
Siauliai, *Lithuania*, 59 G5
Sibiti, *Congo*, 70 B4
Sibiu, *Romania*, 63 H2
Sibolga, *Indonesia*, 42 A3
Sibu, *Malaysia*, 42 D3
Sicily, *Italy*, 62 E4
Sicuani, *Peru*, 30 D6
Sidi-Bel-Abbes, *Algeria*, 68 E1
Sidon, *Lebanon*, 50 C5
Sidra, Gulf of, *Africa*, 66 E2
Sierra Leone, *Africa, country*, 69 C7
Sierra Morena, *Spain*, 61 C7
Sierra Nevada, *Spain*, 61 D7
Sierra Nevada, *U.S.A.*, 24 B3
Siglufjordhur, *Iceland*, 58 P2
Siguiri, *Guinea*, 69 D6
Sikasso, *Mali*, 69 D6
Sikhote Alin Range, *Russia*, 47 N1
Siling Lake, *China*, 48 F4
Simao, *China*, 46 F6
Simeulue, *Indonesia*, 42 A3
Simferopol, *Ukraine*, 63 K2
Simpson Desert, *Australia*, 38 G4
Sinai, *Egypt*, 67 H3
Sinai, Mount, *Egypt*, 67 H3
Sincelejo, *Colombia*, 30 C2
Sines, *Portugal*, 61 B7
Singapore, *Asia, country*, 42 B3
Singapore, *Singapore, national capital*, 42 B3
Sinnamary, *French Guiana*, 31 H2
Sinuiju, *North Korea*, 47 K2
Sioux City, *U.S.A.*, 25 G2
Sioux Falls, *U.S.A.*, 25 G2
Sirjan, *Iran*, 51 G6
Sittwe, *Burma*, 44 B3
Sivas, *Turkey*, 50 C4

Skagen, *Denmark*, 59 D4
Skagerrak, *Europe*, 59 C4
Skelleftea, *Sweden*, 58 G2
Skikda, *Algeria*, 68 G1
Skopje, *Macedonia, national capital*, 63 G3
Skyros, *Greece*, 63 H4
Slavonski Brod, *Croatia*, 62 F2
Sligo, *Ireland*, 60 B3
Sliven, *Bulgaria*, 63 H3
Slovakia, *Europe, country*, 59 F6
Slovenia, *Europe, country*, 62 E2
Slovyansk, *Ukraine*, 56 D4
Slupsk, *Poland*, 59 F5
Slutsk, *Belarus*, 59 H5
Smallwood Reservoir, *Canada*, 23 N3
Smola, *Norway*, 58 C3
Smolensk, *Russia*, 59 J5
Sobradinho Reservoir, *Brazil*, 31 K6
Sobral, *Brazil*, 31 K4
Sochi, *Russia*, 50 C3
Society Islands, *French Polynesia*, 37 J6
Socotra, *Yemen*, 51 F9
Sodankyla, *Finland*, 58 H2
Sodertalje, *Sweden*, 58 F4
Sofia, *Bulgaria, national capital*, 63 G3
Sohag, *Egypt*, 67 H3
Sokhumi, *Georgia*, 50 D3
Sokode, *Togo*, 69 F7
Sokoto, *Nigeria*, 69 G6
Solapur, *India*, 49 D7
Solikamsk, *Russia*, 57 H2
Solomon Islands, *Oceania, country*, 36 D5
Solomon Sea, *Papua New Guinea*, 43 M5
Solwezi, *Zambia*, 72 E2
Somalia, *Africa, country*, 71 J2
Somerset Island, *Canada*, 23 K1
Songea, *Tanzania*, 71 G6
Songo, *Mozambique*, 73 F3
Son La, *Vietnam*, 44 D3
Sorong, *Indonesia*, 43 H4
Soroti, *Uganda*, 71 F3
Soroya, *Norway*, 58 G1
Sotra, *Norway*, 58 C3
Souk Ahras, *Algeria*, 62 C4
Sousse, *Tunisia*, 66 D1
South Africa, *Africa, country*, 72 D6
South America, 18
Southampton, *United Kingdom*, 60 D4
Southampton Island, *Canada*, 23 L2
South Australia, *Australia, internal admin. area*, 38 F5
South Bend, *U.S.A.*, 25 J2
South Carolina, *U.S.A., internal admin. area*, 25 K4
South China Sea, *Asia*, 45 F5
South Dakota, *U.S.A., internal admin. area*, 24 F2
South East Cape, *Australia*, 38 J8
Southend-on-Sea, *United Kingdom*, 60 E4
Southern Ocean, 18
Southern Sierra Madre, *Mexico*, 26 D4
South Georgia, *Atlantic Ocean*, 33 L10
South Island, *New Zealand*, 39 N8
South Korea, *Asia, country*, 47 L3
South Orkney Islands, *Atlantic Ocean*, 33 J12
South Sandwich Islands, *Atlantic Ocean*, 33 N10
South Shetland Islands, *Atlantic Ocean*, 33 G12
South West Cape, *New Zealand*, 39 N9
Spain, *Europe, country*, 61 D7
Split, *Croatia*, 62 F3
Spokane, *U.S.A.*, 24 C1
Spratly Islands, *Asia*, 45 F5
Springfield, *Illinois, U.S.A., internal capital*, 25 J3
Springfield, *Massachusetts, U.S.A.*, 25 M2
Springfield, *Missouri, U.S.A.*, 25 H3
Springs, *South Africa*, 72 E5
Sri Jayewardenepura Kotte, *Sri Lanka, national capital*, 49 E9

Sri Lanka, *Asia, country*, 49 E9
Srinagar, *India*, 48 C4
Standerton, *South Africa*, 72 E5
Stanley, *Falkland Islands*, 33 G10
Stara Zagora, *Bulgaria*, 63 H3
Staryy Oskol, *Russia*, 56 D3
Stavanger, *Norway*, 58 C4
Stavropol, *Russia*, 50 D2
Steinkjer, *Norway*, 58 D2
Stellenbosch, *South Africa*, 72 C6
Sterlitamak, *Russia*, 57 H3
Stewart Island, *New Zealand*, 39 N9
Stockholm, *Sweden, national capital*, 58 F4
Stoeng Treng, *Cambodia*, 44 E5
Stoke-on-Trent, *United Kingdom*, 60 D3
Stora Lule Lake, *Sweden*, 58 F2
Storavan Lake, *Sweden*, 58 F2
Stor Lake, *Sweden*, 58 E3
Stornoway, *United Kingdom*, 60 C2
Stranraer, *United Kingdom*, 60 C3
Strasbourg, *France*, 60 F4
Sturt Stony Desert, *Australia*, 38 G5
Stuttgart, *Germany*, 60 G4
Subotica, *Serbia and Montenegro*, 63 F2
Suceava, *Romania*, 63 H2
Sucre, *Bolivia, national capital*, 32 E3
Sudan, *Africa, country*, 67 G5
Sudbury, *Canada*, 23 L4
Suez, *Egypt*, 67 H3
Suez Canal, *Egypt*, 67 H2
Suhar, *Oman*, 51 G7
Sukkur, *Pakistan*, 48 B5
Sukses, *Namibia*, 72 C4
Sula, *Norway*, 58 C3
Sula Islands, *Indonesia*, 43 G4
Sullana, *Peru*, 30 B4
Sulu Archipelago, *Philippines*, 45 H6
Sulu Sea, *Asia*, 45 G6
Sumatra, *Indonesia*, 42 B3
Sumba, *Indonesia*, 43 E5
Sumbawa, *Indonesia*, 42 E5
Sumqayit, *Azerbaijan*, 50 E3
Sumy, *Ukraine*, 56 C3
Sunderland, *United Kingdom*, 60 D3
Sundsvall, *Sweden*, 58 F3
Superior, Lake, *U.S.A.*, 25 J1
Sur, *Oman*, 51 G7
Surabaya, *Indonesia*, 42 D5
Surakarta, *Indonesia*, 42 D5
Surat, *India*, 49 C6
Surgut, *Russia*, 52 D2
Surigao, *Philippines*, 45 J6
Surinam, *South America, country*, 31 G3
Surt, *Libya*, 66 E2
Sutherland Falls, *New Zealand*, 39 N8
Suva, *Fiji, national capital*, 39 Q3
Suwalki, *Poland*, 59 G5
Suwon, *South Korea*, 47 L3
Svalbard, *Norway*, 52 A2
Svolvaer, *Norway*, 58 E1
Svyetlahorsk, *Belarus*, 59 J5
Swakopmund, *Namibia*, 72 B4
Swan Islands, *Honduras*, 27 H4
Swansea, *United Kingdom*, 60 D4
Swaziland, *Africa, country*, 72 F5
Sweden, *Europe, country*, 58 E3
Swift Current, *Canada*, 22 J3
Swindon, *United Kingdom*, 60 D4
Switzerland, *Europe, country*, 62 C2
Sydney, *Australia, internal capital*, 39 K6
Sydney, *Canada*, 23 N4
Syktyvkar, *Russia*, 57 G1
Sylhet, *Bangladesh*, 49 G6
Syracuse, *Italy*, 62 E4
Syracuse, *U.S.A.*, 25 L2
Syr Darya, *Asia*, 50 H2
Syria, *Asia, country*, 50 C4
Syrian Desert, *Asia*, 51 C5
Syzran, *Russia*, 57 F3
Szczecin, *Poland*, 59 E5
Szeged, *Hungary*, 59 G7
Szekesfehervar, *Hungary*, 59 F7
Szombathely, *Hungary*, 59 F7

GENERAL INDEX

Acknowledgements

Every effort has been made to trace the copyright holders of the material in this book. If any rights have been omitted, the publishers offer to rectify this in any subsequent edition, following notification. The publishers are grateful to the following organizations and individuals for their contributions and permission to reproduce material (t=top, m=middle, b=bottom, l=left, r=right):

© AFP Photos 95bm (Henry Ray Abrams). © Agripicture 55br (Peter Dean). © Craig Asquith 11 projections, 12b, 13, 80. © Corbis 8tr (Dan Guravich), 9tr (W. Perry Conway), 10 (Christopher Cormack), 12tr (Bill Ross), 20bl (Richard Cummins), 21br (W. Perry Conway), 28b (Galen Rowell), 29tr (Eye Ubiquitous), 35br (Bates Littlehales), 40–41b (Michael S. Yamashita), 41br (Keren Su), 64–65b (Tom Brakefield), 65br (Gallo Images), 74bl (Galen Rowell), 76b (Wolfgang Kaehler). © Digital Vision cover globe, 1, 2–3, 4–5 background, 7tr Earth, 14 background, 54–55 background, 74br, 82–95 background, 96–97b, 97tr. © European Map Graphics Ltd 7bm & br, 9bl, 14–19, 20–21 map, 22–27, 28–29 map, 30–33, 34–35 map, 36–39, 40–41 map, 42–53, 54–55 map, 56–63, 64–65 map, 66–73, 75, 77. © Flag Enterprises Ltd 82–95 all flags except Afghanistan, Bahrain, Comoros, East Timor, Rwanda, Turkmenistan. © Stephen Moncrieff 6mr, 8bl globes, 11 globes. © NASA cover background, endpapers (data by Marc Imhoff, NASA GSFC, & Christopher Elvidge, NOAA NGDC; image by Craig Mayhew & Robert Simmon, NASA GSFC), 7tr satellite (JPL). © Science Photo Library 4tr (Geospace), 6bl (CNES, 1988 Distribution SPOT image), 74tr (Worldsat International), 76mr (NASA). © Shipmate Flags, Vlaardingen, The Netherlands 82 Afghanistan & Bahrain flags, 84 Comoros flag, 85 East Timor flag, 92 Rwanda flag, 94 Turkmenistan flag. © Still Pictures 34–35t (Pascal Kobeh).

Managing editor: Gillian Doherty   Managing designer: Mary Cartwright   Cover design by Zöe Wray

ISBN 0-439-68677-6